# Homeward Bound

## Sue Martin

Published in 2012 by FeedARead.com Publishing –
Arts Council funded

A CIP catalogue record for this title is available from
the British Library.

<u>Dedicated to the Memory of:</u>

William Henry Daniel Davis

...my Dad

David Goldie

...a darling friend

Tony Normington

...a treasured neighbour

They left this earth far too soon...and far too young

# PROLOGUE

After spending an entire childhood in Dr Barnardo's Homes; my expectations on leaving were fairly high, to say the least. I was familiar with mainly two types of people in the Homes, as well as School; my peers…and members of the staff.

I presume I suffered the same thoughts as many before me, and since; everything and everybody would be completely different in the 'Outside world'.

'No Way Home' described my childhood journey until reaching my teenage years, and being able to leave the Institution behind me; also my enduring desire throughout the whole of that time, to become an Outsider.

'Homeward Bound' follows the ups and downs of my life post- Homes; the adult bullies because I was Homeless…the angels who helped me, for exactly the same reason…and the unbelievable emotional traumas with which these individually and collectively presented me.

I successfully survived the Homes…

CHAPTER 1

On a beautiful day of high clouds and bright sunshine, the train from London sped on its way into the Kent countryside; the 'clickety-clack' of the wheels adding to my mounting excitement for yet *another* fresh start. I'd already experienced more than my share, having been moved from pillar to post while growing up in Care …but this was going to be very different.

At only seventeen years old, out alone in the big wide world, I was ready to take on every chance and opportunity offered. I had no desire to carry around the daunting baggage of my early years; maintaining my naturally positive, strong minded attitude…I knew I would cope. With absolute conviction, I'd already made the decision to only ever look ahead…my enthusiasm and optimistic feelings were soaring as high as the clouds above me.

As the train travelled deeper into Kent however, I realised I was no longer fully in control of those thoughts; feelings of hope for the future were rapidly becoming overshadowed by the past dark memories of this same County. In1943 I had been placed into 'Babies' Castle' in Hawkhurst; that was the first of many Dr Barnardo's Homes…and where I spent the early part of my mainly miserable childhood.

Although now fifteen years older, I was suddenly trembling inside; recollections were crowding my head in surprisingly sharp focus. Flooding back were memories of the cruel treatment and abuse by the Staff members; tumbling in waves…graphic, disturbing and rather unexpected. In the past twelve months or so since leaving the Homes, I had hoped and imagined my London adventures would have offered the opportunity to 'move on'.

With hands clutched tightly in my lap, I pressed my forehead hard against the cold window, staring out at nothing in particular; aware only of the thoughts invading my mind…and the fear of this sudden change of mood.

I recalled with clarity my first night there.

I was two years old, isolated and alone in this strange place; frightened at the sudden separation from my young widowed mother and five siblings. Having been placed in a cot, I sat up and began to weep uncontrollably; feeling utterly lost I longed for some comfort…but none was forthcoming. Instead, apparently angered by my tears, a uniformed 'nurse' charged towards me; hauling me roughly from my cot she marched me under her arm through the nursery dormitory. Dropping me into a dirty-linen bin, she slammed down the steel lid with all her force; lying on the urine-soaked sheets, terrified by the noise and her anger, I eventually calmed down and cried myself to sleep.

I had immediately learned the first of many harsh lessons; 'never cry again…it will only make things worse'.

The first emotional trauma was the disappearance of my 'Best Friend' Michael; both only three years old, we got on really well. To have just one close friend and play- pal in that bleak place had been wonderful, and for more than a year we did everything together.

At the end of one day, we had said goodnight to one another as always, and went to our separate dormitories; by breakfast time he was not around. I hunted upstairs and down, but he was simply nowhere to be seen and with mounting desperation, I eventually asked a member of staff. Her harshly spoken reply was that he had "gone away"…adding in triumph at my shock… "And you will never ever see *him* again".

With this new separation, I again felt the empty sadness of my first dreadful night; this sudden loss seemed to be almost unbearable for a very long time. I decided I would never have another friend if they were to be taken away from me all the time; however, it also gave me new-found strength.

That was when I decided I hated the Homes people with their bullying and cruelty, and would never comply with their controlling demands. Although not yet four years old…and much to their chagrin…I maintained that decision of defiance for most of the ensuing twelve years. I saw other little kids receiving the same strict discipline, and many were quickly crushed into total compliance…but that was not for me…I would fight them!

Continuing to stare out of the train window, I desperately tried to erase the renewed fears these memories had suddenly presented; even recalling my defiant attitude had not calmed me down. I was shaking; I felt my strength and confidence for yet another new beginning to be waning fast.

Feeling close to tears…I closed my eyes…and breathed deeply to help me settle again.

*Would perhaps these memories never fully leave me?* I asked myself.

I wanted desperately to get on with my life; to leave the Homes memories behind me, and become the 'Outsider' I had dreamed about for all those years. I felt deep down I could make it…but perhaps moments like these would always recur…perhaps I would just have to learn to accept that as fact, and learn to live with it.

That thought made me stronger again.


The beautiful countryside was therapy in itself and my mood lifted as the station names became more familiar; at last it was 'Tonbridge'…I was at the end of this particular journey. As I left the carriage, a tall angular woman sped towards me; fair hair, blue eyes and a warm smile. With outstretched hand she introduced herself as Mrs Murdoch and enquired… "Sue?"

I smiled with assurance, hurrying along in her wake to the waiting car…well van actually. A one-time green battered old Morris, with straw showing from every nook and cranny…I was home…you would only get a vehicle of that description in the Countryside I loved.

She drove the thing as only farmers can; crashing through the gears with a gear stick so long it would appear she was waving at you. The 'dimple' grips on the steering wheel were almost completely worn away; with once-elegant hands now roughened with work, she steered around the corners of narrow lanes almost on two wheels.

Out of the corner of my eye I saw something move just below me…I realised it was the road…I could see it through a hole in the floor! At the same time as driving like Stirling Moss, she shouted her conversation; needing the volume to be heard above the sound of the racing engine, and the variety of numerous bangs and rattles coming from inside the vehicle. To complete the personification of this stereotypical being, she waved and called 'coo-ee' to the few people seen along the way, and looked at every field to comment on the crop.

A mad ten miles or more…but we arrived safely.


The first impressions were pleasing; a warm-looking red brick house set at the end of a small gravelled drive, with lawns and gardens to the front and side. Tall evergreen trees bathed in the late afternoon sunlight, naturally framed this attractive rural scene.

"That will be your room up there," she said, pointing to a small window at the side of the house, while easing the van to a halt.

Then I nearly jumped out of my skin…and she laughed.

Our arrival had alerted the Guinea Fowl "who are more effective than any guard dog" she assured me. What a racket…but as she said, effective; I certainly wouldn't have hung around un-invited with that row going on!

I retrieved my case from the rear of the Morris and followed her around the side of the house to the kitchen door…the whole place seemed very quiet and still.

Without further word she put a kettle on the Aga; with a rather clipped "follow me", briskly proceeded up the stairs to the bedroom already referred to. The steep carpeted stairway, and walls adorned with numerous family photographs, seemed bright and well kept, but it was stark…and appeared to be lacking any feeling of homeliness. She opened the door of my new bedroom;

with the warm smile gone and in the same clipped tones announced,

"There you are Sue, you get comfortable. The bathroom is immediately opposite and you may bathe later…after the children. There are coat hangers and drawer space and all you should need; if anything is missing…just ask. I will be about a half-hour outside, so freshen up and relax after the journey. I will see you downstairs later… I will call you".

I lay my case on the floor and busied myself with the un-packing; trying hard to ignore the subtle but slightly disturbing change in her air since coming indoors.

My room was large; light and airy, with pretty wallpaper and fresh cream paint. The window overlooked both driveway and lawn; high beech hedging formed a natural boundary between the house and the farm land. In the L of this domestic part was another small lawn, with a bench strategically placed in front of a rockery covered in plants. Beyond to my left I could see the hen houses, the other farm buildings, and low-hedged fields for apparently miles distant.

Turning to further inspect the room, I 'bounced' my bed; it certainly seemed cosy enough…which was the complete opposite of the arm chair in the corner...*that* resembled sitting on a stone, very uncomfortable. Under the window stood a small dining room table and chair, at exactly the height to afford a welcome writing surface; I had promised I would keep in touch with the London crowd.

These were the people who had guided me in my first lone approach into the outside world.

On leaving the Homes I had been promised a *proper* family home with my mother; for all my childhood she had been a total stranger. One visit and about eight letters in twelve years had not brought us close...but I held out great hope that it would now work out well for us all. I had three brothers who also grew up in the Homes; one sister I had never seen, as she had been adopted, and yet another sister who had always stayed with our mother.

Our Dad had died very young of TB...she put us into Care because she said she couldn't cope. I soon discovered that was not a 'past tense' statement ...she still couldn't cope...not as a mother anyway. I spent just a few very unhappy months with her; she clearly only wanted me as a Domestic Help...and another wage earner to contribute ridiculous amounts from my pay, to help run a Flat she could never have otherwise afforded.

My brothers were treated in exactly the same manner; for instance, on the day of our arrival, we all had to buy our own beds...to sleep in that same night! Like them, I moved out as soon as I plucked up the courage; an astonishing leap in the dark for a naïve sixteen year old. I had been extremely fortunate to land firmly on my feet, in homely lodgings with lovely people called Eva and Maurice.

While reflecting upon this recent past, I continued to unpack; there was ample drawer space and it didn't take long to sort everything into its rightful place. As I had done at Eva's, I hung my raincoat on the back of the door and that was me, 'home'...but without the joy yet. Looking around I decided; although basic, it appeared very comfortable...a promising start.

After a much-appreciated wash in scalding hot water from the Aga, I returned and sat at the table to absorb all I could see; experiencing again the sheer pleasure of being back in my beloved countryside.

The quietness was almost a silence.

Wherever one lived and worked in London, there was the accompanying noise of traffic and people. I'd

To kill some time and buck myself up I wrote long letters to Mrs Lewis, her sisters and to Eva and Maurice my old landlady and her husband. In the most cheery way I could muster, I got quite carried away telling them about the journey, and the new house. I was pleased the writing had taken so long…the time had simply flown by; stamped and ready to post, it would be interesting to have a little walk after work tomorrow, to find the post box and get my bearings.

I began to relax.

Looking from my window I saw the trees were already silhouetted against the sky, now streaked with the pinks and dark blues indicating a fine day tomorrow. I was glad of this encouragement; *she* was not going to be of much help in the happiness stakes. Ready to make a move to bed, I very quietly opened the door to go across to the bathroom. I stood and listened for a few moments to make sure the coast was clear; I had rattled her on enough occasions for one day I decided.

Once back in my room unscathed, I checked on everywhere to make sure there could be no more condemnation…got out some clean clothes ready for the morning…and wound the clock.

She had already set it to ring at 5.30 am!

Tired and a bit confused about what exactly was going on, I retired early and was almost immediately asleep...in the silent blackness exclusive to the countryside.

# CHAPTER 3

I woke before the alarm; my bed was luxuriously soft and comfortable, and I had slept deeply after the emotional highs and lows of the previous day. Being one of those lucky people who are wide awake immediately their eyes open, I leapt excitedly from my bed and ran to the window.

Quietly drawing back the curtains, I drank in the beauty before me; a deep thrill ran through my body. It was the sunny day the evening sky had promised…but being too early to dress, I made my way back to bed.

Propped up on my pillows, I lay back…and let my thoughts wander.

It felt good being in a new place; I had not enjoyed at all, having to share a bedroom with my sister in London. I had loved the independence at Dollis Hill with Eva, but this was different…I was feeling *very* grown up. It had been a massive decision to leave London; the recollections during the journey had been a bit disconcerting, but I'd soon recovered. It *was* a joy to be back in Kent, with a proper live-in job; but that thought made me reflect more rationally on Mrs Murdoch.

It worried me that she had behaved so strangely last night; her change of mood once indoors was quite alarming. I was going to have to learn to cope; that notion made me feel less grown up and rather small again.

I quickly realised why; I would have to deal with everything that lay before me entirely on my own...no Mrs Lewis, no Eva and Maurice...just me.

With rising anxiety I asked myself...what on earth have you done?

Was she as spiteful as she sounded? *Probably*

Should I have left London? *Definitely*

Was it going to be the right move? *Possibly*

A myriad of other equally unanswerable questions ran through my mind...then the clock disturbed me. I leapt again out of bed; washed and dressed...and got down just before the due time.

Her face immediately showed her mood was as dark as the previous evening; barely looking up as I approached the table, she waved her hand in the general direction of the Aga and said,

"Have a cup of tea and I'll go over your rota".

That was my greeting...in that same clipped style.

"Good morning, I hope you slept well" I responded…hopefully.

No chance…clean over the top of her head!

I covertly studied her while pretending to gaze through the window; she was looking at a bill, or something equally scintillating as 'six-in-the-morning' reading matter, clearly to avoid having to make any conversation. She didn't look as though she had washed herself, or brushed her hair…*you're a mess* I concluded. Perhaps she was not a 'morning person'…a great shame it seemed to last all day in her case! I could not make her out at all, but seeing the children and the way they behaved, this was probably the norm.

*Blimey, the Barnardo's Homes were a laugh a minute compared with this; perhaps I could smuggle them out and get them a dorm at St. Christopher's in Tunbridge Wells, it was only a few miles away…they'd love it!*

She left the table without a word, clattered her cup and saucer onto the wooden draining board and made through the back door; following her lead outside, my duties were explained.

The only live-stock was poultry…boring old 'white leg-horns'; in her clipped tone I was informed,

"You are responsible for all their welfare, the general cleansing of the yards, and basically a common sense approach...if it looks as though it needs doing...do it".

She had been referring to The Farm, but that would appear pretentious from what I had seen; a smallholding yes, as written in the advertisement. She had mentioned a few acres of grass keep, and a grazing meadow leased to another farmer, but hardly a farm *per se*.

Poultry, as with all farm animals, have their particular demands. They hate wet or draughty conditions, and will respond by going 'off-lay'... and no eggs to sell is not the best of commercial ideas. The hen houses were not in my opinion even up to basic hygiene standards...in fact they were at best unkempt.

I had spent sufficient time with my beloved Uncle Tom, who also kept hens, to see how well they should be housed and cared for; this was not the longest apprenticeship in the world, but I remembered everything he had ever said. There had also been a girl at school with whom I had long discussions, simply because of what she was required to do before leaving in the morning. They had Dairy...now that *was* hard, the longest most arduous hours of the whole agricultural industry.

This little knowledge would now stand me in very good stead, I decided.

Mrs Murdoch showed me around the various barns, lean-to sheds and so on, all of which were in the same dreadfully poor condition. The surrounding grass area was also a disgrace; rusting implements scattered around and with anybody's guess as to when it was last cut. Even the apple trees were neglected and un-pruned...almost ranking as a 'heinous crime' in Kent; not known for nothing as "The Garden of England". The lack of any male over-seer was very evident; she had not come over on first impression as being particularly practical, let alone of outdoor stock, but I was truly surprised at the state of what I had already seen.

Maybe she caught my look of disapproval...and quietly she explained,

"Mr Murdoch used to do the repairs but since he fell ill two years ago, I have been coping as best as I can" she confided, in a far more reasonable tone of voice.

I looked at her, and saw as well as heard the weariness and almost despair in that statement; the manner in which she had behaved so far was not very kind, but now I felt rather sorry for her.

"I did woodwork at school," I offered cheerily. "They gave up hope with me in the needle-work class and that was my option…I loved it. I'm not capable of the complicated, but I can repair most of the damage that I've seen so far"

Good grief…you would think I'd just announced I was the 'Messiah'…she was thrilled to bits!

With genuine enthusiasm, she smiled and replied,

"Well let's go and get those children out of bed; after breakfast you can show me what tools you'll need…there's a shed full somewhere".

*What an instant change that had been*!

Her previous attitude was evidently the strain of a frail husband years older than she, being totally unused to the land work, and having nowhere near a large enough flock to make a living for four people. I had tried not to take her manner too personally; now there seemed hope it would be a much more friendly place to be living and working.

Breakfast done with, but no tray this time, I studied the list in my pocket as the poultry had to be attended to first; she was correct in her description of the work-load…blimey, and I had just volunteered to do even more!

After my six o'clock cup of tea I was to be out in the yards to drop down the wooden shutters at the windows of the housing sheds. There were about eight thousand head of laying hens divided into two sections; two thirds deep litter, the rest free range. They were hopeless as free range in all honesty, being far too sensitive to wet conditions; they didn't need the cold rain on *their* feet…these birds would go 'off-lay' just standing on damp grass!

This was the sort of information I had heard and remembered from my darling Uncle Tom, and his wife, known to me as Auntie Dodd.

They had wanted to take out a child from the Homes…and I was to be that lucky child. They lived in Pluckley, also in Kent, and over a period of about two years, between me being seven and nine, they regularly picked me up from the Home in Crowborough and drove me to their beautiful country cottage. Sometimes this was just for a day…but I had wonderful long holidays too.

Theirs was a huge garden.

Besides their gardener growing wonderful lovely vegetables and fruit, Uncle Tom kept hens; these were magnificent sturdy 'Rhode Island Reds' that laid dark brown eggs. I was shown how to collect these, and to feed them the corn and hot mash; "*I loved that smell*" I recalled with pleasure.

He was proud of his birds and cared for them and their surroundings with the utmost attention to detail; he was a military man, and this definitely showed in the precision of all he did…and I copied his every move of course. It was play to me then, but I learned so much without even realising it. Being with them was where I fell in love with the countryside…the peace and happiness from both would always remain synonymous.

I loved to be with them, and would read to Uncle Tom. When I did so for the first time, he said I was a clever girl, something I had never heard before…Barnardo's didn't do compliments. Both they and their Cook had a magic knack of making me feel important, wanted and loved…all uniquely new emotions. It was an absolute miracle when I realised I loved them too…and utter bliss was felt through that trust and belief.

This was the closest to heaven anyone in my situation could ever wish for without actually dying; they were the kindest people on earth, and for the short time spent with them, I was their Princess. Being in their company was the complete opposite of the harsh Barnardo's life. For instance, Auntie Dodd would allow me to look into a mirror when she brushed my jet black hair until it shone; we didn't have mirrors because the Matron called it Vanity…and one of the Seven Deadly Sins.

I felt a lump in my throat and a pain rising in my chest at these recollections;  I could never think about them for too long without that happening. The wicked way I was told I would never see them again was an agony that would never leave me.

To recover, I concentrated hard on my work.

CHAPTER 4

I walked towards the hen houses and immediately realised the food and water routine was going to be difficult because of the lay-out of the place; *why did they only have one tap*? I would tell her I could easily put in another one; that would please her…and me. I reckoned the basics would take up all of the morning…and she wanted help indoors too. I would pluck up the courage to present a compromise…Land repairs and restoration…or house-work; although I loved all domestic chores, I really hoped the outside work would win.

By the time I had 'inspected' all the outhouses I realised the land work *would* win…she had a massive problem with rats! The poor hygiene and dilapidated timber sheds had given these vermin the run of the place…their droppings were everywhere.

*Had she never noticed*?

Maybe the 'blind eye' was the answer, with all the other problems she currently faced. Walking through the country lanes as a child, there were always dogs running through fields, or barking in farmhouse driveways. It was a first in my knowledge to have no domestic *or* working dog or cat on the premises; I thought they were essential, and this problem would surely have been considerably less were they on guard.

This all amounted to a great shame; although I couldn't relate exactly to what she was feeling, she did have my sympathy. I would try very hard to help…and to be more patient with her moods…and the vitriol.

The 'compromise' was resolved at lunch-time; she was extremely relieved at the arrangement because for her, it had been far too much of a worry for too long. She obviously did not enjoy *any* of the outside work, and now all she had to do was the domestics…I would manage the rest.

She was happy…I was absolutely delighted!

Ushered outside I rifled through the precious tools that belonged to the old man; he would love that, I thought…a woman in the wood pile! There was everything needed to do the work; all manner of tools in the shed and in an adjacent barn, an amazing selection of timber, and black tarred felt for the roofs.

I set to examining the worst of the buildings; I decided to carry out the repairs on a sliding scale of need, and on first inspection felt there was nothing I couldn't handle. My immediate list included; broken door and window frames, rickety unsafe steps, complete lengths missing from some walls, and totally neglected flat roofs.

I was in a position of total autonomy; she had not the remotest idea of what to do…and even less desire to find out.

With the sun warming everywhere, and enjoying the beautiful fresh air, I got straight on; I worked hard, and was satisfied with what I had completed in a fairly short space of time. She said so too, when in mid-afternoon she came out carrying a great enamel jug full of home-made lemonade.

To illustrate the enormity of the infestation problem, I pointed out the numerous egg shells I had already come across…there would be hundreds more I explained.

"The houses are so broken in places, it's literally a picnic for the vermin. They take the eggs at will and of course distress the flock when doing so; that puts them off lay…but now the egg count will go up considerably"

She smiled warmly at last, and thanked me before returning to the house. *That's more like it*, I thought, and drank a good draught of the sharp liquid to slake my thirst.

The outside work was something to which I was clearly suited.

As I busied myself, I reflected on the days prior to leaving London; I realised I was already missing none of it. That at first felt like an enormous betrayal as there were many people who had shown me great kindness; but then I adjusted this perspective.

I had been to them what they were to me; I had behaved impeccably with Mrs Lewis at work…and within Eva's home. I had worked extreme hours baby-sitting and house cleaning for the sisters, and was as grateful for my wages as they were for my diligence and high standards. Their memory I would always hold in affection, but I had decided already; however badly it may turn out…*I would never go back.*

I recalled the Maurice quote; "You owe not…nor are you owed"

That summed it up completely, what a wise man.


The Voice was off…yet again.

A two syllable "Su-ue" she yelled, from middle earth or thereabouts.

Recalling previous admonishments, I hurried to the source of this demand. She was right up at the house with young Katie in tow looking as crestfallen as ever. In a voice still much more tempered, she said,

"I need you to take Katie to the doctor for me...Mr Murdoch has a nurse visiting soon and I *must* be here. Only a booster jab today, which she has no qualms about at all...it will give you a break and little walk too".

'*Blimey...polite and considerate*' I thought.

I had a quick wash and changed, grabbed my letters to post, and met them at the kitchen door with Katie in her pushchair.

"Can you show me where to go Katie?" I cheerily enquired of this rather sad-looking little girl; she simply nodded her assent.

It was a warm day but we met no other folk on the way, all busy working I imagined. The hedgerows were beginning to show the approaching spring with new leaves and buds; better days were ahead. I pointed out the uncurling ferns and all the new growth to the unnaturally silent child in my charge; no real response.

I decided against forcing conversation from her; I would wait and see if the problem became clearer with time.

The village was very small; we were in a lane with only two or three turnings to right and left. We came upon more farm buildings as we progressed; but other than the barking of a working dog, and the distant drone of a tractor, there was little to punctuate the still, quiet atmosphere.

"We here now Sue" said Katie, in a voice barely audible even in this peace.

The 'Surgery' was the cottage where-in the doctor lived; we entered the well kept tidy garden through a creaky wooden gate, and a mossy path led us to the front door. The cottage was a pretty little place; weathered stone with roses around the porch door…and a thatch over the upstairs windows that looked like eyebrows slightly frowning.

He was the personification of a village doctor; a middle-aged, balding, short rotund gentleman, with tiny gold glasses that should never have been able to sit on his button nose…but managed it some-how. He was as charming as his home and got the best out of the little girl; not exactly animated but with certainly more to say than was usual. As promised she worried not about the injection; and she 'looked' which is more than I could bear to do at her age!

He studied me as I got her clothing re-arranged.

"So you must be the girl Mrs Murdoch so desperately needed. How are you getting on?"

I replied it was early days...but it seemed to be nice.

"Don't take her manner too personally; she's had a very hard time with her husband so ill...underneath she is alright really"

The 'really' seemed a little revealing, but I ignored it.

"And now *you* must register with my Panel"

My look of surprise had quite obviously taken him aback.

"You are going to be living there so you must have a recognised doctor, it's the Law...and my responsibility," he added abruptly.

The form was already on his desk and I duly replied to his questions; then crunch time arrived. With advice from Mrs Lewis, I had memorised my National Insurance number; I gave him my date of birth, *then he asked for my parent's name.* I did not know what to say.

"You do have a living parent"…and seeing my reluctance said… "or Guardian?"

*Sod it*! *I had not anticipated this.*

When I left my mother to go to Dollis Hill, in her umbrage she had placed me back into Barnardo's Care until I was twenty-one; they were officially until then, my guardians. I never dreamed they would have to ever know where I was living…and now this!

"Well I was brought up in Dr. Barnardo's……." I began quietly.

He interrupted,

"Oh, don't worry about that, with all the Homes in Kent I've had a few of you in here…I even have the address to hand; I'll let them know so you don't have to do anything…except sign here please"

I felt genuine anger as I escorted Katie home; she was out of her pushchair and walking now, and she was sufficiently slow and non-talkative for me to think. How *dare* he say 'a few of you' and lump us together like some alien species? I had never been a 'Barnardo Girl'…I'd only ever lived there…***reluctantly,*** I added to myself.

41

*Were they forever going to be in a position to continually haunt me and interfere with everything I wanted to do?*

I hated them with renewed vigour... I knew I was being silly but I couldn't help it; the real ire was because he was informing them of a true address. I hoped desperately that would be all there was to it; I wanted to...no I was *going* to...live the rest of my life without them...they had taken enough from me already. That resolve cheered me.

We ambled in silence along the dry, dusty lane; around the next bend we came upon what was little more than a shed, which proclaimed on the old wooden door, 'Bicycle Sales and Repair' shop.

We crossed over; my knock was answered by Methuselah...or some-one of a similar age who bore a striking resemblance...his too was a glorious beard.

"Have you got much for sale at the moment please?" I enquired.

He said he had as he led us into the dark interior; he started with an old Grannies' contraption, complete with basket at the front...that made me laugh, and raised my spirits even more.

"Um…I was thinking more of a drop-handle racer maybe?"

He laughed at my clear disgust and said enthusiastically "You look at this then"

I did and it was *exactly* what I would like; good make, full drop handle bars, a five- speed 'Derailleur' gear and with sleek 27 x 1¼ inch wheels…*that* would shift…*and* it looked classy.

I said I would return when I next had some time off; telling him where I lived in reply to his enquiry, he just said "Right".

It had been a spontaneous reaction to look at a bike; I had not previously even considered the idea, but it held great attraction. I was obviously going to be having some time off, this has not yet been discussed but I surely was not expected to work seven days a week. The warmer weather was only just around the corner, and there were many places I could reach with my own transport.

'*My very own bike*'…it sounded absolutely wonderful.

Putting Katie back into the chair I ran as fast as I could to make up for lost time. In the empty lane I swung the chair from side-to-side as we went; she loved it and was squealing and laughing with absolute delight. She was red cheeked and healthier looking by the time we got back, and to hear a bit of life from her had been wonderful.

"Where on *earth* have you been for all this time?" Mrs Murdoch bellowed at me, red-faced and glaring.

I was amazed, and poor little Katie began to quietly cry; I applied my attention to removing her from the chair and taking off her coat.

Mrs Murdoch continued in her rage…really shouting now.

"When I said have a walk, you were only supposed to stay in the village, not go off on some jaunt of your own pleasing".

That is *very* unfair Mrs Murdoch" I responded loudly; outwardly bold and defensive…but it was a façade.

"Doctor was very patient with Katie and then I had to fill in a form to register too……" this on deaf ears as she was striding away as I spoke.

I pushed past them in high dudgeon; stomping loudly up the stairs, I changed into my working clothes, slammed the bedroom door closed behind me, and again resumed my work outside. At least I could escape from her ridiculous temper…*'blooming old cow'* I thought…and immediately felt better!

However, back outside in the fresh air and calming down again…I became so worried I was feeling physically sick. I realised in shock that I had reacted to her tantrum *far* too quickly for comfort or safety; if I did that again, that could be it!

I would find myself without a roof over my head…without a job or any money…and have *absolutely nowhere else to go*. I felt genuinely frightened when the realisation dawned as to how *truly* delicate my new situation was. I had always been capable of the most terrible temper tantrums as a child, but then I had felt a justification. The consequences now though would be very different; HOMELESS…PENNILESS…what frightening words when applied to one-self.

I shuddered at the gravity of these thoughts.

She *did* seem able to fly off the handle at anything that was not perfectly suiting her at the time…she was clearly going to be a challenging handful. I decided I was not going to change *her* by reacting as I just had, so *I* would have to be the one to change…as from this minute.

At the end of the scheduled working day I had completed all that was on my list; with no desire to go up and just sit in my room, I decided to continue with the shed repairs. I dragged out some lengths of 'tongued and grooved'; sorted out hinges, screws, and other bits for a broken door… I turned and there was Marcus.

"You *don't* talk to Mrs Murdoch like that" he sneered…his face angry, as he adopted a posture of sheer defiance.

"I just *did*" I snapped back…and carried on sorting.

I then felt guilty…he was only Jo's age, around nine years old; I turned and knelt down on one knee beside him.

"What's your problem Marcus; why all the sneering and aggravation?" I asked him quietly.

"If you must know…we don't *want* you here"

"And by 'we'…you are referring to whom?"

"All of us…but *especially me*."

"Can you explain that?" I enquired gently…with unrecognisable new-found patience.

"We were doing ok. My Daddy is ill and we can't play so much, but we were doing ok. He doesn't want anyone else in our house…*especially you,*" he added with another sneer.

"And what about Mrs Murdoch, should she not have someone to help on the Land…and give her more time to enjoy herself?"

"She isn't *supposed* to enjoy herself…she's here to look after *us*"

I stood up, "Look Marcus, we are not going to agree and I have tried to help. I am not particularly happy either if you really want to know…which you probably don't because you are too selfish. You go back and see if there is anything *you* can do to help, I want to get this shed done. Just go and leave me to get on…please"

With that he unexpectedly kicked out and caught me a beauty on the side of my leg…I pretended to pursue him…he raced away as fast as his legs would carry him. It was pointless being upset…but the 'especially you' rang in my ears a bit.

"Forget it," I said to myself, the change must be awful for them all.

What a lousy day I decided; the surprise of the Guardian question from the doctor, her temper tantrum and my worrying response…and now a kick in the leg for trying to help.

CHAPTER 5

The days were getting warmer and I was settling in well. Starting each morning at six o'clock, and carrying out he repairs until late evening, left tired as well as grubby; because of the Aga, there was always a steaming hot bath to be had. It was luxury to relax after such a long day… and I happily turned in immediately afterwards.

Eva once asked, where had I ever gone, and what young friends had I made while in London; the answer was none on both counts. The same could be said here but it bothered me not…without the moody Mrs Murdoch this situation would have been bliss!

The work requirements were fairly straightforward, and I loved the freedom they gave; I was even beginning to like these silly, skinny little hens. They were livestock after all; needing exactly the same attention as any other beast, they slowly got to know me, and *vice verse.*

There was always one at least who would run to greet you the moment the door was opened; always one who would look haughtily down at you…or ignore you altogether. And I loved the way they all perched at night in 'their place'…never swapping round...they were all right after all I decided.

I had suffered frequently from Mrs Murdoch's tongue and many a sideswipe from Marcus, but I managed to not rise to the bait. This was proving extremely difficult at times, but after having considered everything, I realised that if I *did* lose my temper…I would be seriously done for. If I wanted to make something of my life I would have to learn many controls…starting with my temper had been a good thing! I loved the work; the outdoor life was wonderful and, with nowhere else to go, I knew I needed the accommodation…and the money that came with it.

It had afforded me my bike.

I was allowed two part afternoons free each week, once all the outside work was completed; this was usually about an hour after lunch and I returned in time to check around and lock up in the yards. As the days grew longer the more freedom I had; the free-range lot only went to roost near dusk, you couldn't lock *them* up when it suited you. I collected the eggs and took them to the kitchen where Mrs Murdoch graded them for the market; that was her only involvement now, she was doing virtually nothing outside and I preferred it that way. It was a heavy, tiring work load, but I loved the freedom to work responsibly alone…and she had never complained. She had not praised or thanked me much either, but I could handle that, she worried me not.

On my first afternoon break, I returned to Methuselah and brokered a deal. He turned out to be a very kind man, even offering to let me have the bike, then pay weekly…I said I would prefer to pay for it…then when I rode it for the first time *it would be mine*.

In the Homes we none of us had things that were 'ours'…everything was shared. Some of the kids had family who sent to them for birthdays and so on; it was they who really had a problem with that as a scheme. I received my gifts from Uncle Tom while I was holidaying there…and they stayed with them. To actually own something paid for with my own money…well what a thing that was to be!

I made the deposit payment with one of the notes so kindly given by Mrs Lewis, and returned once a week with what I felt I could afford; I could have paid it nearly all in one go, except I decided I would always keep a 'nest egg'.

This plan came about one day when cleaning for Mrs Lewis's sister Barbara; I found a quantity of silver change down the sides of the sitting room furniture. Because of my honesty in handing this to her, she had presented it to me in its entirety; a considerable sum of money for me. I decided to keep it to one side, and only use any of it in an absolute emergency; I was aware of the safe secure feeling that 'financial cushion' gave me. No-one can ever know what lies ahead and I was acutely aware of the constant precariousness of *my* life-style; Mrs Lewis had been right on so many occasions and this was her advice too.

Mrs Murdoch had provided the trousers and blouses in which to work; thanks to Eva's clear-out and generosity, I had plenty of other clothes. I did not buy sweets and things so I only needed to buy toiletries with the £1. each week I was paid.

I walked the lane with a spring in my step on the Big Day I had arranged to collect my bike; Mr Methuselah met me with a huge grin...just like mine! He had checked the brakes, greased all round and carried out a good service...*and* given the wheels a special gleaming polish.

"All yours now my dear" he said kindly.

I felt absolutely *thrilled*.

When I rode away down that lane for the first time…the angels turned the pedals.

My case and clothes I owned…but they were donated by the Homes and dear Eva. My bike I owned…but *I had bought it myself*! It was my first real acquisition…I was bursting with the excitement.

Upon my return from that first short ride, I showed my pride and joy to Mrs Murdoch; she had known I was paying off a little at a time…and here at last was the longed-for day. She was suitably unimpressed and with my usual (silent) expletive of '*sod it*', I took it to the garage as ordered.

I went straight upstairs, and with no time left of my break to go back out, I wrote long letters to Mrs Lewis and Eva. I thanked Mrs Lewis again for her kindness; in a previous letter, I explained how I had used some of the money for the deposit. She knew all about the arrangements to pay, and it was lovely to be able to tell her at last it was mine. I knew *she* would have shared in my delight.

The bike was not only my pride and joy…it was total freedom; each day my time off was arranged, I rode for mile upon mile. I discovered all sorts of little villages…and how steep some of the blooming hills were to reach them!

The many roads led to Paddock Wood and all points east; north up the lanes in the Maidstone direction and south to Tunbridge Wells. I purposely avoided the familiar Homes environments; there was no desire at all on my part to return to them. I ate my lunch before these trips; because of the un-predictability of my return time, Mrs Murdoch kindly arranged to leave a sandwich in the larder, which I ate after seeing to the locking-up outside. With the exercise and less to eat, I was soon on the way to being the way I liked to be, strong and healthy; I really had forgotten what 'fit' felt like after the sedentary life in the office in London, but I was improving with every outing.

I pedalled up a steep hill one day and was all set to 'cruise' down the other side. A short distance ahead was a little black Austin driven by a Granddad with his little Granny beside him; he must have been doing all of 25mph!

*"Right, now to try this thing out"*

I stood up on the pedals and pumped hard on the short flat straight, then head down right over the handlebars; I really got a move on as I approached the descent. In no time at all I swept past him at a really fast pace, glancing across to my left as I did so, I caught his expression…*what a picture*; I looked back to make sure he was not getting out because he thought he had stopped!

I loved those days and the feeling of sheer liberation they gave me. I managed to blow away all the oppressive cobwebs of restraint at work, where the atmosphere sometimes was stifling. *This was heaven.*

# CHAPTER 6

The difficult atmosphere continued over next three or four months; this became a burden, simply because of the work-load…and valiantly keeping my temper in check. Mr Murdoch was by now virtually inert and this added nothing to the demeanour of his wife. I tried desperately to understand her, but she was at times impossible; I figured if I had some one as reliable and able as me…I would be pleased…and show it.

She struck me as being completely selfish; now things were not perfect for her, she was sulking. On more than one occasion I thought, *I bet you stamped your foot when you were a little girl.*

I could only guess at the finances, but there were photographs around displaying big cars and smart clothes, and it was she who had placed the advertisement wanting some one to take on the work. I didn't know of course what "Stonegate's" paid for the eggs, but I did know the yield had gone up considerably since I had done the repairs, and strategically placed down the rat poison; surely that would have covered my tiny wage.

The absolute light in my life was Katie.

I had seen a complete change in her after the day we returned from the doctor. She cried when her mother shouted, but it was not just the noise; she saw my disappointment, and was upset for me as well. She had thoroughly enjoyed the outing, especially the running home with the push-chair, screaming with excitement and laughter as we did; met with that angry tirade was upsetting…quite obviously for us both.

Sawing a section for a wall length a few days later, I became aware of 'someone watching'; that spooky feeling that runs down your spine. I turned around in time to see Katie; shoulders dropped and with head down, slowly walking up towards the house. I called out her name…she hurried back towards me.

"Am I pleased to see you Katie…*just* the right time…I could do with a hand if you wouldn't mind. It would be easier to saw if you sat on the end to hold it steady…would you do that for me please?"

Her little face beamed; she sat astride, as if on a playground see-saw with her hands gripping tightly either side. It made her laugh when she saw that the vibration was making her hands wobble. From that moment we became friends; relaxed, with confidence building by the day, she became almost my shadow and chattered away all the time while I worked.

There was something about her that stirred a memory, then I realised she had the same expression I had seen on my little friend Michael's face; he looked exactly like she did whenever he was perplexed.

I had missed him so much for a very long time, and still frequently thought about him…but as they had threatened, I never saw him again. It dawned on me too, that for the first time since those days, I was enjoying the company of a little friend. Although ten years older than she, there was something familiarly similar about it; perhaps I just needed to be reminded of Michael.

Because of the work load, I was devoid of any social life; Katie's presence created a greatly improved environment. I found a little 'toffee-hammer' among the tools; showing Katie how to hold it properly, she would happily bang tacks into off-cuts of wood all day long. She loved to hold the screws and things I needed for each job; carefully counted, put into a tin cup and handed to me when I asked.

When her mother came out with an afternoon drink, we would sit down and rest together…sadly, that was when she fell silent again. She was a dear little thing, but there were times I felt I had a happier childhood than she was experiencing. I at least always had someone to play with; most of the Homes held sixty kids or more.

We didn't have a great deal in the way of toys, but we were inventive. Our Rounders games consisted of two teams of at least twenty; the bat was a worn straight stick, and the ball was a balding tennis ball. There was also a fair selection of board games and jigsaws for the rainy days…we were contented enough.

We imagined of course, that the Outside kids would have all they could ever want, but she appeared to have nothing; no interests, no books or games, not even a tricycle. Her 'place' in the family also seemed strange. Her mother was occupied entirely with nursing the sick father and spoiling the pompous older brother; all too frequently she was left out.

There was a welcome change to her life which benefited us both; the hours sped by with having her company, and she looked and sounded better by the day. With new-found confidence she talked more openly; her body strength improved with all the extra exercise…and she was as a brown as a little berry.

She joined me as soon as Marcus left for school; Mrs Murdoch did once ask if I minded...and showed too much relief for my liking when I said I didn't. We only returned indoors for lunch and tea, but then we split up; a weary but happy little Katie to bed...me back to my work.

It was she who had originally drawn my attention to the awful atmosphere within the house, oppressive would be the most apt description. From a 'normal' happy little girl, chatting cheerfully and banging with her baby hammer, her mood reversed the moment we entered the house; she immediately became withdrawn.

With the pressing need to familiarise myself with everything, and my pleasure at doing what I so enjoyed, I had not fully taken in the now patently obvious. Mrs Murdoch also had to be outside to be anything bordering on polite and relaxed...she too appeared dominated by the pressures from indoors.

I was grateful the rats had come, literally, to my rescue; the long summer days had kept me successfully and happily outside. Even with all the many diversions and constant bad atmosphere, I worked incredibly hard. On the five days I had no time off, I continued to work on the repairs long after supper and right up to dusk if I was completely absorbed.

I was also aware I desperately wanted Mrs Murdoch to like me, and appreciate my endeavours to brighten her surroundings; the difference was already remarkable…but she rarely commented. There was no additional wage on offer…but there was also no pleasure in being confined to my bedroom, which was my only alternative.

On a couple of occasions I had entered the room where the old man sat; other than that I had no idea about lay-out of the rest of the house. Mrs Murdoch provided a hot lunch, and a sandwich or similar for tea; these meals were still conducted in silence as on the first day.

It had therefore been a true delight to have the outside as my almost exclusive territory.

The weeks passed by in a sort of routine; her requirements all day, and the work outside occupying my evenings. Because of these extremely long hours, the wood replacement and other repairs were now complete; general upkeep would be simpler from now on.

On the hen houses I'd replaced missing wall timbers, window and door uprights and new felt roof coverings. The grass areas were cleared of rubbish; the apple trees were immaculate…and I had installed a second tap!

The whole place had a completely different look about it…cared for. I felt rather proud of what I had achieved…*and* Katie told me it all looked better. She was right too; as no word of thanks from Mrs Murdoch was expected, I felt no real sense of disappointment when none were forthcoming.


As sweetly as Katie had developed…Marcus was becoming worse.

He was invariably sullen, bad-tempered and rude; his bullying manner was a constant annoyance. He would taunt Katie in an unpleasant, spiteful way and was extremely jealous of any attention bestowed upon her. I explained he would have better things happen to him if he was a nicer person...he was too much like his mother to see the sense in that.

He was very aware too that I was utterly hamstrung as far as rebuke was concerned.

On one occasion he'd actually punched Katie in the back, hard enough to make her cry; I seriously scolded him, finally telling him loudly to "Push off". He immediately ran up to the house and told his mother…the two-syllable call came and I was severely reprimanded…in front of him!

One particular afternoon, preparing to clear up before tea, I was sweeping and cleaning the back yard; brooms large and small, the hose and the pitchforks were all in use to get the job done properly. Marcus turned up, made some usual rude comments, and because I ignored him, left again.

Now he was back…he picked up the pitch-fork; it was the lighter and smaller of the two, but could still be dangerous if not used correctly. It was long-handled with two thin, sharp prongs; I found it easiest for dragging loose straw off the yards.

"Marcus *leave* it please…*just put it <u>down</u>*" I asked sternly.

It was a most unwieldy piece of equipment at the best of times and although he was nearly as tall as me, he was no size to cope with it.

To my surprise he obeyed, and almost immediately brought it over. However, upon reaching me, he intentionally thrust downwards with his full force…*it went straight into my foot*!

The immediate pain was extraordinary; as I yelled, he disappeared as fast as his legs would carry him. Fortunately Katie had already gone in to wash her hands; she would have been terribly upset to witness that.

I managed to catch a hold of the handle before it fell away from me; immediately and instinctively I pulled the fork out…but resisted the compelling temptation to remove my wellington boot.

I could feel already the stickiness inside that was quite obviously blood; hopping and hobbling around I cleared all the gear away and slowly made my way to the kitchen door where I called loudly for Mrs Murdoch.

"What do you want…what have you done *now*?" she asked crossly.

I struggled to remove my boot and sock from my damaged foot; even I was surprised at the state of it…there was blood everywhere…this was a serious injury. With my footwear removed, the pain had already become more intense.

I told her exactly what her beloved little son had done, but she chose to ignore it; in fact I thought she played the situation down when she said,

"Well you had better change and get down to the doctor ...or do you want your tea first?"

I ignored this particularly crass comment and asked if I could have a rag to stop the blood going everywhere; she clearly thought I was being dramatic, and with an audible 'tut', handed me a tea towel.

I hopped upstairs, but there was nothing I could do about the bleeding; I washed my hands, put on a clean thick work sock, and hobbled back downstairs. With the old man and the children to care for, she could not have driven me; thank goodness the doctor was close by. In only my socks, I pedalled one footed and he saw me immediately.

He removed the already blood-soaked sock by cutting it up the side...and let out a low whistle when he saw the extent of the wound. In answer to his questions, I explained everything while he was getting me cleaned up; he did not make any comment, but he was very gentle and spoke kindly. The worst part was a really painful injection...administered directly into the wound!

"I am truly sorry to hurt you Sue, but that had to done because the damage was caused by a farmyard implement; can you imagine all the muck there was on *that*…besides what was pushed through from your boot and woolly sock? The 'insides' you could see sticking out will return to their rightful place, but not until the swelling has gone down"

He continued in a more serious tone;

"You *must* rest the whole leg up in front of you for at least two days; on the third, I want you to return for a new dressing. If this one becomes bloodied, or you feel at all uncomfortable before then, Mrs. Murdoch *must* send for me *immediately*. I can already see you won't be able to work for at least a week…and anyway, I will need to see you before you resume. Sit quietly now while I write all that in a note for Mrs Murdoch; she will just have to cope without you. It was her son who caused it, and she managed for long enough before…so you must not worry."

I was not going to because he was right; after all the extra hours I had worked for no extra money…a couple of days just resting would be brilliant.

Once done, he supplied me with a little brown bottle of pain killers; I could take these as I needed, but some other pills I was ordered to take for ten days…and that was it…all over.

He forbade me to walk the few hundred yards back to the house; kindly tying my bike to the back of his car, he made a special journey.

"You should think about going straight to your bed; you're already looking extremely pale Sue, so please take care…*and make sure you rest*" was his parting shot.

After putting my bike into the garage, I hobbled awkwardly into the kitchen; Mrs Murdoch at last looked a little more concerned.

"You've been gone for *ages*…was that the doctor driving you home?" she enquired quietly.

I explained it was because I was to completely rest my foot for two days, and not to work for at least a week; I gave her the doctor's note. She read it with a rather puzzling look on her face…but I need not have worried.

As kindly and quietly as before, she said cheerily,

"Right Sue, you go out to the garden bench in the sunshine, put your foot up on the seat, and I will follow with your tea…you must be starving now"

*Blimey, what a turn up*!

I was so relieved at this positive reaction from her…I had fully expected a temper tantrum. With the feeling of nausea gone, she was correct about my hunger; I tucked into the sandwiches and a huge piece of cake.

While having a drink of the lovely home-made lemonade…I turned as she reappeared beside me.

In her hand was my case…*which she had packed.*

Very quietly…but emphatically…she addressed me.

"Your pay for the rest of this week is in your case, along with all your belongings. Now get your bike from the garage and leave…I am not having you lounging around here without working…I cannot afford you."

She lowered my case to the ground beside me.

Without meeting my gaze, she picked up my glass and plate…turned around… and silently walked away.

CHAPTER 7

We have a *solar plexus* in our head…I know…I had just been kicked in mine.

The blow was hard…brutal…and totally unexpected.

It distributed all cogent thought to the extreme edges of my mind; I sat back with eyes closed, waiting for order to restore itself. I seemed instinctively to know that what she had said, she had meant.

I 'came to' staring at the garden ahead, with no idea how long I had been there; the warmth of the sun had gone…already replaced by the early evening chill. It took a further undefined length of time to motivate myself to think, or move at all, but then I picked up my case.

Slowly and painfully limping to the garage, I slumped down against the cold stone wall.

Gazing lovingly at my cherished bike, I felt a deep numbing sadness…so many happy hours and now the means to convey me…*to where*?

Gradually, with the urgent need to do *something,* I was becoming more able to deal with the practicalities of this situation. I looked around the garage to see if there was anything available which would enable me to attach the case to my bike…I couldn't carry it any other way. Farms always have an ample supply of binder twine and the like; there was some on a hook on the wall. I selected a thick long length and proceeded with the arrangement to fix it securely in place.

Dear Eva had given me the case along with the donation of the clothes; it was a cream coloured imitation skin of some sort. The top and bottom were soft and expanded, only the front and other sides were rigid. This had been ideal for the clothes, and now proved the perfect design for tying to the bike frame. I threaded the rope through the metal supports of the case handle, then simply attached to the front handlebar upright, and around the saddle support at the back.

I was deeply aware of extremely slow thought…of focussing and concentrating all my attention on the demands in hand…even my foot did not hurt as badly.

I looked around the shelves and found the 'tea tins' I knew were there; these were pale blue enamel containers with a lid and small handle, used for carrying hot drinks out to the fields, especially at haymaking. With no idea of where I was heading next, I took one of these and filled it with water from the garage tap; at least I'd be able to take my tablets.

"*Where are you going?*" I asked myself anxiously.

I had not yet finished my preparations…so could not answer.

The bandage looked very white and new, and extremely, clinically hygienic; to help keep it that way and my foot in safe order, I pulled out some stripped Hessian sack which was also readily available. I loosely bound two or three lengths from toes up to calf; it looked just like a puttee worn by soldiers in the Eastern desert.

Striving desperately to fend off an air of impending despair, I leaned against the door jamb; trying to breathe properly, and with tears beginning to sting my eyes, I surveyed my handiwork. The case looked ungainly, but was well secured with the water can safely stuffed down the side. My foot looked and felt alright.

It *had* occurred fleetingly, to the shambles which was now my mind, she may come back out with a change of heart; she didn't.

I picked up my bike, now packed and ready to leave; I looked out across the land, to the buildings on which I had worked for all those long hours. With the fresh cut grass and tidy apple trees, hen houses that looked well cared for, and all the yards gleaming,

I could clearly see the enormous difference I had made to the whole place. I would miss my silly, skinny little hens I had so carefully nurtured…fatter now and laying as frequently as they should.

I suddenly felt a nausea rise up from the pit of my stomach.

"God Almighty…w*hat will Katie do?*"

My mind flashed back to a day in Barnardo's when I was four; the morning, I discovered Michael, had gone…just moved away from our Home…without an opportunity to say 'good-bye'. What a horrifying irony that I should now be in the same situation…in reverse.

The additional irony was, for all the time I'd worked for Mrs Murdoch, I had been extremely careful so that just this situation should not occur. I had controlled my temper…never given rise for complaint…and had worked for many hours longer than designed…or paid for...and for what?

I was now without a home…or have anywhere to go…because of the meanness of the woman for whom

I'd worked so hard; it seemed to be just too unfair for words.

With uncontrolled, unstoppable tears now burning on my cheeks, I whispered,

"Good-bye my darling little Katie...please forgive me...it wasn't my fault...don't ever forget me...please be happy".

## CHAPTER 8

In the rapidly failing light, and still in a state of mental inertia, I automatically wheeled my bike out of the garage…down the short drive…and turned right.

*To where?*

About a half mile along the lane was a crossroads; I stopped there and looked all around. I had never felt as alone in my life…signposts have no significance at all if you have nowhere arranged to go. I had recently travelled all these lanes with such joy on my precious time off; now they had to become a destination.

I studied the names again. "Pembury...Pembury?" I kept thinking; somewhere in the back of my mind this 'rang a bell'… then like a flash, it came to me.

About eleven years previously, when I was six, I had been at St. Christopher's in Tunbridge Wells; the Head Maintenance man lived with his family in the grounds of the Home. The 'cottage' where I lived was just over the road from the back of their place. They were kind warm-hearted people, we all liked them…and I well remember going to them for gorgeous teas.

About three years ago at the last Home, Miss Boagey the Matron had read out a sort of 'round robin' letter. Mr Meadows had sadly died; it was suggested that anyone who knew him should write a letter of condolence to his widow. This I did with a couple of the others, and now I recalled the address…well part of it anyway. When I had added my letter to the already addressed envelope, I'd looked hard at the destination; I had spotted the capital 'P'…was it going to where my Uncle Tom lived in Pluckley?

No, it wasn't…it was Pembury!

I turned left into that lane with a less befuddled mind; this was genuine inspiration and my spirits rose…at last a familiar.

I still had no clear idea of what I could do with this recollection, but the improvement in my mood made me want to reflect on the current situation.

Immediately, and inexplicably, I thought of Maisie my estranged mother, who had put me and the others in Barnardo's; I could see her mean features sneering at my dreadful dilemma. A defiant sniff soon ended the tears, and with greater resolve, I set off…to wherever would be my next destination.

The case bulged out on either side of the bike frame; I wanted to rest my foot, but getting on to the saddle was impossible...this gave me no option but to walk. As I made slow painful progress, all there was to hear was the regular 'clicking' of the wheels; this was enormously comforting for some reason. I reckoned, by reversing the times when things had occurred, it must be between 7.00 and 7.30pm.

Dusk and the beautiful gloaming light would be good…and the dark of night would be perfect; inside my head was already black…I wanted desperately for everything else to be the same.

My heart weighed a ton.

Ahead in the distance I could see the steep hill where a short while ago, with child-like jubilation, I had overtaken a Granddad in his little car. I decided to make it to the beginning and then rest; it gave me a goal, and that was a refreshing, uplifting feeling.

It was a longer distance than estimated but I made it; gratefully and gently, I lay down my bike, and relaxed against the thick wooden upright of the five-bar gate at the entrance to a field. I had no idea how far I had already come but I felt fine; my foot was not hurting too badly.

Slowly my thoughts were arranging a more recognisable order; I needed to take the tablets, but must first be able to replenish my tin. Standing again, I saw to my left, an old bath tub used as a drinking trough for the cattle. Good luck was with me as above it there was a tap…as long as it was switched on.

I made my way cautiously over the rutted ground; the freezing cold water gushed out for me. I moistened my face, took the tablets with the remaining water, refilled my tin…and returned to sit for just a little while longer. I was now at the bottom of a really steep hill; however, this was rural Kent at its best, not a house in sight…just fields.

The encouragement of a 'goal' was the ideal solution for me; I decided to reach one field at a time. Leaving my resting place, I resumed the journey…and began my deliberations.

Mrs Murdoch's dismissal of me was an absolute disgrace and incredibly cruel…and yet I felt strange. I concentrated on this to try to reach some sort of understanding…then it dawned; except for little Katie, there was no attached emotion!

Mrs Murdoch had 'used and abused' and had disposed of me like an old rag. I had tried so hard to be empathetic and understanding; had learnt to control my own feelings because of hers…but I had felt nothing for the woman on an emotional level.

With Michael, Uncle Tom and Auntie Dodd, my loss was tragic because I cared so very much. The disappointment of the fiasco that was my homecoming to Maisie mattered less, because I cared not for the people involved. The same thing with all the 'friends' I had met while in London, and now the Murdochs…they had been there for a short period in my life, had made me happy or not, and now they were gone.

I immediately realised the safest way to conduct myself in the future…and up came my barrier…then and there. A conscious decision was made; I would trust only when it was essentially the right thing to do…I would love, but only in response… I would be kind, as that was my nature…but at all times, my barrier would stay in place.

If I maintained that protection… no one would ever break my heart again.

On departing my refuge I felt considerably encouraged and inspired.

The sun was rapidly setting, and the hedgerows and trees were alive with the late chorus; the sky was changing through all the colours from pink to deep indigo. This time of day or the dawn are when you most love the countryside…and to be in Kent. The isolation I'd felt at being so alone in this enormous world was temporarily forgotten, as I allowed every single sound and vision to fill my head.

The darkness rapidly approached, and with it came the stillness and the colder air; my loneliness enveloped me once more. As I slowly walked, tiring now with a throbbing in my foot, I had to decide,

*"What on earth am I going to do?"*

I knew I couldn't walk much further with the increasing pain moving up my leg, making the muscles ache even more; I was beginning to regret having seen the damage at the Doctor's.

He had explained the fork had gone between two bones, in effect separating them for the short while until it was removed. This bruising would be sore he assured me, but not to worry about that. The revolting sight had been the huge swelling, and the insides that squirted out onto the skin from where I had yanked out the fork.

Now that it was throbbing painfully, I could 'see' it all again…and the swelling was growing tight within the bandage.

I was becoming desperate…I would have to stop.

I suddenly realised with that thought…what options presented themselves to me?

*None…* was the chilling exact answer to that.

While I had been walking, I was *going* 'some where'.

If I had to stop…*I had nowhere to go.*

CHAPTER 9

The total desolation I now felt made me shudder; with no other options available to me, I concluded…I would just have to sleep in one of the fields. The physical situation worried me not…but the lonely isolation thrust upon me by some bitch, who KNEW I had nowhere else but where I lay my head…*that* now made me angry.

That anger gave me strength.

With the decision made as to where I would sleep, the next plan was how to go about it? I mentally went through my possessions. The mackintosh I was wearing when leaving the Homes was a real waterproof…that would make my groundsheet. From Eva I had an assortment of jumpers and cardigans with which I could cover myself and form a pillow. I was wearing the thick 'working' corduroy trousers; they would keep me warm.

My pace had slowed considerably and I walked with enormous difficulty, but suddenly I realised I was nearing the village; the road now had cottages at irregular intervals. This made me want to go on a bit further; I wondered if there was a pub…and if so, would they know where Mrs Meadows lived?

At last, I was at the top of the hill and as I turned left, I saw the pub, but it was in complete darkness…shut. I knew little about such places but I seemed to think it must be gone 10.30, and their closing time. It made little difference except it had taken me all that time to go about three miles…no wonder I hurt and was tired.

I passed two possible fields on my left, but both had the strong pungent smell of fox; I did not fancy being in such close proximity to Mr Reynard. He was not my greatest bucolic friend, and that smell on my clothing would have been utterly repugnant.

I limped painfully onwards along a narrow pavement; leaving behind the main part of the village and the unlit houses to my left. On the opposite side of the road…there it was …the perfect place. Not too large…high hedges for shelter…and no smell of fox.

I crossed over the road and in through the gate.

I hobbled awkwardly across the rough meadow, just a short way alongside the tall, thick beech hedge; desperate to sit down and stop the pain from my foot, I found a flat even space. Gently laying my bike on the ground, I opened the case…firstly to check my 'nest egg'; it was safe in the cardigan pocket in which it was always kept hidden.

I found my pay in the usual brown envelope…not a word added…just the wages.

"*Miserable cow*" I muttered.

I decided I could only do the rest while sitting on the ground…what a beautiful relief it was to get off my foot. The 'groundsheet' was a bit on the short side, but everything else seemed adequate. I managed to fold some small items of clothing into a bundle and wrapped them inside a skirt…the perfect pillow.

Eva had given me a very large, long heavy cardigan, which I would now turn into a wonderful blanket. Managing to wriggle my legs down the ample arms, and bringing the bottom hem right up my back, I was enshrouded…and could still do up the enormous wooden buttons. I reckoned that if my already aching legs got cold, I would never sleep.

It was hardly camping; but I had somewhere sheltered to rest behind high hedges, it was cold but dry, and successfully coping was a lift to my spirits. Feeling exhausted, but at last feeling more comfortable…I stopped for a moment, and two thoughts occurred;

"*What the Hell must I look like*?" was the first.

Then I surveyed the scene…the Case, the Bike and Me…and a Maurice wisdom came to mind;

"If you can't have what you want…want what you have".

*Yeah…right Maurice…I'd try and remember that*!

I even managed a quiet chuckle to myself.

About one in three of the fields I'd passed had working taps; my water tin was full, so I took more of the tablets. Before getting into my cardigan, I had slowly unwound the Hessian dressing; I realised it had been a brilliant idea as although it was fairly wet, the bandage beneath was dry. I did not dare loosen that off, reckoning the swelling would reduce now I was off my foot.

I combed my hair; rubbed my face and hands over with a still-damp flannel, and squeezed a little toothpaste onto my tongue to freshen my mouth. Pleased with what I had achieved, I lastly dabbed on some '4711', the perfume used by my Auntie Dodd; this always reminded me of them both, and I had never been without a bottle since I first earned enough to pay for it.

I snuggled down under the black sky and the stars, lying very still in the silent darkness; the tablets seemed to be taking away the pain, and I was slowly becoming cosy and warm.

With the familiar perfume comforting me, I was deeply aware of being in the same County as the two dearest people God had ever put on His Earth.

When Auntie Dodd and Uncle Tom had arranged with the Homes to take me for outings and holidays, they gave me the only truly happy times I had in the fourteen years spent in Care. Although only about seven years old, the impression of their affection was staggering; they were loving and generous…and had eventually applied to adopt me.

Barnardo's apparently approached my mother, a woman I had never seen since being placed in their care; she refused…and I was never allowed to see them again. That decision broke my heart…and the dreadful pain was a constant thing. I closed my eyes and allowed my thoughts to wander comfortingly but painfully back.

A few miles away to the East of my field, in their beautiful cottage in Pluckley, I could now recall in detail, 'my' white bedroom, with an entire pink night ensemble always laid out waiting for me on my visits.

Their bathroom; with my special pink soap and, framed above the bath, the 'Mabel-Lucie-Attwell' poem I learned by heart.

I could see and hear Cook waiting to hug me in greeting.

The "Charlie Smirke on Tulyar" framed photograph that hung between hall and dining room.

The sound of their laughter, the beautiful diction when they stopped laughing and talked to me; directly to me…just me… Oh how Special was that?

The gentle of Auntie Dodd's hands and smile… and the rough of Uncle Tom's 'Harris Tweed' jacket I could feel on my bare legs when he picked me up and cuddled me.

The visible outwards signs of being their little Princess; the knowing and feeling, for the first time in my young life, that I was not just loved…I was adored.

The realisation that I loved them…what a revelation that was for me; and the wonderful, lasting effect this had on all of my childhood.

The warmth of their cuddles and kisses 'Goodnight'…never again to be experienced after they were gone from me.

The despised Barnardo's, Boagey and Maisie, had physically wrested these loving people from my life, but their memory, even with the dreadful lasting pain of that severance, stayed undimmed with time.

In that instant I knew exactly what I was going to do. I had to keep unchanged these visions, within my head and heart forever; never to fail with the frailty of age and eventually die away. These were the perfect and only 'Treasure' I had ever owned…or indeed had ever wanted to; if I never loved, nor was loved again…I had my all here with me.

No-one else had known, or ever would in the future, exactly what these people were to me…they were Life itself.

The agonising pain of these memories overwhelmed my entire emotion, and finally exhausted me; I allowed the tears to come and cried myself to sleep. I knew that if my memories remained unchanged, Uncle Tom and Auntie Dodd would never ever leave me.

With their love and inspiration as my strength…I knew; I could take on the world tomorrow…and get through whatever happened.

CHAPTER 10

A sudden flash of light…full in my face…woke me with a dreadful shock; I snapped my eyes tightly closed again and barely moved a muscle…*straining* to hear who or what had disturbed me.

Silence…the dense black empty silence of rural Kent.

My thumping heart was settling again; I very slowly opened my eyes. It was a flash of light alright…from a shop exactly opposite where I was camping; Human Beings…Civilisation.

"*Good Morning World*"…I yelled in my head.

What a stroke of luck!

I moved onto my side, and from my vantage point at ground level, by peering under the hedge I could clearly see what was going on.

A man inside appeared to be working on his own; as I watched I heard the sound of an approaching vehicle. Within moments, a large van pulled up; the driver and shopkeeper then carried bundles of newspapers into the shop. From the lights on the van, I could make out the name of the place "Bo-Peep Stores". I bet *they* would know if Mrs Meadows still lived in the village.

I found myself suddenly propelled back into very centre of the real world. The previous day had been a surreal, agonising experience…but my bedtime decision and gut-wrenching tears had washed away the worst properties of that particular.

I turned my mind to matters practical, and decided I had better make a move while I still could, under the cover of darkness. I did not know the exact time but the paper man was busy preparing to open his shop; already the sky was displaying the milky black that precedes the dawn.

My foot was not hurting too badly as I sat myself up, but then I had another surprise…I was absolutely soaked through; my hair, all my top clothing and my case…thoroughly drenched in the dew of the night and early morning…but I had stayed warm.

Dragging my case towards me across the wet grass, I found some clean underwear and a dry jumper. I managed quite well to 'wash' with my now soaking wet flannel, left fortuitously on top of the case, and I changed without too many problems.

I dried my hair as well as I could; it was very thick so I didn't do it particularly well, but once combed it was alright. I repeated the toothpaste on the tongue as of last night and that was me, fit to take on the world…until I stood up.

As soon as my foot touched the ground, the pain seared upwards through my leg; using up the last drop of water, I quickly took my tablets and sat back down to give them the chance to work.

Rapidly now the day was waking up around me; I could see all sorts of comings and goings opposite…obviously people collecting papers on their way to work. I continued to busy myself to take my mind off my foot. Still sitting I stowed away everything, even the damp stuff, into my case…to be ready for whatever and wherever today may take me.

I was aware of no qualms or worries about what the day may hold…I simply held a feeling of growing optimism. Thinking about Uncle Tom was always going to be hard but I knew this forward-looking inspiration was of their doing. They would both have been so proud of the way I had conducted myself yesterday and last night; I felt proud too.

The milky sky was beginning to take on the developing lightness of the new morning; the birds were in full chorus, and the rabbits were making their way from the hedgerows to play.

"*I wonder how many of you came over and looked at me last night*?" I thought.

I attempted again to stand but it was only slightly easier; I was not yet able to move about well enough to tie the case back on to my bike. The shop was well into their new day so I decided; leave everything in the field, lean on my bike for support, pluck up courage…and go!

Giving myself a final check over, and deciding I would have to do…I lifted my bike…and struggling like hell made it over the road, parked on the walkway and entered the shop.

The expression on the shopkeeper's face made me immediately realise I could not look nearly as good as I felt…there was a discernible tremor in his voice when he greeted "Good morning". Poor man, but as I could do nothing about the situation immediately, I tried to ignore it; with greetings exchanged I cut straight to the matter in hand.

"I am really sorry to trouble you…but do you know if a lady called Mrs Meadows lives in the village?"

He looked at me kindly but in silence; I realised I would have to be more informative as to who *I* was.

91

"Look…I know this must seem extremely strange but…."

I started to tell him about the night in the field and what led up to it; with only the beginning of this situation explained, he interrupted me.

*"My God*…you must have a cup of tea…I'll get you a chair…I'll just get my wife…you sit there…I'll be back!"

He was quite clearly shocked at my revelations and returned in mere moments with his wife… and the promised welcome hot drink.

"Right…start again and tell us both" they encouraged…and I did.

When I had finished they had amazing news; Mrs Meadows *did* still live in the village and I had walked right past her house last night…*that close*! It was literally a couple of hundred yards away…one of the unlit houses I had walked past last night!

"You come through to the back parlour with me Sue. John will get your bags and stuff from the field…you must be starving".

I assured her I wasn't, but she insisted on something 'to take the tablets with' as she put it. The shop had held the same warm friendly atmosphere as their small neat living room, in which I was now standing.

"Now you sit yourself down there…here's a stool for your foot…I'm going to make you some more tea…and please try and eat a round of toast, your tablets will work twice as fast I promise you."

She bustled away to the kitchen; I took stock of just how fortunate the morning's events had proved.

*Could this be an omen…will things be so much better*? I decided "YES" to both questions.

She returned and sat with me while I consumed a veritable feast of doorstep thick hot buttered toast, with home-made marmalade…she laughed at my clear pleasure!

"This is so kind of you both…I really do appreciate it, very much indeed; I was beginning to lose faith in people…but there is always a good for an evil isn't there?

"And she is an evil for what she has done to you…how *dare* she. If you were mine I'd have the police on to her"

We continued with small talk and I drank the tea-pot dry…twice; purely killing time until it was a civilised hour to approach this lady's door. When it was deemed appropriate, John popped his head around the door.

"Feeling better now darling? In about ten minutes old Cyril will be up for his paper, he's got a little pick-up truck. One of the paper boys has got your stuff over and I'll ask Cyril to pack it all, and your bike, and drop you down the road…you must not damage that foot any more".

A huge lump came to my throat and my eyes were stinging; their kindness to a complete stranger was over-whelming. She came over and wrapping me in her arms allowed me the few tears needed to dissolve away the lump…if not all the hurt of Mrs Murdoch.

"You'll be okay now Sue…we all know Mrs Meadows and Bill. They will know what to do for the best and once that foot is better…you come back up and see us. You will always be welcome."

"I could not believe my luck when I woke up to your lights going on. I am glad I plucked up the courage to come over and ask. I'm thrilled to be seeing her again even if it's for a short while…but I'll come and see you, whatever happens next."

"Cyril's ready to go now dear" called John from the front of the shop.

94

With a chorus of "Good-bye and good luck" as a send off...I sat beside Cyril...to begin my next adventure.

# CHAPTER 11

With all my possessions safely in the back of Cyril's truck, and a wave to my saviours, we were off; trundling the short distance to Mrs Meadows.

"You'll be looked after now dear" said this kind man; he looked just like the doctor…but his button nose was very much more red!

He almost carried me across the road so painful was my foot;

"I'll knock…you hold on to me."

Mrs Meadows opened the door…I was thrilled and beamed a smile at her. She was silent for only a few moments after I said "Good morning Mrs Meadows"…then she let out a squeak, clapped her hands to her face and with a beaming smile, excitedly said,

"Good Lord above! It's Susan…Susan Davis…what are *you* doing here…what's happened to your foot…come on in…and you too Cyril…well well well".

Then turning and looking up toward the stairs behind her, she shouted,

"Bill, come and see who we have on OUR doorstep".

Cyril stood behind me; we were in a tiny hall with two front rooms to left and right...the stairs went straight up from the middle. I looked at her son coming slowly towards us, but then an odd thing occurred.

The stairs were becoming narrower and steeper by the moment...however many steps Bill came down...the further he was away from me.

Then all the lights went out.

*A warm comforting feeling enveloped me, which was odd as I was standing in my field; maybe the sun was out. I laughed as Mrs Meadows frantically chased the baby rabbits...but got annoyed at Bill for riding my bike down the stairs...and it felt like an elephant was standing on my foot.*

Then, for the second time in twenty-four hours, I 'came to'.

I had been in a dream because in reality I was in bed; they were all in attendance...including my Doctor! He had removed the bandage, which caused my foot to suddenly hurt more again; he gave me a warm smile as I opened my eyes, and then sat by my side.

"Well, I didn't think I would see you like this young lady. I cannot *believe* what has happened to you…why didn't you come down to me?" he asked kindly.

"It didn't occur to me at all I'm afraid…I had only met you briefly and just felt I had to get on with it."

"Like you have done all your life in the Homes," added Mrs Meadows, wisely.

"Well…you are in a terrible mess I must say; we'll sit you up and you can see the problems for yourself".

With great care from them…and no help from me, I eventually could see all around me. Cyril and Bill said their 'goodbyes' as they had to continue with their working day.

"They have been marvellous," said Mrs Meadows, "But I'll tell you all about that later".

The Doctor continued from his initial observations and showed me the damage…it had looked bad last evening…now it was *dreadful*.

He'd removed the bandage to reveal the wound; it had inflamed my foot, to what seemed to be double its size. The skin was bright scarlet, and stretched so taut it was shining…and burning like mad with the bandaging off. The same redness traversed my ankle, up my leg and thigh; it was travelling towards my groin…I was feeling sick just looking at it.

"You cannot put that foot to the ground at all for the time being Sue, but I have already spoken to your good friend; you can stay here…isn't that right Mrs Meadows?"

"*Most definitely*", she replied enthusiastically…I responded with a big grin of utter relief.

"I'm afraid now you are looking at some weeks Sue. You must not get out of bed for one whole week at least; I can't risk the poison getting any worse. I'm going to give you another injection now, some more tablets, and will call in daily".

After dealing with everything, with a gentle pat on my head, he was gone.

Alone now, Mrs Meadows sat on my bed; she cuddled me so tightly it made me cry…more big tears again. We seemed to stay like that for ages, until all the misery had left me and I could feel her affection flowing through me.

"Good girl Sue; you dry your eyes now while I go and make us a lovely fresh pot of tea."

Hearing the homely sounds of crockery being prepared in the kitchen, I took the opportunity to survey my surroundings. I was lying on a bed settee, under the window in a small bright room, with pictures and a large oval mirror adorning the walls.

On my arrival, I'd walked through a tiny front garden with a small wall; I could now hear the footfalls as people passed by on the pavement.

It was already a warm sunny day, but it was the comforting warmth of the blankets that made me realise how cold I had previously been. With a big smile and an even bigger tray, Mrs Meadows returned.

She drew up a table, and with great ceremony poured out our tea; handing me the most enormous piece of cake ever seen, she said, "Eat and drink the lot…the Doctor feels you are under-nourished… as well as being too tired for words".

At her request, I gave her a brief resume of my life in Barnardo's, Maisie and London, and all that had happened recently; leading up to my being on her doorstep. She showed clear disgust at Mrs Murdoch's' treatment and went on to tell me what had happened after I passed out in the hall.

Bill and Cyril gently lifted me off the floor; apparently, I was drifting in and out of consciousness.

Once they had the bed out, Mrs M (that was what I was to call her) managed to undress me.

Having spoken with the shop owner, Cyril knew exactly which Doctor would have seen me, and as there was no 'phone in the house, he drove to get him. He came immediately, not having even started his Surgery; when the events were explained, he was furious. Apparently Mrs Murdoch *did* have a reputation as a 'hard woman', but he would not have believed her capable of what she had done to me.

Besides the foot, he was certain I was anaemic and took blood samples while I was only half-awake. I was in fact out of 'his area' now, but he would stay involved because of the situation.

By the end of the tea, cake and long conversation, I was feeling exhausted.

"You snuggle down now Sue dear, and get some much-needed sleep. You have been working far too hard for far too long; even though young, you have to restore your strength. I'll do us a light lunch, and then have supper with Bill after work. I expect the Doctor will come then…they always turn up the moment the food is on the plate…however well you think you've timed it"

I awoke to the gentlest touch on my shoulder…it was the Doctor.

"I thought you weren't coming till after supper," I said in surprise.

"Well, I make it 6.30pm, Bill is home and waiting for you to wake…you have slept soundly for at least eight hours."

I was suitably amazed, being someone who liked to see in the dawn and enjoy a long day. He proceeded with another inspection of the wound; I looked on as well, rather reluctantly.

"There is virtually no change, except the livid is reducing to a healthier colour. You are going to need to be a patient patient," he added, laughing.

"This will take some time. How you managed that hill and those miles is beyond me, but well done for your resourcefulness. Now I have some good news for Mrs M, 'bye 'bye for now…I'll see you tomorrow."

I could feel the emotional surge always experienced in these circumstances; the extremes of kindness shown by virtual strangers. It was as overwhelming as cruelty, the other end of the spectrum…but something I would to learn to cope with. I seemed to be creating a list of things I would have to adjust to!

Before I'd even left the Homes I knew my emotions were a mess; the sexual abuse and other physical cruelty I handled in my own way, and coped with not too badly.

My mentality, sense of humour and social manners were far superior to those of the staff, this being a direct result of the 'Uncle Tom' effect…but the enduring emotional frailty was Barnardo's damaging legacy.

When Mrs M returned I was crying, simply because of all the kind tenderness…but she soon cheered me. The meal was ready; she and Bill brought mine on a tray and then followed suit. We chatted away with ease; it was amazing to think I was just over eight years old when we last met.

The 'good news' the Doctor had referred to was explained.

He had gone to see Mrs Murdoch…told of the further damage to my injury…expressed his horror and disgust at her 'unspeakable' behaviour…and then presented Mrs M with a 'reasonable' sum of money to pay for my keep.

"Blooming good job I didn't go down there," said Bill gallantly.

"While we are talking of money, I have some I could give you." I said. I then explained about my 'nest egg'…and how I bought my bike.

"Not at all," said Bill. "If Ma needs more because your recovery is longer, the Doctor will visit again; he has already told her that. I think she is very lucky the Police aren't involved…he told her that too!"

We all laughed at that remark and lifted the mood again.

I hobbled to the bathroom, thankfully just beyond the kitchen on the ground floor, and managed a thorough wash…bliss after the last 'spit and lick' in the field, but absolutely exhausting.

Once back in bed Bill brought in his daily paper…with a promise of the Telegraph the next day. Although I had not seen a paper of any sort at the Murdoch's, I'd told them how Maurice kindly gave me his each day.

"Got to keep the grey matter stirred with the crossword," he joked.

He stretched out beside me with hands behind his head; we chatted for ages.

time. The effort was well worth it; they were pleased to see me properly healing, and I was invited to have tea and a welcome seat.

Cyril had popped in frequently to see me and had kept them informed of progress; he told them how wonderful the Doctor had been…they thought Mrs Murdoch having to cough up some cash, was Justice indeed.

"I said I'd have had the police onto her if you were mine. She was responsible for you as a minor in her employ…her actions amounted to neglect and abuse of that situation", my host said with feeling.

My visit today though was for advice; which was the best paper for work advertisements was my question. Ironically they suggested the "Kent and Sussex Courier", the same one in which Mrs Lewis had first seen the Murdoch job.

"Oh, don't you worry about that, there can't be many more like her out there. You come up on Thursday and we'll have a look together", she offered kindly.

I was still not fully fit for work, but after a couple of more visits when I was…there was the new job.

A similar situation to the one I'd just left;

"Live in – Poultry – Milking Cows - House-work"
…but no child care.

The one drawback…it was in Crowborough.

I had some *very* painful memories of the Barnardo's Home there, but I would just have to get on with it; I had stayed too long with Mrs M, it was not fair to encroach now I was fit. I rang the advertised number and, with her blessing, went for the interview.

It was a long bus journey and the farm was a good half-mile from the bus stop, but I made it without too much discomfort. I approached down a beautiful lane; narrow with high hedges and tall trees, this arrangement keeping contained the unique smells of hedgerows and fields. The flora and fauna were there in abundance; cattle grazed in every field, peacefully in the early afternoon sunshine.

*"Oh! How I love the countryside"* I thought…*"It's so **good** to be back"*.

My first sight of the farmhouse was memorable.

Turning left off Harlequin Lane, a steep path took me down to the front door; the house nestled closely into the bank behind. It was a low stone-built building that had clearly once worn a thatched roof, but was now covered in red slates, that seemed burnished in the suns' rays.

A large cheerful woman, who turned out to be the cook, answered my knock; she showed me through to the Sitting Room. There I was introduced me to Mrs Walker; a middle-aged woman of small stature…but who's strength and energy exuded from her.

Once comfortably seated, she asked me a few questions. I described the work I had undertaken at the Murdoch's, and found I had no option but to explain why I had been 'sacked'; she made little comment. The blooming Barnardo thing again reared its ugly head, but there was even less response to that, which really pleased me.

I was with her for no more than a half hour, but was told immediately the position was mine; I was to start in two weeks, when the other girl had left. She rang a bell for cook to escort me out…and that was that.

Cook was a warm friendly lady and grinned with pleasure when I told her I had been successful. She chatted cheerfully as she made a pot of tea and explained about the time of the bus I needed to catch home; with not too long to wait, I made my way back up the hill, reflecting as I walked.

It seemed to me now it had all been very brief.

I had learned from Mrs Walker there were ten thousand head of deep litter hens for me to care for…and quite a bit to do indoors as well. Most importantly for her however, were six Gold Medal Jersey cows. She became exuberant and animated when telling me of these, she obviously *adored* them. I was to be up and ready for milking at 5.30am; she would teach me to milk and care for them, so adding further to my experience.

I had noticed an orchard of fruit trees down to the right, and the hen houses beside and beyond, but had not been shown around the Land or house; however she seemed happy with me…once more I would just have to hope for the best.

One bit of really good news, my pay was double to two pounds; I would be glad of that for my bus fare to go and see Mrs. M…it was too far away and with too many hills to cycle.

Upon my return, my news was greeted with great joy…although, for me, a feeling of uncertainty prevailed. While helping with the vegetables for supper, Mrs M explained that it was due to the experiences already suffered, besides the absolutely normal trepidations of a new position.

Bill came in from work; we all sat around the table discussing this new event.

"Personally I would find the 'living in' part very difficult", Mrs M said with genuine feeling. "It's a completely different thing from being able to just walk away home when you've had a bad day…and we *all* get those I promise you!"

"What I found most odd was the briefness of it all; she didn't show me around anywhere…I haven't even seen where I'll sleep. To be fair though, with the other one, I only spoke to her over the 'phone before moving in. Cook seems very kind, so at least I won't feel too worried about things. It seems a long way away from you too…but I will come and see you in my time off, whenever that is to be"

Bill spoke sagely and with sincerity in his voice.

"You make sure you are not too over-willing this time Sue; you were anaemic and exhausted when you first came to us. Be less worried about 'being liked'. You are a great hard-working kid; you stand alone with your sense of humour and your kindness…just don't let them bully you this time."

111

I lapsed into thought for the rest of the meal.

"Right" said Mrs M "Come and help me with these dishes madam…we have some plans to make before you go!"

She told me she had a little of the Murdoch money left over; we were going to do things with that which would help my settling in.

A few days later we bussed into Tunbridge Wells.

We trawled the shops; I ended up with some new underwear, strong cotton blouses and trousers for work…and a new outfit I was to wear on my first visit back to see them. Then I got more stationery and stamps; new toiletries completed this little expedition.

We had a real treat in the 'Cadena Café'; fresh coffee, from beans ground on the premises in what looked like a red, upside down concrete mixer! When I was at school in Crowborough, I used to go a little further up from there, to the 'Monson Road' swimming baths; I easily recalled the magnificent smell from that place…and now I was actually drinking the wonderful beverage.

"Well, I must say, that is an outing I really enjoyed" enthused Mrs M on the bus home. I agreed…and then was surprised to hear of yet more arrangements!

"Everyone who has got to know you in recent times wants to come and wish you "Good Luck" before you leave she explained.

"On Saturday we will have a little gathering indoors…there are quite a few who want to see you. And the following Sunday you will travel to the new job ready for work on the Monday."

"Blimey, that's soon come round" I said quietly…and with a degree of anxiety.

The idea of the party sounded good though.


It was less a party…more a 'popping in and out'…even on a Saturday, people had work to do. Everyone I had met during my stay called during the afternoon; all came with useful little gifts to take on with me, but the Doctor gave me the best gift of all…a 'Clean Bill of Health'…plus his very good wishes. Mrs M was marvellous, with a permanently fresh teapot, and simply *piles* of sandwiches and cakes.

"*God, she's a good woman*" I thought "*I have been so lucky*".

The last visitors were the kind folk from the Bo-Peep Stores, they called in after six o'clock; it was late by the time they left so I helped Mrs M clear away.

After sitting for a short while to comment on the pleasure of it all, and to offer my sincere thanks, we were all ready for an early night.

But I could not go off to sleep; the extremely kind actions from all these people had been really 'getting' to me…it was not what I was used to in my life…I was finding it more and more unsettling.

In London, after leaving the Homes and my mother's place, Mrs Lewis and my Landlady had been very kind to me, but this was a different level again.

Mrs M and Bill had offered me their home and done so much, and the events of the day were overwhelming me; I felt that awful breathless pain in my chest and just wanted to cry with it all…so I did…very quietly.

"*It was so much easier being threatened and attacked*" I thought…I could deal with that virtually standing on my head.

Eventually I realised…I was bound again by emotion; through sheer luck I had found these people, they had cared for me so very well, now I found myself inexorably caught up with them…and I hadn't felt it happening.

The strength from anger is there in the immediacy…a response to protect oneself; that is what

I was more accustomed to doing, but how was I going to cope with this?

The surge of pain deep inside my chest reminded me of the feelings I had when recalling Uncle Tom and Auntie Dodd… I really did not know what I would do.

*"Bloody Barnardo's! Giving me a life that was now such a mess…even the good things felt bad…no wonder I despise you".*

# CHAPTER 13

The due day arrived and I felt a surprising calm…nothing more.

I had settled myself emotionally for the parting from Mrs. M and Bill, but could find no enthusiasm for where I was heading…I was positively 'flat'.

I have always hated 'good-byes'; that stemmed from not bearing to watch Uncle Tom's car go down the drive, once he had returned me to the hated Home after a visit to his cottage. This parting was not on that exact level, but it was close; I'd cried many tears when alone in bed…now I was ready to face the world for whatever was ahead.

We both found it hard to say anything while standing at the bus stop; I just held the hand of Mrs M…and waited. At last the old green 'Southdown' bus pulled up; I squeezed her hand more tightly and turned towards her…she stood there…with tears in her eyes…I just crumpled.

"You'll be alright Sue darling; just remember all Bill has said about not doing too much to impress. You'll work hard and well because that is your way…just don't try *too* much. We have loved having you with us and seeing you do so well, coping with the injury and pain…physical and emotional. We both know how absolutely *dreadful* the night in that field must have been for you; I don't know of anyone who would have managed with such aplomb and strength, especially in your poor health and pain. We admire you Sue, we both do; we have grown enormously fond of you for the person you are…and never forget that".

Then she gave me a big hug; in a haze of tears I boarded the bus…to yet another new start in my life.

The travelled route was one I knew quite well; at Tunbridge Wells I changed to the Crowborough bus …another familiar place from my childhood. Going through Eridge reminded me when Uncle Tom had taken me to the Castle; later I had gone to the tiny village school run by the Headmistress, Miss Rothwell.

Beyond was Groombridge; I recalled a Barnardo's outing that left from there, which for me at least, had gone horribly wrong.

We all were waiting on the platform to board a train; as it appeared around the bend, I leapt into the air with great excitement. What I had failed to realise was, I was standing directly beneath the great green station sign. My head connected with it at some speed …I very nearly passed out…and had to forego my trip and be escorted back to the Home!

This reflection lifted me; I even managed a chuckle to myself.

"*Gosh I'd been a boisterous kid, I must have driven them barmy sometimes*"

I was surprised at my clear recollections of scenery, cottages and so on that I had not seen in years; I must have been so tense on the day of my interview, I had barely noticed any of it. Now, besides it bringing me a relaxed, comforting feeling, I was also becoming very aware of the rather daunting…'well this is it and it's too late to go back now'.

Not much further along was my Stop.

I walked down 'Harlequin Lane' in the late afternoon, with enormous trepidation and 'nerves'; I just longed for the first meeting as a new employee to be okay. I turned left into the lane that led down to the Farm, trying to put a 'lift' in my step; concentrating hard on feeling optimistic.

I had almost reached the front door when it flew open; there facing me was Mrs. Walker, wearing such a warm smile. I smiled genuinely in response, and welcomed the vigorous shaking of her outstretched hand.

"*Thank you God*!" I thought…with *such* relief.

"Here…let me take that case for you…I am so glad you got that bus…the Sunday service is awful…we will have a cup of tea…Cook left a roast for you to heat up when you want it…you must be hungry as well as thirsty… here we are, this is the kitchen. Oh! Do you need the toilet first?"

I assured her I was more than comfortable, in a sensible measured tone; hiding so well the screaming laughter going on inside me …I had never heard as long a sentence in all my life…it sounded like a machine gun!

As she filled the kettle and sorted out cups, I watched her, and quickly decided she was a darned sight more nervous than me. My relief at her welcome had been immense; I think her relief was just that I was actually there!

"*Perhaps she thought I wouldn't turn up*" I thought.

"You sit there Sue, facing the window is good; you can see right up to the paddock gate…that's where My Girls  assemble for milking"

"*My Girls? Blimey, she really does care for them*"

We drank our tea at yet another long Pine farmhouse table, in the bright Aga-warmed kitchen; we both tangibly relaxed, and in a strange sort of way, each seemed to be aware of this happening.

She was very concise in her description of what she expected of me; I responded by assuring her I would work hard...it was in my nature. She explained her husband was 'a dry old Economist'; he was published on the subject and wrote for many journals and I wouldn't see much of him apparently. He always worked an eight hour day, only leaving his office for meals.

"There is some housework as you know, but one place you will *never* go near is that office. Fortunately, there is so much paper strewn over every surface and the floor, there is no space for the dust to land!"

She threw back her head and laughed heartily at this, as much in her relief at the relaxed situation as the joke.

"Now Sue, I have things to do but you are not 'at work' until tomorrow; is there anything you would like to do now?"

"Well, I would like to take my case to my room, but mainly I would love to walk around outside and see where I am…just to get familiar with it all."

She genuinely enthused at this; after clearing away our tea things, and with her instruction to leave my case in the kitchen, she showed me to the side door. I was directed to go across the small lawn in front of me, turn left and go past the small orchard, then follow the trees and path around to my right and I would find myself by the hen houses. Just carry on following the hedges and I would be back from where I started…full circle.

"Take all the time you like Sue; let me know when you are back and I'll show you where you will be living. We can see the rest of the house tomorrow"

I thanked her and we went our separate ways.

It was a calm, warm late afternoon; the sky was already changing colour and the birds were assembling for their evening chorus. I made my way very slowly, wishing to take in fully my new surroundings. I felt a great contentment at being outside, but realised too that her welcoming attitude was a large part of this. I could not help but make comparisons with the other place; so far the difference couldn't have been greater.

The other striking difference was the tidiness of everywhere.

I had just passed the kitchen garden on my left; the rows of vegetables were straight and neat and hoed, not a weed in sight…it occurred to me that it may become my job soon. Ahead was the orchard…all the apple trees were in just as good condition of care…and then I saw the hen houses.

Great wooden buildings in perfect condition, freshly painted in the dark wood preservative I had previously used when working so hard for Mrs. Murdoch. I felt confident this place would be a far happier environment; I was already looking forward to my start in the morning.

It was too dark now for there to be a sound from the hens… though they would make up for that tomorrow morning when I first went in. From the big orchard that traversed the length of the path behind the hen houses, I turned right, and walked the steep gradient of the paddock; at the top was where the cows would gather for milking.

Everywhere was lush and green, the colours seeming more so because of the fast-failing light; it was all so still…I could *feel* the silence. Opening the five-bar at the top and going onto the path, I had completed the circuit and made my way back to the house.

I was approaching the small lawn when I heard a strange noise in the lane to my left; intrigued, I walked up to investigate. I had almost reached the entrance to a field when I was greeted with a gentle whinny…it was a horse!

A seemingly enormous beast with a greying dappled coat; she became so animated at my approach, I laughed out loud to her. She nuzzled her soft hairy face into my neck and made quiet 'blowing' sounds in her horsy conversational way…she was gorgeous…it was love at first sight! I decided, if I was ever fed up or just needed a friend, I would go to her.

I realised I had now been outside for some considerable time; I said a brief 'goodbye' and ran back down to the house. Mrs Walker was in the kitchen and I was greeted with;

"So you have met Sally…that's her name…I heard her call you as you were coming back; she really *loves* people and you may always go and visit her, but she's too old now to ride."

Almost as though she had read my mind about the need of a friend, I said I most certainly would.

My thoughts went back to Uncle Tom's Hunter, another magnificent beast; I was about to mention him, but choked on the words. I swallowed hard, realising I still could not think about them easily yet.

I quickly composed myself and told her I liked what I had seen of the land; I was looking forward to the morning and working again…this she greeted with clear pleasure. I imagined I was going upstairs to see my room…I was longing to see where I would sleep…but she had been busy.

She had already mentioned that Cook had left me a roast; while I was on my wanderings, she had put this in the Aga. It was now piping hot, ready to eat and smelled great. I sat at the table and consumed what must have been one of the largest plateful I had ever seen, let alone eaten; it was absolutely delicious.

# CHAPTER 14

She had said to call her once my meal was finished; I gently tapped on the middle door in the hall, from where she had come earlier.

"Right then Sue…let's get this case upstairs, then you can sort yourself out, maybe have an early night and be ready for the morning"

We crossed the spacious hall; on the way I said how much I had enjoyed my roast, but would have to ask cook not to make it such a large meal next time. She laughed, but agreed it was a good idea as we walked up a narrow wooden stairway…and the door to my new place.

"You won't usually come this way Sue; this is just my access when I need it. Your entrance is outside, next to the side door from where you left for the walk. There is a tiny vestibule before you go up your stairs; to keep your floor clean, I would like you to leave wellies and outside coats down there."

We had reached the door, which she threw open with a flourish.

"Right Sue, there you are. You have a bathroom on the right; there is always ample hot water so you can bathe daily, you will probably need to. The bedroom door is opposite; the bed is made up and all else is ready for you so I'll leave you to it. Goodnight…I hope you sleep well."

I was aware she had a hurrying scurrying way about her, a bag of nerves really, but this seemed to be an incredibly brief introduction to my new accommodation; it made me a little dubious in my approach.

Justifiably so as it turned out.

Beyond the doorway was a long dark corridor, at the far end of which were my stairs down; the floor was just bare concrete…as indeed were the bathroom and bedroom.

The walls were plain red house bricks…with no rendering or paint. The small-paned metal casement window was ill-fitting and obviously draughty; it may have been painted once…*about a hundred years ago*, I thought. Hanging lifelessly in front, were the thinnest pair of curtains imaginable; the vaguest outline of printed flowers just showed through…but a long time dead I guessed. I peeped quickly into the bathroom; it was very cold and old, but clean at least.

My bedroom I must say was a shattering disappointment; I returned and sat on the edge of the bed…and just stared at everything in a rather mindless fashion.

The bed was a 'Barnardo's' style tubular metal thing with a hard, lumpy mattress, but lots of blankets. In the left alcove on the opposite wall, was a narrow five-drawer chest. The other side housed a piece of dowel upon which I could hang my clothes; I assumed that was the idea as, hanging there rather drunkenly were a couple of rather tatty old coat hangers. Nothing could have been more far removed from being a wardrobe.

Actually, on looking around again…there was nothing more far removed from being a bedroom!

I will admit to a feeling of extreme disappointment; it was as if everything else was spoiled because of it. My mood crashed down and my shoulders slumped but after a few minutes of misery…I shouted to myself,

"*It's better than being in that blooming field kid…get on with it*"

That worked!

The bathroom provided some genuine amusement, mainly because of my strong sense of 'silly', and I couldn't see the point in making it an issue.

I only stood knee-high-to-a-grasshopper...definitely of the vertically challenged variety...and I had to climb up to sit on the loo! It was altogether a very old contraption; the chain was so high and the string was so short, I had to stand on the seat to reach it.

When I turned on the tap to wash my hands, it just 'burped' and blew at me for a few moments, and then the water spat out, rather sporadically to say the least. I decided if I was going to bathe, I'd better start now! The bath taps repeated the same procedure as the basin, but eventually they settled down and the boiling hot water gushed out. It was rusty to begin with but I reckoned it would do.

Goodness knows when any of that lot had previously been used; during the War I guessed.

Returning to my *boudoir*...I decided that was going to be my name for it...I started getting things put away; I seemed to have accumulated considerably more while being with Mrs M.

Once I'd managed to open the drawers without the whole works coming forward on to me, I did quite well.

The dowel…um, wardrobe…was so flimsy, I was glad there was not much to go up there.

I had already noticed the hook on the back of the door…and continued the now ritualistic hanging up of my mac…and that was me done.

I put the fairy ornament given to me by the people of the 'Bo Peep Stores', on top of the chest of drawers.

Cyril had presented me with a beautiful picture of a horse with hunting dogs; this was hung ceremoniously, on an old rusty nail already in the wall.

I placed very neatly on the bedside cabinet the pens; the Collins Dictionary and a Roget's Thesaurus given as my leaving present by Mrs, M and Bill…"To help with the crosswords" was written inside. They were leather bound in black with gold lettering, and were my pride and joy…they would be well used I knew.

I had, in the meantime, remembered to turn off the taps; now I was off for a longed-for soak. What I hadn't allowed for was the bath bottom…it was as rough as sandpaper.

*"Mine will be too if I slide down there"* I chuckled to myself.

Mrs. M had supplied new flannels, with some beautiful matching perfumed soap and talcum powder;

there was a hand and bath towel already in my room. I didn't dare wash my hair as it was thick; it wouldn't have been dry by the morning, so I left that.

When finished, I felt like Cleopatra, or some other posh bird who would have definitely smelled as nice as me!

There was a clock by my bed. *"Blimey...it's gone ten o'clock"*

I decided the warmth from the bath would soon send me off to sleep; checking the alarm was already set for five in the morning (it was!) I slipped into my horrible lumpy bed...and after saying *"Goodnight Boudoir"*... went out like the proverbial light.

# CHAPTER 15

Awake before the alarm, I lay quite peacefully with my hands behind my head, wondering what this day and new life would offer.

I'd decided it was already a darned sight better than the Murdochs' place; nothing surely could ever match that for an 'Experience'. I'd slept well despite the awful room and lumpy mattress, and was very grateful for the weight and warmth of the blankets; it was still only the autumn, but it made me wonder to what temperature my *boudoir* would drop in winter.

The clothes on the dowel…even I couldn't keep calling it a wardrobe… were surprisingly still in place. The light was just about showing through the apology for curtains so, already wide awake, I got up. I felt quite happy and relaxed about the day, especially at meeting Cook again; she had seemed so friendly at my interview.

I manoeuvred safely down the concrete steps…there was a new pair of wellies in the floor well; goodness knows how she had gauged my size, but they fitted. On the back of the door hung an old wax jacket, and shoving that on…I walked across the yard for the first meeting with 'My Girls' and the new boss in  working mode.

Her smiling greeting gave me a warm feeling; she noted the time and that I was early…and said how much she appreciated that.

I was in the cow byre; three stalls each side on opposing walls were ready for the six Girls. Clean straw upon which they would stand, a 'mineral lick' on their front- facing wall…and the place was *immaculate.*

There was not a spot of mud, or anything else, to be seen on the washed floor; the high ceiling and walls were free of the great 'stringy' cobwebs one associates with such places, it was a revelation.

These were most definitely uniquely, favoured animals.

"Right Sue…we are ready now. You stand in the shadow of the door while they make their way up, they soon get spooked you know. You will see each of them saunter in and go to their own particular stall…they never ever change the routine. Once they are settled. I'll call you in and *quietly* introduce you to them and the rest of the procedures."

When she said 'saunter', she was spot on…if they'd gone any slower they'd have been going backwards.

These were most definitely the *prima donnas* of the 'Jersey Gold Top Club'!

This was the closest I had been to cattle; they were gorgeous…with the black shading around their eyes…and those eyes! They melted your heart.

Once all stalled up, I was allowed inside; I walked quietly up the 'milking' side as she put it and while talking to them, gently stroked their backs and the fluffy hair between their eyes. They were extremely docile; I was overjoyed they appeared to have taken to me.

I was instructed to place the heavy tether chain around their great necks, and to get the hot water ready. Each one had from the tail down and the udders, thoroughly washed; I wouldn't have batted an eyelid if she'd asked me to apply some baby powder as well! It was a balming cream instead, to insure they suffered not from the ardours of our hand milking…they were relishing all this of course.

She told me to get ready the milking stool and pails, adding for that first morning, I was just to watch. When she had finished the first three however, I boldly asked was there one of a sufficiently docile nature that I may be allowed to try.

At first her expression was that of a mother whose baby was about to be taken away for slaughter, but she then obviously decided I wouldn't have asked if I didn't think I could do it.

I sat down on the stool...that was the easy bit; I then pressed my head into the flank and, using the pressure in my hands as I thought she had been doing. It worked first time and she told me I was a 'natural'.

I don't know who was more surprised...me...her...or the cow!

Once all done and safely back out in the paddock, she sorted the milk in the great 'coolers'. I had a fine old time cleaning through and hosing down the floor; with a broom almost as big as me, all the water and debris was swept down the gullies. Then the new spread of straw was laid ready for the next go, and I was done, ready for breakfast.

As we walked towards the house together, she thanked me profusely for my aptitude and willingness to learn...but most importantly, for the affinity I had with Her Girls...she was genuinely pleased. So was I.

Mrs W went to the front porch; I took off my wellies and coat at the side kitchen door...and walked into the kitchen, full of the smell from freshly cooked bacon.

With a simultaneous "Hello…how are you?" Cook hugged me like an old friend…what a perfect start.

"You wash yer 'ands love while I just serve up theirs…then we can 'ave ours over a good natter. You've got an hour off now you know…so don't rush."

She was soon back, and with a new approach to 'portion control' I sat down to a splendid breakfast; I had been at work for three hours, so I was ready for it.

I thanked her for my delicious roast.

"Don't you worry about that darlin'…Mrs. W is a stickler for meals…and meals on time too. She wouldn' have let me go home without platin' one up for you first"

She had a lovely warm tone of voice and was quite clearly 'a Treasure' to Mrs W; I knew we were going to get along just fine. I helped clear away our things while she went in for their tray; I washed while she put away, watching where it all went for a change of role on another occasion.

She chatted on about her family…six children, all grown up and working on farms, even the one daughter was a farm secretary. Her husband drove a tractor.

"You'll meet 'im end of next week; you'll be loaned out to his boss to help out with all the extra work on their 'arvest…its bloomin' ard work too I tell you."

"I've never minded hard work, but can you tell me what my duties are in the house?"

She then in detail explained my day.

After my breakfast hour I would go down to the hens. The wooden window flaps were dropped down to give them fresh air…deep litter always stinks of ammonia from the droppings, so it is essential. All the eggs are then collected and brought up to the side shed for grading and boxing up; that was the sole contribution to the farm by Mr W, who found it relaxing and a break from his writing.

*Then* it was to be indoors; Mrs W would explain daily what she required…there was no particular routine…it was up to her. I would be responsible for the care of the kitchen garden…I KNEW I would…and Cook would ask me what was ready for table; I would pick and bring that to her.

By then it was lunch time; I would have another hour off but would be guided daily again as to what further was needed. I would help with the evening milking and clear up; lastly to collect the eggs again and close down the houses.

Lastly that is, until 8.45pm when I would take in their supper tray, say 'goodnight'…and could *then* go to my room.

"Is that ALL?" I asked in amazement.

"It's a long bloomin' day love I know; she aint too bad to work for, but she does like her pound's worth. I've been 'ere for years; but that's cos I don't take no funny business off anyone. He can be a moody soul but 'e don't mean no 'arm really…and she just leaves me to do my job…I know it better then 'er anyway!"

"Well, I'd better go up and make my bed; I only pulled it back to air when I got out this morning. By the way…please may I take a glass for water with me?"

"Course you can love…it aint much of a room is it? I hope you manage up there alright. I should 'ave mentioned too…'as she told you about yer time off?

You'll 'ave two afternoons…from about three o'clock, Sundays an' Wednesdays. You'll 'ave to do yer clothes washing and clean yer room on one day…she won't 'ave you doin' it any other time. I'd do it on a Sunday cos the buses are rubbish. That only leaves one day to go out…but it's all she allows I'm afraid."

I didn't respond at all, except to thank her for my glass…I went upstairs.

# CHAPTER 16

*"Well stone the blooming crows!"*

Bill's suggestion I don't show too willing, nor do too, much should have been addressed to her!

*"Five thirty in the morning till nine o'clock at night? Blimey that was a long day. And only allowed to do my own washing and so on in my own time? I may have been the ingénue, but I wasn't* completely *daft!"*

While fetching a glass of water, I reflected on the condition of the cow byre, and thoroughly cleaned the bathroom…and decided I would do so daily. To check up on things was why she needed the back stairs…and she would, as sure as God made little apples.

I sat back on my horrible bed and, not for the first time in my life, considered what on earth was happening to me; when for instance, would I ever get to see Mrs M and Bill? Leaving at three…and with the bus taking ages…to catch the last one back hardly gave me enough time to be with them.

I would write during my lunch hour to explain, and see what they suggested; perhaps they could meet me in Tunbridge Wells.

I asked myself; *Surely, I would never have to do all that work for all those hours?*

"*Yes you will girl*...you need the roof over your head...*that's why*"

The glaring truth hit me hard for a moment, before reality set in.

I was over seventeen now but until I was twenty one...when certain wages *had* to be paid...I was at their mercy; I had to have *somewhere* to live and this situation was my only option. I honestly didn't think I could cope with a second dose of misery as inflicted upon me by Mrs Murdoch; I had been constantly within a whisker of having nowhere to go...and I shuddered at that recollection.

"*I suppose I could be working in a Chinese Laundry...and sleeping on an ironing board... so this aint that bad!*" I told myself for cheer, but it didn't work.

I splashed some cold water on my face, put on some comforting 4711 perfume...and went back down to the sweat shop.

"You okay love? You look a bit low."

"Oh I'll be alright Cook…it was learning of the work details…took me off my feet for a minute…but I'll be fine."

"I'm sure you will Sue but you've got to be back out now…go and meet 'er in the byre again…you got five minutes."

I straightened my back; with shoulders and head held high, I returned to join this twentieth century slave driver. She was as charming as ever; full of smiles she showed me around the hen houses and described the work.

It was very straightforward, but I got her to explain in the smallest detail, what she expected; I knew instinctively she would jump on me for the slightest of errors.

We sorted out requirements together, me following her every move with absolute concentration. There were hundreds of eggs; these were placed into baskets, and transported up the hill to the grading shed in a specially adapted sort of wheelbarrow…the weight of which was a surprise in itself. Mr Walker wasn't there at the time, but Mrs W repeated what cook had already told me.

"You will only see him up here; he likes to get away from his desk and do the grading. If you don't see him before, you will when you bring in our supper tray."

He was beginning to sound a most mysterious character.

It was time to do the stint indoors; on our way she showed me the shed for the kitchen garden tools, explaining that a few minutes every day would keep it "as I want it". There was a definite stress in the "I"…mental note taken!

I was to do all the rooms in stages; today was the rarely used Drawing Room, but all the rest would get their share of my attention. The most memorable detail to strike me was the comparison between the main house and my appalling abode…*my boudoir*!

The entrance door was a low, wide solid oak affair, which closed with a very expensive 'clunk'; It was a large, rather dark room, that looked down toward the kitchen garden; Chinese rugs covered the most beautiful oak parquet floor, and rich blue velvet drapes hung at the lead-light windows.

The furniture was clearly valuable antique, and it would have all been beautiful, except…*it reminded me of the Barnardo's Homes*…especially "High Broom", just a short distance away.

That was a huge country pile, full of the same dark wood and parquet floors; beautiful if you weren't 'imprisoned' within. Miss Boagey had been the matron there; she hated me and the feeling was mutual.

The earlier physical abuse had been shattering, but when she 'punished' me in the tower of that place by abusing me for her own sexual gratification…I thought my life would end.

*"I'm really pleased I'm in my hovel to sleep…I couldn't have stood this"* I decided…and felt considerably better.

I dusted and polished at the only pace I knew how to work…swift; I was just finishing off the floor when Mrs W opened the door.

Casting a critical eye quickly around, she announced;

"You have done well for the first occasion, Sue; finish off now and you will have about a half-hour to hoe the rows in the kitchen garden. Cook will know where you are; she will call you when lunch is ready."

On my way out I called to the kitchen to get a glass of water; cook explained there was going to be no other refreshment between breakfast and lunch. I wasn't allowed a tea break, as that was when Mr and Mrs had a cup of coffee and caught up for a while; I couldn't see what that had to do with it…but I kept my mouth closed.

Cook called; I had time to wash my hands and then sat down with her to the most brilliant lunch. It was a far more sensibly sized meal, but even then I could not have eaten a dessert; I didn't have a sweet tooth anyway.

I helped cook clear away before returning upstairs; keeping an eye on the time, I wrote to Mrs M. I gave her my work detail without any added comment, and then explained about the arrangements for my time off. I told her Cook had given me the bus times…that in all honesty I could never see me getting all the way out to Pembury…and asked if perhaps she could arrange to meet me in town. I added that I didn't expect it to be on a regular basis, but that I could see no alternative. I looked at the clock…time up!

Returning downstairs, cook offered to post my letter for me on her way out; very kind of her…but I wouldn't have had time myself anyway.

On my way out to the yard, I looked back at the house to try and see where my room was in relation to the whole building…I was flabbergasted when I realised it wasn't even *in* the main building.

There were two entrances at the side; one into the kitchen, and adjacent on the left, the one up to my room. These were both reached through a narrow covered alleyway, beside a sort of car port attachment with big doors covering up the front; I was in the space above.

No wonder it was so rough and basic; it was little more than an upstairs shed!

"*Oh well…nothing to be done about it*" I shrugged.

The afternoon was largely taken up with clearing both chicken feed sheds and the cattle loft. There was to be a delivery the next day I'd been informed; the off-loading of the lorry and the stowing away was clearly my responsibility.

By the time I had finished to her instruction, you could have eaten a meal off the floors; there was never going to be a vermin problem in this place…*they wouldn't dare,* I decided with amusement.

The cattle were now assembling at the gate in the top paddock; I joined her and the morning procedure was repeated. She finished off the last bits and pieces, while I went out to collect the eggs and close up the houses.

Meeting her in the grading room, she explained I would meet the dog the next day; he was called "Mappie" because of a distinctive pink map of Ireland on his otherwise black nose. He had been two days at the Vet's with some sort of infection, but was recovered now. The place was almost over-run with cats, so to have the company of a dog would be good.

"Well, all is finished out here Sue, so you go on now; you can have a bath and change, but I would like you to sit in the kitchen, should I need you. Cook has left her paper for you…do you like anything particular for yourself?"

"I love The Daily Telegraph, mainly for the crossword"

"We have that, and The Times, but neither of us does the crosswords, I'll put them on the table for you, we have finished with them now."

It was a pleasure to be back upstairs without the pressure of the clock-watching. On the way, I had looked in to the kitchen; the paper was on the table, along with a doorstep of a sandwich for me.

The bath was hot, deep and welcoming; I washed my thick hair, hoping it would dry in the warmth from the Aga. I changed into a skirt and blouse, dabbed on some more 4711…and went down for my first evening.

The day had gone well, I reflected, consuming the food with welcome pleasure; there was also a full kettle on the Aga, and all the accoutrements required for making a cup of tea. I delved into the papers and, truly before I realised, the time had come to take in the tray.

I gently knocked the door; the Gentleman of the House opened it for me. In a loud, jolly voice, and with a sweeping flourish of his arm, he welcomed me in.

He was tall, slightly overweight, but with a kind face and boyish smile.

"So, you're the little stranger I have managed to avoid for the past twenty four hours; I have seen you working hard young lady, you don't dawdle much do you?"

This all said in the most jocular of fashion; I chuckled with him, and then gratefully took my leave.

Back upstairs, I lay on my bed with hands behind my head, thinking.

*There was no doubt this was a 'Curate's egg' situation – good in parts.*

I went over almost every minute of the day and was *very* aware of just how much I had achieved on the work front; aware too, it would be no mean feat to maintain on a daily basis.

I had got on well with all concerned, eaten like a little piglet, managed to write my letter to Mrs M…and enjoyed a lovely bath.

My bedroom was more welcoming now after the 'Barnardo's' reminders from downstairs.

The warm kitchen and the daily papers were an added bonus; as I got undressed and into bed, I decided…*I'll be alright*.

# CHAPTER 17

I enjoyed another excellent sleep as the hard work and hot bath had tired me out.

The morning was also a success, repeating the same as on my first day, with no problems; I had only just finished eating my breakfast however, when a lorry trundled down the lane.

"Sue, he's a bit early, but that's the delivery; sorry love but you'll 'ave to meet 'im in the yard. Mrs. W would expect it, but don' worry; the drivers are here regularly and they know the ropes. He'll show you what goes where; I'll clock the time for you an' add it on to this hour once you've finished."

With no apparent choice in the matter, I made my way outside again.

"Hello titch…what's your name then?" the driver enquired with some humour.

I laughed at the slight on my height. I told him my name, adding that this was only my second day so I would rely on him to tell me what to do; he was great.

He was delivering feed for both the cattle and the hens.

He took off the hens' stuff first; that was to go into the two small sheds I had cleaned the previous day. The bags were made of very strong but shiny paper; this made them too slippery for me to get a good grip…and they weighed twenty eight pounds each.

The driver asked, with apparent disdain, whether I would manage; I knew I was showing off really, but decided I would prove his manner wrong. Forty bags had to be stored in each shed; four side-by-side rows of ten bags high. I started slowly, realising the degree of difficulty; upon completion he was suitably impressed…as indeed was I!

Waiting on the ground were eight hessian sacks of cattle cake; having already explained where they were to go, he bade a cheerful farewell and drove off to his next farm.

These sacks were large and very baggy, which made them infinitely easier to handle; any benefit stopped there however, as they each weighed 'a hundred weight and a quarter'.

I dragged them one at a time, to an adjoining shed with a high loft; this was reached by climbing a ridiculously narrow, tree-pruning ladder. This contraption was broad at the base, narrowing at the top to fit between small branches. I managed to wedge the base between jutting bricks covering the floor; all I had to do now was hang on like grim death.

Once on the first rung, I gripped the sack in my right hand, letting it hang down beside me; all was fine, until I reached level with the floor of the loft. Holding on hard with my left hand, I managed to swing my other arm with enough force to get the sack above shoulder height and land on the loft floor; I felt relieved the driver had gone as this was a dreadful struggle.

Once finished I was breathless and shaking, but had managed to get everything correctly stowed away. My hands were bright red, and the tendons in my right palm were hurting with the strain; my arm and shoulder muscles were 'trembling' from the sheer physical effort required.

With difficulty, I swept up where the lorry had made a mess, and gratefully returned indoors for a little respite.

"That was hard…*very* hard", I said to Cook as she ran some hot water, saying I could clean up there to save me going upstairs again. She brought a fresh pot of tea over and gave me a little hug; with a sympathetic smile she confided, almost in a whisper.

"I don't think its girls' work at all…and that lot only will last about ten days. Now you just have a cuppa and relax; you still have forty five minutes before you go back out. I think she's expectin' far too much…and there aint nothin' to you either".

"At this rate there soon will be…but I'll look more like Tarzan than Jane though!"

We both laughed at this; it was so good to have her to help through these initial potentially difficult times.

"Look Sue, I don't want you to worry, but your next challenge is the harvest next week. My husband has heard all about you from me; he'll really keep an eye open for you, but I'll warn you now…it's more really hard work darlin'. His boss is a lovely lady, very firm but fair; she'll make absolutely certain that everthin's okay for you."

We had barely sat down with our drinks when we heard another vehicle in the drive; she told me it was the vet's van with Mappie;

"That's the end of peace and quiet for a while" she wryly observed.

She was right. The dog had a high-pitched yap, rather than a bark; he was exercising this awful sound at the most amazing rate…he couldn't have been drawing breath!

He was greeted with two simultaneous sentences;

From her; "Oh! My *darling*…you're *home* again…*come to Mummy.*"

From him, "Will someone shut that *bloody* dog up…*I'm trying to work*"

Both were greeted by us with muffled laughter; Mrs W was so embroiled, she didn't even realise we were there, let alone hear us. We shot back into the kitchen…then laughed our heads off.

"Good grief…she's so *stupid* wiv 'er animals…I sometimes can't believe 'er!"

"I bet she wouldn't let him sleep in *my* room" I suggested boldly.

Cook nodded in knowing, silent, agreement; we spent the rest of my break nattering about daft pets…and their even dafter owners.

I resumed work with my first Order from the kitchen garden, to be brought in once I'd done the hens; I felt already, there was a little routine becoming established.

I'd never liked routine for its own sake, but this was providing me with a sense of belonging; being part of the whole…I found that very comfortable. My work until lunch was to cut the long grass growing tightly to the apple tree trunks; the mower would otherwise damage the bark.

Thinking of 'bark'…Mappie had discovered me; a dear little white wire-haired terrier type creature, who was clearly never going to leave my side…or shut up! It was an unbelievable, almost painful noise; I stopped my work.

Kneeling on the ground, I took his collar and pulled him gently towards me; he sat down immediately and gazed at me, with soppy brown enquiring eyes. In a very quiet voice…which became quieter the closer I got…I told him he had to be quiet; almost by now, directly into his ear. I repeated it over and over again.

At the same time, I gently stroked his neck ruff, and stayed like this for a good three or four minutes. He was calming all that time; his eyes were nearly closed in a quiet, trance-like bliss. Very gently I let him go; as quietly too, I stood up…and he *immediately* jumped around like a mad thing, and continued barking!

"*Okay... it didn't work then, but it will; give me time and it* will *work Mr Mappie*".

I was delighted when it did; over many days, the procedure was repeated and eventually it happened. It was rather sporadic at first but; when it got to the stage where Mr W told me he had noticed the change, I knew I'd cracked it.

Mappie was the only dog; I couldn't have counted the numerous cats…excepting Rupert. He was a beauty and I saw him everywhere; one of his favourite places was up in the paddock with Sally. I would, as often as possible, go up to see her and have a nuzzle into that lovely warm neck; invariably she and Rupert would be close to one another, almost as if they were in conversation.

Another favourite of his was to be around during milking.

He would sit just to the left of my milking hand and, without any warning, I would squirt a line of milk towards him His mouth shot open and he swallowed the warm milk…he never missed! This was repeated until he'd had enough; fat and full he'd find somewhere cosy to sleep it off.

The day for the harvest dawned and I felt rather nervous; firstly meeting another group of farming people, but also hearing the warnings of the work involved from cook. She was a genuinely warm, kind person and would not set out to exaggerate or worry me…but I *was* worried.

Up at the usual time, I completed the milking routine; I was to have a speedy breakfast and be ready to be picked up at nine o'clock. Promptly at the given time, a Land Rover arrived; cook gave me a hug and with "Good Luck" as her last word, I went to make the most of my first day on another farm.

The sun was well up, and surprisingly warm for the time of year; that was a good start, I decided. The driver was one of the farmer's sons; he didn't have much to say but I wasn't in the mood for conversation anyway. Their place was only a couple of miles away, so not a long time to endure this rather icy atmosphere; that changed the moment we arrived.

Everything was hustle and bustle, with men all over the place sorting out tractors and machinery.

My boss for the time being was a pleasant young-looking lady called Joyce; she greeted me cheerfully. She explained that the hay was already cut, dried and baled; my role was to do exactly as directed on the field, to aid the collection and storage of these bales before they got dampened by possible inclement weather.

I was immediately more relaxed, with the clearly conscious effort on her behalf to put me at ease. I looked around to see if I would know which was cook's husband; there were too many people though…and that was when I realised I was the only girl!

We all trooped off and I just followed the leader; once at our destination, I was told exactly what my duty was.

The tractors would slowly follow the line of bales; I had to be in position, with said bale on this blooming great pitchfork, and hurl it on to the flat-bed trailer being towed. I had used that type of fork before; it was a slightly larger version of one that had been forced through my foot by the Murdoch boy! It was even more unwieldy; it was heavy *before* anything was on the end.

As the tractor drew level, and with all my might, I hoist the bale aloft.

It missed completely and all the men around me laughed; a derisive laugh I thought. I felt my cheeks go red.

All then went very quiet…because of a booming shout from another tractor.

"Don't just stand there laughing you *blithering idiots*! Sue…stay there a moment"

It was cook's husband Tom. He was all of a-bluster as he approached; the men now standing around looking very sheepish and guilty.

"Right you lot, lets get some sorting out done here; for goodness sake, can't you see she hasn't the height or strength to reach? From now on Sue, you go up on the trailer and receive the bales…Mickey here will help you…just do exactly what he says"

With that, he lifted me up bodily on to the flat-bed; Mickey gave me a reassuring wink.

Firstly, on both hands, he put what looked like fingerless gloves. Made of leather, and a bit big for me, he assured me they would help protect my skin from tearing when lifting up the bales. He then addressed me seriously, in what exactly I was to do.

I had to slip each hand under the binder twine around the bales and throw them over to Mickey; he would stack them up as that was the really heavy bit. Even dried as the hay now was, he reckoned each bale weighed between twenty five and thirty pounds. It was hard work but infinitely easier than the first role.

Everything suddenly came to a halt and quietness descended; engines were switched off and the men made their way up the field…it was time for lunch. I felt nervous again…about eating in front of strangers…but I was starving!

I need not have worried as Tom came swiftly over and explained; we were each provided with a paper bag full of individually made sandwiches, a billy-can of hot or cold drink, and an hour off to rest.

"You sit down on that old Mill-stone darlin' while I'll go and fetch ours; you and me can catch up while we're eating"

There were a couple of discernibly cold looks from some of the men; I felt well protected though with Tom there.

We sat and consumed the tastiest of sandwiches on lovely fresh bread; Tom was more than happy to eat the two I just couldn't cope with. I was so hot, and my throat was dry from the dust and sheer physical work, so I chose to have lemonade. He suggested I have tea during the afternoon break, explaining the hot drink would cool me down more.

He also informed me, his wife stayed on to give me a cooked meal as we were working until eight in the evening; his daughter would do his for him.

The afternoon was *excellent*; I may have struggled at first, but I had the strength to deal easily with my new task, and the food and drink had helped. Then came a moment to remember, when Joyce stopped us all for a much welcomed tea break; I was absolutely *gasping* to quench my thirst. I couldn't face drinking the tea as suggested by Tom; instead I chose a jug full of cold, cloudy lemonade. With it was a huge piece of absolutely *delicious* home-made fruit cake.

Because I was so dry, the lemonade worked a treat...the cake was sheer bliss...and for ever after I could only consider having the two together...on the rare occasions I ate cake!

I was relieved but happy when the machinery ground again to a halt for the final time...all done...that was it!

Tom came over and put his arm around my shoulder;

"Well done Sue love, bye for now, I'll see you in the morning...sleep well...*you will*!"

Cook heard the returning Land Rover, and stood waiting for me by the door.

"Good Lord girl...look at the state of you! You must have worked so hard darlin' but I've took the liberty of goin' up and runnin' you a bath"

She stroked my hot cheeks and put a protective arm around my shoulder; kissing my fore-head she ushered me upstairs, saying my meal would be ready for me as soon as I had finished.

I went upstairs…but lay on my bed and broke my heart.

Tom had been so kind to me all day…and now Cook; I felt a deep overwhelming emptiness inside.

My Uncle Tom's cook had been constantly on my mind since the day I'd arrived; I missed them all so much, and she too hugged me with those same squidgy arms.

There were many other comparisons with the two ladies, but especially their kindness and warmth. I felt a sudden pang of envy for this cook's daughter; I'd *longed* to have had the good fortune to have parents like hers. I knew I was tired, but the pain of that emotion was just too great to manage without tears.

*God*! *I wish I could handle these changes… its like riding on a switch-back*!

Trying to come to terms with it all, I decided that I wouldn't *really* want to change anything; at least it illustrated I *did* have people around me who genuinely cared. I just hoped the day would soon come when I would be able to accept it…without the accompanying pain.

I ate my supper in the warm kitchen, with cook chatting to me; there was good news too as she said there was nothing else for me to do…not even the tray.

She added that Joyce had already 'phoned Mrs W with glowing reports of my day…and I would be required for the rest of the week

When I arrived back the following day, cook gave me a letter, obviously a reply from Mrs. Meadows.

"Blimey…that was *quick*!" I said.

Cook replied, when that happened at home, Tom always said…

"They must 'ave re-shod the 'orse!"

No matter how tired or fed up I was, that dear lady could *always* make me laugh; her soft Kentish burr added to the way she spoke, and kindness oozed from her. I had liked her from the very first moment we had met for my interview; I'd felt I could trust her and I was right.

I tore open the letter from Mrs Meadows; it was of no great length, but she explained she wanted me to have a reply as soon as was possible. She was telling me that Cyril and Bill would drive over to Crowborough on Wednesday. I was to meet them outside the main store, 'Webb and Longstaff's'; we were to have tea out…and they would bring my bike. I did a great whoopee!

Then I saw cook's face.

"Oh darlin'…that's tomorrow…you're doin' the 'arvest…oh what a *shame*."

She groaned as she came round and gave me a hug.

I wasn't quite sure how to react; I really couldn't believe my bad luck and was *bitterly* disappointed…but I also knew that work would have to take priority. I felt sick at being so thoroughly trapped; because my need was for a roof as well as a job, I had no alternatives but to comply with the boss.

"Good grief…*tomorrow*...how can I let her know I can't be there?"

"Look love, I'll tell you what I can do. I'll go up the 'phone box and ring 'em this evenin; I'll explain for you."

"Ring them…what, on the 'phone…they haven't *got* a 'phone" I blurted out in panic.

I tried hard to think.

"*I know*…the Bo-Peep stores…they've got one, *and* they would give Mrs M the message. They were lovely when I was ill; I know they'll do it"

"And we'll get the number easily cos they're a shop…good idea!" she added.

I realised the short notice was as a special surprise for me; I'd said I was off on a Wednesday and hadn't
164

seen them for what seemed like *ages*. As well as meeting up, they knew I would love to have my bike with me; what a rotten disappointment for us all. I would write again before going to sleep, post it en route to Joyce's farm tomorrow, and explain all about the extra work that had precluded our visit this time.

Before I left the next day, cook had arranged it all.

"An' I sent 'em your love too" she added, kindly.

We had been lucky with the weather all week; "All is safely gathered in" I found myself thinking! The harvesting experience had taught me a great deal, other than how kind the men had eventually been…all of them.

I'd learned how to relax with so many people around me, and watched and learned from each of them; seeing how the bales were dealt with, and the skill of the tractor drivers, had been a marvel to my eyes. It *was* as hard as cook had warned, but I found myself far less tired by the last day.

Youngest son was waiting to take me back for the last time when I heard Joyce call me to her.

"You young Sue, have been a little marvel; if you ever find you need, there is a job waiting for you here…and I'm not joking either…I mean that. Now you take this as an extra 'thank you' from me, and off you go!"

We actually passed the short journey with small talk, which made a pleasant finale; with a cheerful smile he was gone, and I went in for supper.

My bath was run and, after a quick hug with cook, I ran upstairs; I couldn't *wait* to see what Joyce had written. I opened the envelope and out fell a £1 note; blimey half my week's wages as a 'thank you'…I was thrilled to bits!

When I told cook, she admitted Joyce was a far nicer person than was Mrs W; *and* she knew the money charged by her for my assistance, most definitely did not get shared with me.


The routine soon re-established normality but I found a subtle change in myself; quite simply, Mrs W didn't frighten me any more. I had held my own with experienced workers far older than me, and I had proved effective enough to be offered a potential future position; that gave me enormous comfort and confidence.

She was okay really and the farm was hers after all; surely she had the right to demand what should happen there-on…sometimes it was just the way she said things that was so disconcerting. However, when I did get a bit cheesed off, my mind returned to the Murdoch's…that had the immediate effect of me changing my mood!

She did do some very odd things; as with her soppy way with 'her Girls'- and Mappie as well as the cats.

I walked past the lean-to shed one day and the door was slightly ajar...something I'd not seen before… I peeped in. Although pretty dark, I could see a pole, set horizontally across, with bits of fluff or something hanging on it.

I was going in for lunch and mentioned it to cook; what she told me nearly put me off my meal. Rupert had what was a veritable harem out on the land; when the many kittens were born, Mrs W drowned and skinned them…to send off to make *Fur gloves*! That was the row I had seen suspended…and they were directly below my *boudoir*!!

I looked at cook in utter disbelief and astonishment; she assured me it was absolutely true. *"Urgh*!" was my reaction.

Cook realised how sick I felt about that, so cheered me completely with another story while we ate out lunch.

Mr W liked to go out once a week for a drink at an Inn a couple of miles away, but he tended to have a bit too much. On more than one occasion, folk had been out looking for him when he failed to appear within a reasonable time of the place closing. On one such occasion, he was found asleep in a ditch; that was when a plan was decided upon.

A local chap was engaged to train Sally!

He coached her to stay patiently in a very small yard at the side of the Inn; as soon as she heard Mr W, she would go around to the front door, wait for his friends to help him into the saddle, and slowly get him home.

Once there, she gave him time to dismount (mainly he just fell off!) and then she made her way back to her field!

"She's too old now to do it, an' he's old enough to know better, but it was a joy while it lasted"

# CHAPTER 19

At long last my visit to Mrs M came around; Bill and Cyril had arrived with my bike about three weeks before but today was the first time Mrs M could make it into Tunbridge Wells. I spent the entire bus journey reflecting upon the wonderful way she had cared for me; she had been so very kind and I was *longing* to see her again.

She was waiting for me as we pulled up; I ran towards her grinning from ear to ear with arms outstretched for a welcome hug but she was 'distant'…I could see and feel it.

Rather embarrassed I said a really cheery 'Hello'; she did respond, but barely.

"Is everything alright Mrs M? Are you okay? I'm really *really* pleased to see you"

"Well I hope so; it has taken you a long enough time to manage it"

"But Mrs M, I thought I'd explained I couldn't help that! I *had* to do the harvest; I *have* to do my room and washing on Sundays and even today I didn't leave work till *nearly three o'clock*. I work *so* hard, honestly I do"

"Well I thought perhaps you had been out on that bike of yours, now you've got it back; I worked hard too you know when you were ill. I helped you get this job and I don't think it's as hard as you make out; I might write to her and see what she says"

"Oh please *don't* do that…she can be *such* a funny woman and wouldn't like that, I *know*" I was pleading now and very confused.

She then suggested the 'Cadena' again to have some tea; it wasn't going to be happy like the previous time. We made totally unmemorable small talk; try as I would I could not raise her mood, she seemed determined to maintain her attitude…I was hurting inside and could not make it out.

"Please understand Mrs M, I honestly *am* tied to the farm; I *do* work long hours…and I can't change that"

"And what do you call 'long hours' then? You must have time off for yourself; I think we have a case here of, 'Off with Old and On with the New', I think we have all served our purpose"

I was stunned at this harsh attitude; I explained in full detail my working day, but I could see a vague look in her eyes…she clearly didn't believe me!

I hadn't believed it myself in the first few days; cook was always saying the hours were far too long.

Mrs M had nursed me through the horror of being thrown out before, and had been disgusted; she of all people knew there were no alternatives for me.

*It was where I lived…I had no other place to go.*

The rest of the visit is impossible to recall; I well remember sitting in deep gloom on the return bus trip, trying to work out this most amazing turnaround.

I didn't sleep at all well; for the first time ever, when the alarm went off, I didn't want to get up. I could feel a dreadful dragging pain inside, but I still managed to join Mrs W out in the byre on time. I couldn't *wait* to get in to talk things over with cook.

I could see from her expression she could tell all was not right, but she still asked in her usual cheerful manner,

"Well…'ow did your day out go…did you enjoy the break?"

Although very sad, I felt anger at the distinct sense of injustice; this was the over-riding factor and was keeping the tears at bay. I explained all that had occurred; she was visibly shocked. I said too that I did not have any idea of what to do next…or how I truly felt.

She brought over the breakfast and we sat and talked at length; the solution, as far as she could judge, would be thus. Write Mrs M another letter; say I felt things appeared not to be good at the moment, and how much I wanted to see everything how it once was. Explain again about the hours, and how much I *would* like to visit, if only I had more free time.

"Give 'er time to reply love but don't expect too much. There is a lot of jealousy out there and perhaps that's it; maybe she really *does* think you've found better things to do. Bloomin' sad though that she couldn' believe you…that is *very* wrong. You were right to put 'er off writin' to Mrs W though…that would 'ave really put the cat among the pigeons…she'd 'ave been livid. You get on now…oh and I need some greens for lunch when you're ready please love"

I was fairly distracted with it all, but continued working in the usual way; the routine was well established and it wasn't hard…just too much of it in one day.

I slept well for the rest of the week, but when Sunday came I was really looking forward to my time off; I was used now to going straight upstairs to do my cleaning.

Cook supplied clean bedding, I just stripped and remade my bed and put the dirty things in the box by the kitchen door. After the first week of struggling with my clothes washing, cook had given me yet more good advice.

I was to leave the Saturday night bathwater in the bath, and put my clothes in to soak; the next day they would take no time to wash through. After wringing them out, I'd press down with my hands to flatten out the creases; when they came in from the line, or from hanging over the Aga, they didn't even need ironing... brilliant!

Everywhere else was swept and washed down thoroughly, because that was how I liked it to be, but I also knew very well she *did* check round. After I'd gone back downstairs and eaten the sandwich left by cook, I often fancied a ride out on my bike; I soon realised I was too tired to build up any enthusiasm. Returning to my room I'd lay on my bed reading...drifting in and out of sleep until bedtime.

The disappointment with my visit to Mrs M was still crushing; it was proving hard to shift the glooms.

Each morning I hoped cook would produce a reply to my letter; by Wednesday, almost a week later, we both felt it was going to be a futile wait. She had written by return the other times; it looked highly unlikely I was going to hear. I thought this realisation would be hard to bear; in reality it wasn't at all.

"Well, you've already 'ad a lot of disappointments in your life young lady; you're gettin' older and more used to it now. Wiv a sweet nature and an 'eart as big as a pillow, you'll get 'urt all the time. Don' let 'em bovver you though love…they're the losers!"

She was a great philosopher without any doubt.

At lunch time I was back in the kitchen, nearly exploding with hidden temper.

"It's a good job I didn't arrange to do anything like go to Mrs M today…*do you know what she has just told me to do?*"

She stared back, bewildered at this overt display of anger.

"There's a blooming cow out there, apparently due to drop her calf at any moment; I have *got* to stay here in case she needs my help! She didn't even *ask*, I was *told*"

"Oh Sue love, that aint right. Blimey, you've had no time to yourself at all; an' you're right…Mrs M would never 'ave believed you…all over again. You are gonna have to find somfin' definite to do *every* Wednesday…a Club or somfin' where you *'ave* to attend. We'll get our finkin' caps on"

By the next morning she had the answer, or Tom had apparently…join the Territorial Army!!

The following Wednesday…I did just that.

CHAPTER 20

I managed easily to get bathed and ready and catch the bus to Tunbridge Wells, then I caught a second one out to the TA Hut; it was a fair distance, but a great way to relax.

Once enrolled, I fitted in immediately; I became W/402434 Pte Davis, 42nd Mixed Signals attached to the Kent Yeomanry. Full uniform was provided and Sgt. Major Glazier instructed us regarding expectations of its care, and our resulting smartness. She also instructed us in Drill, and other military skills; even a suggestion we go on the Firing Range one day.

I loved the whole thing, especially being in the company again of girls and boys my own age; that was a first since school…which seemed to be ages ago.

The conversation was more adult of course and we shared many a joke; it was my turn to make them laugh when I described the army as…

"Barnardo's…with saluting…and very shiny buttons"

On top of all that, there was a small remuneration.

*"Blimey…a Club that paid me for going!"*

At last my breaks were now as regular as clockwork; I felt a million times more content. I'm not sure Mrs W was particularly overwhelmed with enthusiasm, but cook managed to get Mr W very animated by it all, so she had too much competition to make any complaints. With that simplest of matters sorted out, and the opportunity to mix with own age group, I felt happier than I had for a long time.

Then I had a *very* black day indeed…we all did…Sally was going to be put down.

Mr W was positively distraught, almost beside himself with impending grief; the gloom hung in an ominous pall over the whole house. I had spent hours collectively with dear Sally; always the same slow amble to the gate, her great head pushing into my neck and shoulder. With the unforgettable smell of her coat, and sweet breath from the grass, I would gently stroke her cheeks and muzzle; she would stand there, stock still for ages, relishing every moment.

Now it was to end.

At breakfast break Cook told me to go nowhere near the field, as Mr W was up there; she did not know what time the man was due, and kindly went on to explain what Humane Slaughter meant.

"She won' even 'ear the bang Sue; she'll know nowt about it at all"

I believed her, and did as she bade;

"Go down to the hen houses… keep busy…and you won't hear anything either"

But I did.

I didn't actually *see* her go down…but I did in my minds eye; that beautiful, once magnificent beast was now over on her side…dead.

I put my face in my hands and wept for her; another darling friend was gone.

Only a couple of weeks later, another horrible experience, for me at least; everyone else took it in their stride.

My favourite of the six cows was due to drop her calf; she was a seasoned Mum and all went well. I was allowed to go into the 'Nursery Pen' as Mrs W called it.

In the dim light, I was met with her dark beautiful eyes that seemed filled with pride as I looked at her calf. She was diligently washing and grooming and then the calf began to suckle; I quietly departed and left them to it.

On the third morning, during milking, everything was as before; the same at breakfast…but then a change.

I was going between hen houses when I heard the most horrifying bellow from the top of the Yard. Knowing better than to intrude on Mrs W, I went in to see cook; in response to my anxious enquiry she told me.

Apparently the calf was male; this was a Dairy Farm where there was only room for a milking Herd… they had just removed him after three days…to be VEAL!!

I was terribly shocked at the heartlessness of this.

She had been allowed to care for and suckle her baby for long enough to strip the essential life-giving 'first milk'; this was unfit for human consumption anyway. Then he was removed from her care to be slaughtered, for the expensive meat to be served at only the Best of Tables; her milk would also be of a superior quality for a long while because of her calving.

This information was delivered by cook in the most matter of fact way, which I found as utterly tasteless as the Veal itself.

*I would never go near the stuff*, I decided, and would relate that episode to all and sundry to deter them as well.

That poor beast bellowed for a night and two days, almost unceasingly; I don't know if cows actually shed tears, but she had lines of wet down the sides of her face.

For quite a time afterwards, when she came in for milking, she would swing her head towards the Nursery Pen. My heart went out to her; it was a dreadful experience, but one that was so common even lovely cook was inured to it.

Nothing awful at TA though; I was having a great time. I was about the only one who not only enjoyed the Drill routines but *relished* in it; it was all just perfect as far as I was concerned!

We would 'work' under Instruction for the first session; after a tea break we then invariably played some sort of game or another. Once again, my sporty background came into its own; how I found those reserves of energy I'll never know.

Most of us travelled back into town to get various buses home; before we caught these, we all met up in 'Fortes', the Coffee Shop. Set on the High St, the brightness from the fluorescent lights reflected out onto the pavement, and bade us a warm welcome; we would fill the place, crowding into every available seat. The poor lady waitress was bit of a sweetie; we got away with murder as long as we made not *too* much noise.

On one such occasion, one of the girls announced that her sister was getting engaged; we decided to donate a gift.

In each cup and saucer was placed an aluminium "Apostle Spoon"; we gathered a dozen of these together, wrapped them in a 'Fortes' napkin, and made a very grand presentation.

She *seemed* pleased!


At tea break…and also when in the café…I found Brian always sat beside me; it seemed to be not accidental. He then didn't pay me any more attention than the rest, but I was aware he liked me. I had never 'been out' with a boy as the others called it; when would I have had the time to start with?

The winter was well set in, and by January the nights were very much colder; Kent and Sussex definitely knew how to be cold!

I remembered from my childhood spent in those vast Barnardo's Homes, just how bad it could get. I prayed it wouldn't snow, firstly because my *boudoir* was already like an ice box…but mainly I wouldn't be able to get the bus to attend TA…disaster. That made me realise how much I would miss the company of my new friends once a week…but especially Brian.

This feeling became greater after one night at the bus stop; he very gently kissed me…on the lips. I was so surprised to begin with…but when repeated, felt myself almost overcome with tenderness.

The nicest thing was, he didn't get 'soppy' about it, and neither did I. It was repeated often but mentioned not at all…perfect.

On the bus home after that first time I was rather perplexed; I had read books, magazines and so on, but I felt nothing could possibly illustrate how one would *actually* feel.

I liked what had happened of course, but I immediately felt an underlying threat; I still could not trust, and immediately all my barriers surrounded me yet again.

Fancy words would fall on deaf ears; the Homes had been bad enough, but even since I had experienced sufficient let-downs to last me a life-time. For me to be able to trust would be a long time, and with someone very special indeed; and anyway…beside me constantly were my Uncle Tom and Auntie Dodd…that was *real* love.

I had a rough idea of how babies were made and what led up to that, but my morals were the most perfect of all birth control…bar none. I would not…*under any circumstance in the world*…have gone into another Home…especially one for 'Unmarried Mothers'.

# CHAPTER 21

The grey cold days of the winter months were slowly passing, but Mrs W made sure my hours were not reduced at all; she simply switched my housework duties from after lunch, to the evening…so she could have me outside for all the daylight hours.

I was beginning to feel a sense of total injustice in my life; it appeared, mainly from TA conversations, nobody else seemed to be in the same over-worked, tiring position.

Always uppermost in my thoughts of course was the *desperate* need of the roof over my head; it was a condition of my work that she would provide this…but I was beginning to think she was taking total advantage; then a catalyst.

I had enjoyed breakfast and the usual cheering conversation with cook; I then admitted to her that I was *so* weary, I really didn't want to go back out into the dreadful chill. I also told her, the evening work seemed to be taking a lot more out of me; it seemed harder now than when it was split up throughout the day.

Cook sat down, caught hold my hand, and made an amazing announcement…in very hushed tones.

"Sue, I was sworn *never* to tell you this, but I can' bear to watch on any longer…*listen.* You're the first girl she's 'ad to 'live-in'; before you came she 'ad *two* women to do your job! They both lived in the village; one came in for the Land, an' the other did the 'ousework. They earned *each* what you earn, and neither did the job as well as you. That's bad enough…but this business where you 'ave to sit till late and take in their tray is utter nonsense; I used to leave it in the Larder and one of them would sort it out. It jus' panders to 'er Slave Master Mentality…that's what Tom says anyway"

I'd never seen myself with my jaw dropped open…but I'm sure it did then; I was speechless too…which was a very rare occurrence!

"Cook I *knew,* just from the way the others go on about it at TA. None of them do my hours BUT they don't live-in either; if I don't go along with absolutely everything she asks of me…I'm out on the street again…*that's* my dilemma"

"Ah! But she *knows* that Sue, that's what she's playing on. I feel awfully disloyal to 'er in a way; I've

185

been 'ere years, but this is just plain *wrong* love. Tom an' I 'ave talked *hours* about it"

Although in reality it would make little difference, it was an enormous comfort to have been confided in at that level; I felt much of my frailty and naiveties disappear…I felt considerably matured.

However I also realised,  knowing all that was going to make it far harder to be tolerant of the situation; but it helped just knowing cook and Tom felt it was unjust…and that put them on 'my side'.

These things invariably have a way of working themselves out; that is exactly what happened in this case. It was Tuesday afternoon, just after lunch; Mrs W approached as I worked in the garden.

"You cannot go out tomorrow Sue; I have a Ministry man calling and he will be here for hours. You shouldn't have *all* the milking to do, but you will have to start it off for me"

"I'm sorry Mrs W, but I can't do that; I have my first Army exam tomorrow…I have worked and studied hard…and I want to pass"

I had responded boldly; but only on the outside…I felt *extremely* shaky on the inside…she still scared me.

"Well! I beg your *pardon* young lady…*you* are here to work and do exactly what I tell you. You do *not* question or argue with *me.* I have told you to be here… *and you will*"

"I will *not* be here…I *am* going to TA…*and the sooner I get out of this flipping dump the better*" I added…shouting loudly now.

She at first looked a bit nonplussed, but quickly recovered; she came slowly towards me and prodded her finger, hard into my chest. With her beady eyes staring, and an ugly sneer on her reddened face, she said in a low, threatening whisper.

"You *can't* get out of here dear girl…*you have nowhere else to go*"

I was stunned; turning away I slammed the spade down and left in a fair old temper. That was my first outburst there…ever.

What really choked me was…she *was blooming well right*!

I had a dreadful night of fitful sleep, going over and over again what was said; I was sick with worrying.

During our tea break the next day at TA, I told them I had defied her orders to be there, and I broached the subject of my dilemma; they were very kind and even

Sarge came over to join in. A variety of criticisms were aimed Mrs W, before the topic of what could be done was seriously discussed.

I told them I'd once had the job offer from Joyce, but that it worried me; it would be living-in yet again, and anyway Cook's husband Tom worked there, it all seemed a bit close-knit. They agreed an alternative would be better; almost all said they would give it some thought.

They were so encouraging; I began to feel more optimistic immediately.

Later, when we were at the bus stop, rather mysteriously Brian said he had an idea, adding that he would have to leave it until the next TA meeting. He looked down at me smiling; I was so comforted, just leaning into him with his arms around me; he smelled so good and was lovely and warm. I was *dreading* leaving him, I felt safe…and was going to *hate* returning to that place; the thought made me shudder.

When the bus arrived, he didn't kiss me 'goodnight', but hugged me tightly instead; it seemed perfectly right and all the nicer for that.

The journey back to the farm was horrible; my imagination ran riot as I went through all sorts of different scenario.

The worst one by far was…as at the Murdoch's…she had packed my case and it would be waiting for me in the drive.

Nothing like that had occurred, but the ensuing days were pure Hell; she set out to be a Bitch…and achieved that aim with flying colours!

Whatever I did was wrong, even though it was exactly the same as before.

She would 'disappear' after milking; leaving me alone to sort out all the cleaning etc. but I made absolutely certain I would give her *nothing* to complain about. I had my own high standards to which I worked; these were hard to maintain under the circumstances, but *she* wasn't going to push me to change.

When she addressed me, she was bordering on being rude; I barely spoke to her at all…I honestly couldn't be bothered.

One morning I met Mr W in the hall; he hesitated in front of me as if he was about to say something, but then clearly changed his mind. He gave me an extremely odd look; not malicious…not particularly friendly…just odd. It conveyed nothing of its meaning to me at all.

Thank God cook and I could talk, which we did frequently and with animation; even more so since the revelations about the other previous staff and their hours. Apparently, when she told Tom how I'd stood my ground against Mrs W, he roared with laughter.

She then went on to say; she had known Mister W for long enough to realise that *he* didn't have much sympathy with her either.

*So that's what that look meant,* I thought to myself.

There were no orders for me to stay behind the next TA night.

The bus journey seemed to take double its usual time, and two things preyed on my mind. Firstly my exam; I thought I'd passed because it hadn't seemed too difficult.

Secondly, I wondered had Brian found a solution to my predicament; if not he, had anyone else in the group?

By the time we pulled up at my Stop it was dark, freezing cold and raining hard. I left the steamy, humid warmth of the bus and with shoulders hunched high, stepped onto the pavement…and nearly knocked Brian for six!

"Going anywhere I might know?" he laughed, as he caught my arm and spun me around to face him. I just looked up into that handsome smiling face, and felt like a million dollars.

"Right…*Plan A*. We have to go in for the first session to get our exam results tonight. *Plan B*. I'm going to ask Sarge if we can leave immediately afterwards; you have something to do and see before you go back to the Workhouse!"

"Oh Brian, tell me, please tell me…*now*"

He waited until we were on the next bus; what he related then I could hardly believe.

After the discussion of last Wednesday, he approached his Mum and Dad; he had apparently already spoken about me and the difficult working situation in which I found myself. They likewise had already said it was a disgrace; taking advantage of a homeless girl was about as nasty as it got.

His proposal to them was…would they consider allowing me to 'lodge' in their front room? He explained this was now only used at Christmas, and it was such a waste; they had readily agreed...but there was one condition.

"We cannot be any closer than at the moment; they seemed to think our friendship was more of a relationship, I told them that would be fine" he added, looking at me quizzically.

"Oh of course...you can be my big brother!"

We chattered and laughed all the way, I felt as though *two* enormous weights had just been lifted from my shoulders; one was I may have a new room, and as importantly, I knew *exactly* where I stood with Brian. I already realised how much I liked him, but was terrified of getting it wrong...or it becoming more than I could cope with; I did not really know what that 'more' was...but the ignorance had worried me greatly.

We both went over to Sarge and Brian explained; we were to get the bus to Rusthall, I was to meet his parents and see the room, then get the bus back to Crowborough.

"Good Lord! You *will* be pushing yourselves for time. Look...I'll do the exam business immediately; GET FELL IN YOU 'ORRIBLE LOT!!" she shouted, laughing.

We all passed…I was in the top three with my marks…higher than Brian!

Sarge came over with her congratulations.

"I've got a lance-jack out there who is ready to take you to Rusthall; he can't wait around to bring you back, but that will save you a good bit of time. Good luck Private Davis…you'll do all right" she added, with a wink.

"Cor! If it weren't against the rules Sarge…I'd *kiss yer*!" said Brian.

Laughing yet again, away we went; we were at his house before we would have even *boarded* a bus.

"Come on in you two cold, soggy people; you're lovely and early"

That was the welcome as Brian entered the kitchen from the back door; a welcome as warm as the room itself. We explained about our lift from TA; she beamed as she took my hand and led me through the narrow hall…on the left was 'my' door.

The room bore a strong resemblance to the one at Mrs Meadows; larger and brighter but just as homely looking. The walls were freshly papered and a dark red carpet covered the floor; in front of me, under the wide bay window, was a 'put-u-up' bed.

"Well, what do you think Sue?" she asked.

"I truly can't believe it...it's absolutely *wonderful*!" I replied with enthusiasm.

I caught the blissful expression on Brian's face as we were led back into the kitchen; over large cups of steaming hot tea, she continued.

"I won't go into the pounds, shillings and pence of this now, but I had some *marvellous* news today. If we can get you out of that blooming awful place before the weekend…you've got a job on Monday…as long as it appeals. I think it could be ideal"

On the bus back, I reflected on everything required of me to make myself a successful new life; we had discussed in depth the details of Brian's plans…as long as they worked.

Again I barely slept; bubbles in my tummy kept me awake.

Brian's mother, Mrs Chandler, had been so welcoming; I knew I would be comfortable in my new room…*and* the walls were plastered! I was very excited about living with a proper 'family' for the first time, especially going to and from home for work; Dollis Hill seemed such a long time ago when I had last done that.

It would be strange at first…but 'firsts' had never really daunted me.

With further excitement building I wondered.

"*As well as my new room…I wonder what Mrs C has in mind for my new job?*"

At long last the dawn came…and with it the beginning of my anticipated final day on the farm!

I went to the byre with a renewed spring in my step; trying hard to stop the grin which, without my self control, would have spread all over my happy face.

Mrs W was as rudely silent, as she had been for the last few days;

"*Oh if only you* knew" I kept thinking.

The work went smoothly; I had not felt this energised for simply ages.

"You look like the cat that got the cream"

I was washing my hands ready for lunch and cook was laughing at me; I had a feeling she knew *something* was going on, but was too polite to ask.

I would tell her of course, but in my own time…when I was ready. I immediately realised how shocking was my sense of trust in people; I was determined I would not breathe a word, until I knew cook was not in a position to tell Mrs W.

*"That's a disgrace Susan Davis"* I told myself; but I couldn't help it, I couldn't take the risk.

As we finished our meal, Mrs W came in with our pay; cook's envelope was a little fatter than mine though.

"I don' know why she does it Thursdays, every one else seems to get theirs on a Friday"

"Well I don't know if you realised cook, but I didn't get any on the first Thursday; I had to wait till the following week…but still didn't have any extra"

"Typical bloomin' farmer watchin' every blinkin' penny; they'd do you out of that an' all, if they thought they'd get away with it!"

I went back out to my afternoon duties; I was working up the lane, clearing out the ditches. She had instructed me to do them then, knowing full well I would get caked in mud from all the recent rain…but she would never know how perfectly she had played into my hands.

On her way home at the day's end, I stood up as cook approached; she nearly jumped out of her skin!

"Sssh...I want to *tell* you something"

"Oh my *Good Lord*!" was all she said when I related to her my plan, well Brian's actually.

196

"All I can do darlin' is wish you all the luck in the world, you bloomin' well deserve it. It's been a pleasure to 'ave you around, you're an absolute little treasure. Should you ever need 'er, just remember where Joyce is; I can unnerstand why you wanna be further away from 'ere, but don' you forget… now give me a big 'ug"

I returned to my ditching with a heavy heart, and tears in my eyes as I watched her walk to the top of the lane; she turned and waved, blowing me a kiss.

She was an amazing lady; had really kept me going through all the hard times.

She had made me decide too, to try and trust people; I had a dreadful feeling of guilt because I had not allowed myself in her case.

"*It'll come in time… or not*" I decided.

After cook had gone I suddenly felt vulnerable; goodness knows why but I felt extremely alone.

The day dragged on but at long last, all was done… *finito*!!

Mrs W and I went our separate ways…she to her sitting room…me upstairs to have my bath.

And…*pack my case*!

197

CHAPTER 22

By now I was breathless with anxiety and shaking like a leaf; I had seen her for the very last time...*and she didn't even know*!

Brian had asked what time the tray went in; his Dad had instructed me to leave a half hour before.

Thank goodness there was a clock in my room...at least I could work less frantically.

I was under enormous pressure from realising that without any doubt whatsoever; absolutely *nothing* could be allowed to go wrong.

Finally, under the dowel, I placed the working clothes she had provided; everything else was folded and neatly packed...I was ready to go.

Once completed, I returned to my 'post' at the kitchen table; on the stroke of eight o'clock I went quietly out of the kitchen and through the hall to their door.

The radio was turned on as loudly as usual.

Silently retracing my steps, I left from my own side door, hurried to the shed and got my bike. Still acting with extreme caution, I walked quietly up the steep path to the road, keeping to the grassy side so as to be as quiet as possible. To ensure it was completely hidden from view, I gently laid my bike in the ditch.

It was by now pitch black; I was absolutely terrified of stumbling or making any noise, but I made it safely back down the slope to the house. With enough time to comfortably go up my steps…I collected my case.

With a last glance around that dreadful cell, I made my 'under-the-cover of darkness' escape…to a new freedom.

I waited in the lane, for what seemed to be an interminable length of time; I could hear my heart beating in my ears.

The panic was real and painful and I was swimming in emotion.

Then at last…in the all-surrounding black, overwhelming silence…I heard a car.

Nothing came down this lane at night;

"*Thank God…It's them!*"

But it drove straight past!

The white of the headlights turned to little red dots…it was going away from me…I really panicked now…and was shaking all over.

*"How the Hell will you get back indoors if they don't come?*

*Do you want to?*

*Would you dare, when she will have seen the empty room?*

*She will know you have run away.*

*Where will you go now…*to Joyce*?*

*I'm not sure if I'd find it in the dark…she'll be in bed soon anyway.*

*Suppose they've broken down?*

*Perhaps they talked it over; maybe they'd decided it wasn't going to be a*

*good idea after all.*

*Maybe they don't want me there… and probably* **never did**!!"

Then the white lights returned…*they must have only gone to turn round*!

The car slowed to a stop and two chaps jumped out…*it was them*!

"Oh Yes!...*Oh! Thank you God… I honestly* mean that!"

200

"Hello young Susan, I am pleased to meet you, and even more so under these circumstances; does she know you've gone?"

Still in a state of complete panic, but now mixed with relief, I just grinned in response. Brian's Dad gave me a brief warm hug; he was as excited as me.

I decided we'd have had a *great* time at the 'Gunpowder Plot'…and we'd have made it work…most *definitely*!

They told me to get in while they hurriedly but quietly, stowed my stuff; we drove away very slowly into the dark night; to yet *another* new destination for me.

Inside I was shaking with excitement… and total, utter relief.

"You have nowhere else to go" she had said.

"*Yeah… right*".


Part of me began to relax as we travelled the road to my new home; the other part was wound up with the most explosive sensations, recalling what we had all just done!

"Well done Sue, sorry I called you Susan before, *very* well done indeed. Were you frightened at all?"

"Yes…I was terrified at times throughout the day; to cheer myself up I kept on thinking what I'm thinking now"

"George dear…where is that **stupid** gel…our tray is **late**…how **dare** she treat me like this. *I pay her for gawds sake!*"

My shrill mimicry of the exaggerated posh accent, made them both roar with laughter.

We seemed to have travelled a very long way, but the time sped past because we didn't stop talking; we were tripping over each other to say our piece.

"We are nearly there now Sue; all I can say is we all hope very much that you enjoy being with us…you don't have to be mad, but it does help!"

"Cook used to say that Mr Chandler, it always makes me laugh; thank you so very much…I'm *longing* to make my new start"

Brian was sitting in the front by his Dad, but he pushed his arm between the seats; he found my hand and gently squeezed a silent message "It's all going to be great"

There was absolute bedlam as the car pulled up; Mrs C and the other two boys were there as a welcoming committee…and what a great job they did!

"Cor! Smart bike Sue, bet that goes well, can we have a go tomorrow?"

"For goodness sake boys, just take it to the shed and let's get Sue in first before we do anything else! Come on love, the men can bring your case in, let's get that kettle on"

Suddenly I felt the dreadful pain return to my chest… I simply couldn't breathe!

The sheer magnitude of what I had just done, coupled with the kindness from these virtual strangers was too much; I was completely overwhelmed.

Because I'd not responded, Mrs C turned round; I could see from her expression she knew what I was feeling. She walked back to me,

"Oh my baby, it's all too much; you haven't told Brian everything, but we can read between the lines. Come on darling, get a breath, there's a good girl"

With that the men came down the side path; there wasn't enough room to get past. Mrs C was cuddling me in her arms, but let Brian and his Dad take over, saying she would make the tea.

They both stood there, either side of me and let me quietly cry out my pain.

"I'm *so* sorry to you all; the mad thing is, I'm so happy deep down"

"Don't you worry young lady, beside the normal emotion you must be so tired; you have had the most worrying of weeks, wanting every day to hurry by and then look at today! Gordon Bennett...I'd be exhausted too!"

That made me laugh and in better spirits, we joined the others in the kitchen. Brian's brothers were twins; they asked me to relate the daily farm routine to them...Brian had already given them an idea, they just couldn't believe it. They understood when I told them what cook had said...that two people did it before me. To keep the happy mood on a high, I then recounted the many humorous things that amazing lady had said.

Then out of the blue, from one of the boys;

"Were you at St. Christopher's Sue?"

The unexpected question rocked me a bit; this was one of the Homes just a few miles away in Tunbridge Wells, and where I had lived when very young. I shot a quick look at Mrs C...I couldn't handle that at the moment.

"Look, I think we should help Sue to get sorted in her new room now; you all drunk your tea? *Come on then slowcoaches*"

With that she leapt from her chair and 'raced' the boys down the hall!

I opened the case and we all dived in; clothes were in drawers and hung on hangers before you could say 'Jack Robinson'. They were intrigued with my books from Mrs M…and the fact that I did crosswords.

"You and Dad will have to fight for that then…he does the Telegraph too"

"When Sue gets this new job, she won't have to fight over a paper; she'll be able to afford her own. Now if all is put away, I'll take the suitcase to the cupboard under the stairs. You two boys go and have your wash and get ready for bed; we'll go back through and discuss this job, you've got the interview on Saturday morning if you want it Sue"

We went together into the cosy kitchen where Brian and his Dad were on the settee along the wall by the door; they invited me to sit between them. Mr C squeezed my hand and Brian gave me a kiss on my forehead; Mrs C sat at the table under the window opposite.

"Right then…this job. We have a good friend out on the Langton Green road that has a Nursery. She and grows all sorts; it's where we get tomatoes in the summer, and most of our other vegetables throughout the year. How would you fancy working there? "

"Oh Wow…I can imagine doing that! I was responsible for all that stuff on the farm; it wasn't as big as a proper Nursery would be, but I've a good knowledge of what to do…like side-shooting tomatoes for instance"

"Well she will be delighted. She's only in her late forties but already suffers quite badly with arthritis; she would want you to do most of the heavier work from what I can gather. I can't see it being more than you've already done mind you"

I explained to them about the feed delivery; the size and weight of the bags, and the struggle to get them put away each time.

"Blooming people who expect that from a girl need locking up" was Mr C's response to that, and we all agreed!

At my question as to whether I could go by bike, I was assured it was only about six miles away; not right into the village.

"That's not too far for me, I love cycling…if it's possible to make arrangements, I would *love* to go and have a look"

"We've actually made the arrangements Sue; we were only going to ring her if you *didn't* fancy the idea. Now, I go to Tunbridge Wells on Fridays; if you would like to come too you would be more than welcome. Dad gets the early train to the City, so I think we should all get sorted out for bed now…and he always goes first"

The three of us sat and chatted in such a relaxed way; they had put me entirely at my ease…I told them so with grateful thanks.

"Well we're *all* going to get on I'm absolutely certain" said Brian. "The boys are fascinated by you already"

"If you don't want to talk to them about the Homes Sue, it really doesn't matter. They have a boy at school whose Dad was in there that's all, there are so many in this area I suppose"

"Oh no, I don't mind at all, I can tell them the funny and weird bits; it was just a bit raw tonight with all the emotion going on. That's the only damage Barnardo's did though; because I am so aware of that, I can usually deal with it, but not when I'm taken completely by surprise"

Brian drew me near and again kissed my forehead; Mrs C got up and did the same.

Although virtually out on my feet, once washed and into bed I could *not* go off to sleep; the day had been one of the most amazing experiences ever.

It had only just happened, but it already seemed impossible that all had gone so well; leaving without her knowledge was scary…but the waiting in the lane had been worse.

Then I smiled to myself remembering dear cook and her clear delight in it all…and almost laughed out loud when I pictured Mrs W's face when she found the tray on the table…but the kitchen empty. I wondered…did she go straight upstairs to see if I was there…or go into him?

I would never know, but the differing possibilities rolled round and round my head...being out of there was the positive joy for me.

Already feeling warm and cosy in my new room…and tomorrow going out to town with Brian's Mum…I at last turned over; full of happiness and hope I drifted slowly off…to a beautiful peaceful sleep.

What an amazing start to my new life;

*"God I'm so lucky"* was my last thought.

Somewhere within the mist that was my mind, I heard a very gently spoken call, almost a whisper.

"Sue…Sue love…I think it's time to be up"

I always sleep flat out on my tummy, someone once said I resembled an ironing board; I lifted my head, and there was Mrs C with a cup of tea for me. The house seemed very quiet and still, and the late winter day was light and bright already...I turned over and sat bolt upright.

"Good grief Mrs C…what on earth's the time?"

She laughed, and then told me it was nearly ten o'clock; I had slept for eleven hours minimum. I couldn't believe it but I was wide awake now.

"Gosh, I hope I haven't held you up; I haven't heard a *thing,* but I do promise you…this is by no means what I normally do, I'm an early bird"

"Well I suggest an egg on toast is better than the worm! If you get a cardi on for now and bring your tea through, I'll get some breakfast on the go"

She was plump and a little taller than me; she had a bustling manner, while maintaining a tangible gentleness which was so endearing. She was clearly a contented, well loved lady; no wonder her family adored her, and I had seen already they most obviously did.

I sat with her at the table under the window, enjoying the welcoming homely atmosphere; tucking into my breakfast, I broached the subject of my 'keep'.

"That's not my department Sue, Mr C will organise that for you; however, nothing will be expected before you have your job. Brian was out of his mind with worry about what was happening to you at the farm; our one aim was to get you out of there. You go for the interview tomorrow but then discuss with Mr C if you would"

I stressed how extremely kind that was; I did have a little money saved from unspent wages and the harvest bonus. I promised I would sort it all out once I had the job.

Then she outlined the plans for the day.

"Once done here Sue, you pop in the bathroom; the bus stop's just at the top of the road, let's get ourselves into town. I'll show you where I always go; the Market, that sort of thing, but is there anything you need love?"

I told her from whom I got the majority of my clothes; I thought they would do for now, except work stuff. If I got this new job I would have to buy some tough trousers; a skirt would be ridiculous in that situation.

As we walked to the stop, and on the bus, we kept up a constant conversation; she explained how having a girl in the house was going to be bliss for her. To be able to wander round the town and just window shop would make a real change.

As we were heading for Tunbridge Wells, I mentioned Mrs Meadows. I told her the gist of the story; how surprised I was at her eventual actions and that I'd never seen her since. I had never managed to work out what I could have done wrong.

"Probably nothing if the truth be known love; she obviously didn't understand the inflexible demands of farming in general and of Mrs W in particular. Some people think they own more of you than they actually do. You have the unique capacity to mix great boldness, to make your way in life alone, coupled with extreme caution to protect yourself; Mr C said that to me last night and I think it sums it up. You did all you could to set matters right Sue; if your all is not enough, the fault is hers not yours…but just in case, we *won't* go into the 'Cadena'" she added, laughing.

I was so relaxed with this lady I could feel it was doing me good already; I carried the bags, which were increasing in number at an alarming rate, then we stopped for a tea and cakes.

"A little luxury for you Sue, certainly not what I do every day, but this is Special; you will probably be at work this time next week so enjoy it while you can. And talking of work; we'll go and have a look at some trousers for you now. Don't worry about buying shirts though, with a house full of men, I could kit out half the girls in the 'Land Army'!"

Those Mrs Walker had provided were heavy corduroy; they were uncomfortable because firstly, they were too big, but also they were far too hot…I'd been more than happy to leave them behind.

We looked at loads and eventually opted for some strong cotton, in a lovely girly, pale blue colour. She suggested I pay for one pair; very generously she would buy the others until I could re-pay her from my wages.

By the time we had finished we were well laden.

"That was the nicest shopping expedition I've had since Christmas; there's no need to ask if you have enjoyed yourself, you keep grinning from ear to ear!"

En route home, at my request, she outlined what I could do to help her in the house. At night I'd be last in the bathroom; I was to make sure I cleaned up after myself, to be ready for Mr C's early start in the morning.

She went on to say that once washed and into nightclothes, I could sit and have a last hot drink with them. I would also make my bed and clean my room; but other than that she would ask me as things turned up.

"Blimey…cushy or what…I've never had so little to do in all my life!"

"There is one other demand that will be made of you I know; the youngsters think you're smashing, they would love to spend time on your bike and so on. There are times Sue when an hour to myself after tea, when the evenings get lighter, would be absolute heaven"

"Deal" I said…and we shook hands.

# CHAPTER 23

I didn't sleep in for long the next morning; when I did wake, I was relieved to hear sounds from the kitchen and went straight through. Mrs C greeted me with a cheery but muted 'good morning' explaining that every one else was still in bed.

Mr C had no weekend work. Brian was a trainee butcher and went in at lunchtime on Saturdays; and the boys were 'at the age when they could sleep for twenty four hours…turn over…and do it again'.

We sat and had a cup of tea, but I declined breakfast.

"Yesterday was a treat but I don't eat it normally; at the farm I had already worked for three hours, so by half past eight, I was more than ready"

I went through to the bathroom to get ready for my interview; I was excited more than nervous and had high hopes my experience would stand me in good stead. Mrs C had given me directions and the procedure once I arrived; at nine fifteen I was on my way.

It was as easy to find as she had said; a pretty whitewashed cottage on its own, on the right hand side of the narrow country road. As directed, I went up the path and through a high heavy door by the garage.

To my left was a bell attached to the rear cottage wall; I was to grab the rope, give it about six rings and she would appear…it worked perfectly.

A small well-tanned lady walked towards me through the gardens; she wasn't slow to move, but an awkwardness in her gait was plain to see. She greeted me with a broad smile and firm handshake, told me to call her Meg, and ushered me into her kitchen.

I had made excellent time by racing a bit, but now the sweat popped my brow; she saw this and offered me an ice-cold drink before we sat down to talk.

She asked what I had done as far as work was concerned; when I told her, in all the detail I could muster, she was pleased…and said so.

"I went over to see Elaine last week; she told me the disgraceful state of affairs at the farms you were on. Those sorts of people give farmers a bad name; it's so wrong of them, but I'm glad the plans worked out. It was a risk to take, but by far the best way to get you out of there; I bet it was pretty scary for you though. I try to be fair here, and wouldn't ask you to do anything I felt was too much. In a minute you'll meet Lenny when he comes in for a break; he wants to go to Horticultural College when he leaves school in September and he works here Saturdays to get a bit of learning experience. He's a lovely kid and strong as an ox; he will always do any really heavy stuff. There's an old boy in the village I can also call on, but in truth he's a bit slow now; if you are as good at woodwork as you say, I would far rather you did it"

I looked at her but felt unsure yet of quite what to say; I swallowed hard and blurted out,

"Does that mean you want me to work here Meg?"

"It most certainly does Sue; you are as charming as Brian described you, and you most *certainly* have all the experience and attributes I'm looking for"

"Wow! I'm honestly over the moon Meg; I promise I'll work hard and never knowingly let you down…*oh I'm so pleased*"

We were doing a sort of jubilant jig when Lenny walked around the corner; poor kid, I think he thought we were bonkers! Meg introduced us and after his break was over, he showed me around the land.

It was enormous; amazingly deceptive after the size of the cottage and the frontage of the place. It spread out sideways on both side and seemed to go back for

216

ever; that is where the three long, narrow greenhouses were sited.

Most of the flower planting was bulbs, daffodils and such; then there was a large area for kitchen garden vegetables. There was a lot of fencing which acted as windbreaks; I could see what one of my immediate paint jobs was going to be!

Lenny was tall and thick-set, with a mop of hair as black as coal; a slow, quietly spoken sweet kid who looked much older than his fifteen years. He was extolling the virtues of working with such a clever lady.

"You'll like it here, she's good and kind, and loves to explain what's what; I've learnt so much to take to college, thanks to her. I've been coming here Saturdays for three years; she's never lost patience with me, not like they do at school. My Ma says I aint the sharpest knife in the box, but that aint no cause for being nasty to me. By the way, don't tell her I told you, but sometimes she aint arf in a lot of pain; she's got a bone problem and it aint gonna get any better. But she's a lovely lady, never moans; she just goes quiet sometimes…and that's when I know"

"And don't you worry about school bullies Lenny; I was brought up in Barnardo's so I know all about them.

You go your own way, do what you want to do; you'll be fine"

He responded with a warm broad smile and we completed out tour; Lenny went back to work and I rejoined Meg who was now sitting on the low wall at the back of the cottage. In response to her question I told her of the shopping expedition to buy the trousers.

"You don't do that here love; I'll pay you for those. Leave them here to change into, and each Friday, they'll go off with everything else to the Laundry. Get Elaine to give me a receipt for the business, and I'll settle up when I next see her"

I gave her the explanation for not needing shirts, and that made her laugh; hers was a really funny infectious laugh…and set me off with the giggles.

I felt absolutely marvellous on my return home; my tummy bubbles were joy this time…not fear.

"Well I don't have to ask how *you* got on young lady, I can tell from your face; oh Sue I am *thrilled* for you. Now come on in and tell me all about it"

"First of all, I think Meg is a lovely woman and I can never thank you enough for this opportunity. I start on Monday at 8.30am, but 7.30am when the mornings are lighter; I finish at 5.30 now, and an hour earlier when the morning time changes. There could very well be overtime then, especially if she has lots of orders to get out.

By the way, she would like the receipt for the trousers; she will pay for them *and* have them laundered. She will provide me with tea breaks morning and afternoon, and something light to eat at lunchtime…AND Mrs C…I am going to be earning more than DOUBLE what I got on the farm!!"

"Sue darling, that sounds wonderful and you are clearly so excited; well done love…you deserve it. Those horrible jobs, places, and people, will all have been worth while; the bad experiences will stand you in good stead, something good often comes out of the bad. But you look hot after all that cycling; why don't you go and have a bath and wash your hair…and we can natter while perhaps you'll help me with the supper"

There was a buzz around the table during our meal; everyone was pleased for me. Brian mentioned my being on the road in the dark…so the boys had already designated 'jobs for the weekend'.

"We'll give your bike a proper service Sue; brakes and a grease round, but especially the lights. Then we'll give it a road test just to make sure it's okay"

"You cheeky little beggars!" said Mr C.

The dishes were washed up cleared away quickly, with all of us in mood of happy contentment. We played cards after supper, they showing me many games I didn't know; Brian and I played Cribbage alone when the boys went up to bed.

He was obviously fond of me and likewise, but I was very contented with the arrangements as they were. We would travel together to TA and join the others in the coffee bar afterward; then come home…where I was already feeling like one of his family.

# CHAPTER 24

When I awoke that Sunday, I was surprised to hear voices; the two boys were in the kitchen with Mrs C…clearly no lie-in for *them* today.

"Hi Sue, we're going to have early breakfast cos we've got *loads* to do today" was their excited greeting.

"Good *grief* boys, let her get through the door! Here's a cuppa love, are you going to eat anything now?"

I declined and happily sat down, still in my pyjamas, as they related their plans; it was going to be a great day, I could feel it already.

Mr C was already in the bathroom; after his breakfast he also wanted to come out and help sort my bike. Then he wanted our help to clear the shed out; the sort of job that was right up my street.

I left them to it and started by helping Mrs C with the vegetables for a roast lunch.

"Gosh it's nice to have some female help Sue; by the time you've shown the men what to do, you could've done it all yourself"

This banter continued until she was satisfied all was ready; she informed me lunch was always at 3.30 on

Sundays as everyone lay in and had a late breakfast. Brian appeared in the middle of all this; Mrs C saw to him while I carried on.

"What a scene of utter domestic bliss" Mr C chuckled.

That was something I had already felt; this 'family life' scenario was new to me…and I found it rather unsettling…I kept choking up and feeling close to overwhelming tears.

The first trigger had been the constant hearing of 'Mum' and 'Dad' being spoken by the kids; my brothers had said Mum when we all first came out of the Homes, but my Dad was long dead by then.

Mrs Meadows and Bill lived a happy life, but even that seemed very different from this. It was going to take many emotional high jumps to get fully used to living amongst this beautiful domesticity; but it was *not* going to be a chore!

At last we were all fed and fit and ready for the fray.

The bike was attacked first; there was not much wrong save the odd adjustment here and there, a good polish followed, and that was it finished. Next, everything was hauled from the shed; that's when we discovered the old wireless.

"Cor! Can we have it on Dad? Mum only has the talking people, can we find some music? One of the boys at school has got a radiogram that plays records; he's got an Elvis Presley his Auntie bought him"

Mr C laughed, and with a pretend moan, brought it down from the shelf; it was an enormous thing, with the sun's rays in wood on the brown canvas speaker at the front. He gave it a good wipe over with a rag…plugged it in… turned the tuner around until all the whistling and buzzing stopped…Hey Presto, it worked!

Brian intervened then and found a station playing Pop music; I was converted instantly! I played violin and *loved* the Classics, but this was something new for me.

We heard Cliff Richard, Buddy Holly and Elvis. There was also Russ Conway…but they immediately took the mickey out of him, by dancing round the garden with pretend pianos and silly grins on their cheeky faces.

"Oi you lot…he's my favourite" shouted Mrs C, coming to the back door.

We all groaned in a very loud exaggerated manner!

The music happily played away, and made the clearing up very straightforward; Mr C didn't seem to throw much away, just put the rubbish back in a tidier order! It was a large shed and we had created lots more space; it would be easier to park my bike now, and would lessen the chances of scratches.

Mrs C called my name;

"Sue, can you come in now love…and you lot have got no more than twenty minutes to sort yourselves out. Brian, put that bowl under the outside tap, I don't want all their muck in my new bathroom"

I was allowed to wash in the kitchen sink; then under her instruction, I set out the cutlery for my very first 'Chandler Sunday Roast'. It was hard to believe the kitchen table would take us all; I had dragged it away from the window wall, and then fetched extra chairs from my room. I voiced my concern about occupying their Dining room, but was assured it was only used thus at Christmas.

It was a bit 'elbow to elbow' but we made it; Mr C carved for each of us and Mrs C served the veg with a promise of "more in the oven if anyone wanted." Once 'Grace' was said we all tucked in; it was a perfect meal.

I had to sit still for a moment, needing desperately to 'feel' the atmosphere; I wanted never to forget this wonderfully happy family experience.

Throughout the meal the boys kept on about riding my bike; they did have one each, but they were apparently far too small for them now. They had asked for anything *but* for Christmas; now it was a case of waiting for the next one…or for the birthday present.

In response to Brian's question, I said I didn't mind them going out at all; then he outlined a plan. We would all 'muck in' and get the clearing up done quickly; he would then get his bike as well, and the four of us would go to Happy Valley…up to Toad Rock.

"You won't have time to go there *and* back before its dark; what do you think Alan?"

Mr C agreed with her and came up with the best solution of all.

"I suggest what we do is this; leave all this washing up malarkey and forget using the bikes altogether. I'll go down and get the car…we all pile in…and go off and jolly well enjoy ourselves"

"Oi…you just hold on a minute to all that cheering and whooping about! There's one condition; when we get home, everybody mucks in and does their share"

To unanimous assurances this would happen, we were all ready to go; the car wasn't small, but it was a bit of a squeeze. We drove just a short distance out of Rusthall, and there we were; what a fantastic place!

There were lovely coppice of trees, and long walls of smooth stone and rock clung to the side of the pathways. We followed these paths, wending their way up and down, and then we reached 'Toad Rock'...and what a sight! It really was exactly like a crouching toad...I was absolutely fascinated.

It was lovely to have the space and opportunity to really let off a bit of steam; for too long I'd been harnessed to the rigours, decorum and discipline, of adult life...so I went a bit loopy! I charged around chasing the boys, who were amazed when I caught them.

"Blimey, you can run fast Sue...bet you can't throw though!"

Mock disappointment followed when I showed them I could; we slumped on the ground to get our breath back.

"That was one of the good things about Barnardo's; there were sixty of us in one Home, with enough space to run and play all sorts if games"

That opened the door to the conversation I knew they were itching to broach; they chattered all the way home. I learned about their friend at school, but his Dad's was not a name I recognised.

"It's like at school really; you only know the people of your age or in your class"

Brian and I washed up; Mrs C saw to the boys getting ready for bed, while Mr C garaged the car down the bottom of the road. When he got back, he returned the table to under the window and we all flopped down to relax.

"Well, what a day. We try to get out and have a bit of fun on Sundays Sue; everyone works hard all week, one way or another, it's nice to unwind and have a laugh"

"It's been absolutely wonderful for me and I cannot thank you enough; you have all made me feel *so* welcome and I loved the outing tonight. I'd never been up there before…I think it's a marvellous place and I'd love to go again"

With that the boys came over and threw themselves onto me; I had a double cuddle and a kiss 'goodnight', and then they were away to bed.

At the suggestion of Mrs C, I was next in the bathroom and made my way immediately to bed; it was my first day with Meg tomorrow...I wanted very much to be in good form

# CHAPTER 25

As lovely as Sunday had been…Monday dawned cold, wet and windy; but nothing could dampen my spirits about the new start. I left with time to spare as I was going to have to battle against the wind; I also needed time to change out of the wet things and into my work clothes, all ready folded in my saddle pack. Mrs C had put in both pairs of blue trousers and four clean shirts; she also gave me an envelope with the receipt for Meg.

Meg's greeting was cheerful, but with sympathies about the state of me after the ride…I was soaked! Once into her warm kitchen I soon felt better; I was in plenty of time to dry my hair a bit and get changed. Over a welcome hot cup of tea, she explained my first day.

Lenny had done a brief tour with me, but Meg and I set out to really see where everything was; she chatted as we went and brought up the subject of her disease.

Inherited from her mother, she was first diagnosed in her mid-thirties.

"I couldn't have chosen a worse career than horticulture; this place was my Dad's though, and I remember spending many happy hours out here with him, he taught me so much. He was older than Mum; once he was turned sixty, he reckoned he'd done 'his share' as he put it, and they upped sticks and went to Eastbourne. My brother could have come in with me, but he was the brains of the family; he does some old stuffy job and works and lives in London. Can you imagine leaving here to do *that*?"

I agreed that I couldn't; our chat had lasted all the way to the greenhouses.

"These three are used only for growing tomatoes Sue; come on in and see what we do. You can see there are no pipes; I won't put in heat to force them on at all, I could make more money…but they wouldn't taste as good. That's why people come here; the taste of everything is superb, cos I grow it all like my dad did"

We walked the long narrow concrete path that led to door at the other end; that was a good idea…two doors would save a lot of trekking to and fro. There was a counter either side of the path; underneath was stored the shallow wooden seed trays, and an assortment of watering cans.

"What on earth is *that* stuff?"

She laughed and explained; the counters were covered in a layer of soot, it was what she grew the tomatoes in! Everyone had at least one open fire in their houses, and the chimneys always needed to be swept; she bought the soot from the Sweep, as her Dad had done before her.

"It's wonderful stuff; he always said it was what made the fruit so red and juicy. The other huge advantages are; it doesn't grow weeds as normal soil would, and it needs little water to keep it moist. I do a natural feed once the flowers are on the vine, and that's it"

This was going to be a fascinating place to work, I decided.

"Over to your right are the flower beds, to your left is the kitchen garden area; those fences need your magic touch, I can't think when I last dressed them, but it will be a priority once it's dry enough"

We both looked to the sky as she said this; the rain had now returned as a downpour. The first job I was asked to do was to pull out the hundreds of trays and brush them out, ready for pricking out the seedlings.

The second was to tear through the rain down to the cottage; collect the basket on the kitchen table...and tear back.

"I need a blooming cup of tea...*this very minute*" she said, laughing.

The basket contained the wherewithal for making such; she showed me the way she did it, and we sat down on two upturned galvanised buckets, to enjoy our break.

"Tastes like nectar out here, dunnit Sue?"

The whole day continued in the same easy going fashion; that did not mean there was any slacking however...I worked hard.

As I was ready to finish, she told me I had...and that she appreciated my efforts.

"If it goes along like this Sue, I will be thrilled. For too long I've struggled on, but I just can't do it alone any more. You'll make an enormous difference to my life; for instance, before today, I would be bathed and in bed within an hour of finishing work. I was in so much pain after a day out here; I could bear it no more. I just want you to know what it means to me, and then if I get the grumps because I'm hurting, you'll know it's not a personal thing."

I was changed into my now dry clothes, and ready for the ride home; I waved as I left and I reckoned the smile on her face was easily as broad as mine!

I set out for home in almost dry weather, but then the rain came down in *sheets;* I just took my time, even I couldn't battle those elements.

"Never mind love, it means that spring is on the way when we get these heavy showers" was the welcoming assurance from Mrs C, presumably to cheer me; that may not have worked, but a ready run bath did.

"You look like an orphan of the storm" retorted Brian; so I chased him through the hall, flicking rain water over him.

While enjoying a hot supper, I talked over my first day at work; they asked questions and all showed an interest, which I found charming. Once I'd helped clearing up the kitchen, I spent an hour with the boys doing their English homework, explaining I'd thoroughly enjoy that subject…but maths was a complete 'no-no'!

"Don't worry about that Sue, Dad is the one who does maths with us, but he can't spell for toffee, and he's *rubbish* at grammar; how he manages the crosswords, we'll never know!"

"Well I'm rubbish at all of it…that's why I'm going to be a butcher"

"Bringing home the money you do lad, plus the extra bits the boss gives you…if that's rubbish, it'll do me son"

The atmosphere was perfect; it seemed to prevail throughout all my waking moments I felt it was the quiet skill of Mrs C; she was such an influence on everyone, but took no nonsense, she could give full vent if she needed.

"When I say **now**…I blooming well mean **now**…in **my** time…not **yours**"

That was her favourite; the boys would immediately respond, looking very sheepish.

Once tucked up in bed I reflected upon the fact that, a mere *four days* previously, I had escaped the Walkers and their farm; the comparison in my spirits was almost unbelievable.

It was hard to take in my good fortune of finding yet again, another group of truly kind people to counter-balance the bad.

I kept reminding myself of just how very lucky I was…but I wasn't really going to forget.

# CHAPTER 26

It was Wednesday already; Meg had made absolutely certain I would be away on time to get to TA without having to rush. Brian worked strange hours; an extremely early start but an equally early arrival back home. When I got there, he was washed and changed into his uniform; Mrs C had a cold supper already served for me and in no time at all I joined him.

I loved my uniform, and even under the difficult conditions at the farm, had managed to keep it pressed. Mrs C had let me use her iron on the previous evening, so I was looking extra smart. We stuck out like sore thumbs on the bus; but once assembled in the hall we looked a well turned out troop.

Sergeant Major Glazier was a Regular soldier and an absolute stickler for correctness; she could not *bear* a half hearted approach to anything. A brilliant Instructor…if you didn't learn from her…well you wouldn't learn at all.

She set as well as marked, our test papers; we would do these frequently enough to stay on out toes. When we were having the break before relaxation, I asked if I could see her in her office.

She was a straightforward lady; so I told her about the evening, when Brian and I had left early. She had been included in the discussions about my dilemma with the farm; I told her in detail about the escape…she looked at me in utter amazement…then roared with laughter.

"You young Davis are a class act; you will go a long way in this life…and if that is to be the in Regular Army, I would back you all the way. You have the makings of a really fine soldier; I say that to very few people who come through this door…so don't forget it! Now, I need your new address for the records"

When I was a bit younger, I wondered about a career in the Army; a lady came to my school and discussed various professions to help guide any decisions. All I wanted to do then was get back to my mother; history shows was an unmitigated disaster that decision had been!

Two of my sports teachers told me they thought I could get to Loughborough University to train to teach the subject; I would have been almost old enough now. However, the demands of working and avoid being homeless; the struggle to keep both job and roof over my head…these factors had formed my career decisions.

But I felt I'd done alright up to now; I had a beautiful contented mix of a happy home life…a job I enjoyed with enough cash to begin to fund life's little extras…and a circle of friends which was increasing all the time.

But, a couple of months further on, a disaster struck that turned my life upside down.

Sgt Major Glazier had set a hard routine of Drill for the first session; the weather was fine and getting warmer by the day, but by the time we were due our break, dusk was already moving in. Given the choice of leisure pursuit, we unanimously elected for 'indoor cricket'; we had played on many occasions previously, the hall was sufficiently spacious, almost the size of an aircraft hanger.

The game had proved as rowdy and boisterous as ever; my side was chasing the runs set by the first innings. I was always incredibly competitive, and tonight was no exception; the excitement was building. Having gone in at number three, I had seen a couple lose their wickets, but we had batted brilliantly. We needed just one more run for a glorious win…and I wanted to get it.

I faced the new bowler; a skinny kid, who seemed about eight foot high in my state of anxious determination to win this game! I'd seen a good gap in the field, and hoped that was where I could place the ball.

In truth, I had already selected the shot without the ball being bowled; too late I saw the spin. My bat was already in place, so the only correction I could make was to hit the thing with all my might, hopefully to counter the spin and travel far enough for me to make it to the other end.

I was away down the wicket as fast as my legs would carry me; *stupidly*, I then quickly glanced to my left, and towards the potential catcher.

A fraction of a second later I heard the explosive sound of smashed glass; a fraction of a second again, I felt the pain.

The far end wall into which I had just collided held a half-glass door; with my *ridiculous* lack of concentration I had veered to my left, and leading with outstretched fingers had gone straight through the pane of glass. I finished off the job by bringing my wrist down against what was now, a razor sharp edge in the opening; I was trying not to fall over.

Immediately, there was blood everywhere; the whole unit quickly gathered round, making varying noises of shock, sympathy and "urrgh!"

Sarge took over very quickly;

"Stand exactly in the spot you are now…can anyone see the tip of a finger?"

That was a rather disturbing way to learn of this detachment, but one of the girls *did* find it; Sarge stuck it in place and wrapped plaster around from the ample First Aid tin already accessed.

She secured my wrist with a crepe bandage, informing me it was a terribly deep wound that would need to be stitched. The whole process only took a few minutes, but the Ambulance had already arrived; they drove me with Sarge, to the Kent and Sussex Hospital.

When the lady doctor cut away the jacket sleeve to expose the injury, I heard Sarge merely 'breathe' out… "Christ Almighty!"

I looked too, and was immediately violently sick.

My wounded foot had been one thing…this was *definitely* something else.

The doctor's deft fingers gently worked on removing glass and stitching me up; there was a moment of light relief was when she said;

"Well done for finding that little piece of finger Sergeant; it's a shame it's been put on upside-down!"

"I'm a soldier...not a blooming doctor!" responded Sarge.

We laughed hilariously...as much to calm the nerves as anything else.

It was really late by now; poor Sarge had to get me home, and then go all the way back to write a report for Head Quarters.

"I'll be out in the morning at some time; you'll have to verify what I write and sign it for me, blooming good job you're right-handed!" she declared, laughing. She put in my good hand the bag Doctor had given her, saw me safely indoors, and was gone.

Brian and his parents were anxiously awaiting my return.

"Goodness gracious darling, you've been *ages*; before you tell us what happened at the Hospital though, let me just tell you this. Brian rang Meg from the telephone box on his way home; he caught her before she went to bed and explained what happened.

When he said you probably wouldn't be in for work tomorrow, she said you're not to worry; she wishes you well…and she wants you to go back in and soon as you are fit enough. Now then, what on earth have you done love?"

"Well…I had a lady doctor and she was brilliant; she's made a right mess of my uniform though, but Sarge says that will be replaced for free under the circumstances"

"Forget your blooming uniform; tell us what happened!"

I then explained I had been given three local anaesthetics in the wrist and palm of my hand. Describing what she was doing to me all the time, she had to scalpel out the flesh to remove the dusty glass and other small bits in the wound on the wrist. I had managed to cut clean through a muscle or tendon; that was now pushed under the wrist joint.

After all the stitches were in, she put in place a strong splint. It ran beneath the arm from the elbow, down under the wrist and palm, and was supporting my little and ring fingers; she said she was doubtful my knuckle would ever go back into its rightful place, but it was the best she could do.

She repeated the cleaning procedure with my index finger...that was a real mess; I'd got seven stitches in that too. Once she was satisfied with her art work, she crepe bandaged the whole from above the elbow and all over my hand...I looked utterly ridiculous!

"Well Sue love...what drama!" sympathised Mrs C.

"You were *determined to* get that last run kid; I could see the expression on your face! As a matter of interest...you weren't caught. The ball went high, right up into the roof void; on its way down, with the fielder directly underneath, it just scraped one of the beams. It deflected enough for him to miss it; so you were *in*...and you've gone down as a Win"

I grinned with delight at that bit of news and thanked Brian; he was a lovely chap and knew how pleased I would be with that result.

"Sue, you're beginning to look suddenly very pale; I think we all ought to go to bed now. Skip a wash for tonight, there's no blood anywhere so they cleaned you up well. You go through...but if you can't get undressed...I'll come and help you."

I coped okay with getting *out* of my clothes, but made myself laugh trying to get my pyjamas on; I called Mrs C for help…we were absolutely collapsed with the giggles once it was done.

"It's going to be a real burden having your hand sticking straight out in front like that Sue; but we'll manage. You've got to go back to Hospital on Friday according to the paper you had with you. They'll see then if the splint is going to work, or if you'll need a plaster; they can't tell till the swelling goes down.

I've brought in the tablets; take the pain killers now…and there's a sleeping tablet just for tonight. I'll leave water by the bed for you, but I imagine you'll go out like a light"

Getting comfortable before settling down had created even more problems.

If I could have managed without getting the giggles, I would have done so much better…but I could *see* myself slowly getting into a pickle.

Fortunately, I still had full movement in my shoulder and elbow joints, but getting over on to my tummy was where the real trouble began.

I turned to left and right before completing the first manoeuvre; by now I was throttling myself with my own pyjamas! Once in a comfortable position, I couldn't get my hand to move, it had got stuck underneath me somewhere… and so it went on.

At last I settled down and, with the help of the tablets, enjoyed a deep contented sleep.

I woke of my own accord, to the accompaniment of an orchestra percussion section banging away in my wrist and the end of my index finger… I will admit to swearing under my breath and feeling fully justified!

I went through to Mrs. C in the kitchen; she made me some toast and I took more, most welcome painkillers.

Difficulties presented themselves during every procedure that day, but I soon realised this was going to be the established norm for a while. Getting out of bed was only slightly easier than getting in had been…putting on my clothes was something I could have done on a comedy stage…and going to the bathroom is best not remembered at all!

Mrs C was as helpful as she could be; I knew I'd manage eventually, and as I said,

"I've got all day to do it anyway"

I kept my appointment at the hospital, managing to go on my own; Mrs C offered to accompany me but I felt I was already being a bit of a nuisance. A nurse removed the dressings and when the Doctor examined the wound, she was satisfied with the progress.

She explained the swelling would soon go down, and it would then be less painful; there was no need for even a lightweight plaster cast, just carry on as I was, and go back in ten days.

"And of course young lady, work of *any* sort is out of the question, at least until the stitches come out"

*Damn it*! I could think of all sorts of jobs I could have done for Meg.

Now the health issue was decided, I was suddenly frantic about finances. I spoke to the nurse who had done the dressing; she was so kind and told me where to find the Almoner.

She explained I may be entitled to what she called a 'Sick Payment'. I would have to go to the office in town…and the sooner the better she'd added. Although feeling a bit wobbly from the doctor's fresh poking around, I felt I had to get there immediately.

First of all they gave me a form to fill out, telling me to post it back as quickly as possible. In some alarm I explained I couldn't take that length of time to sort something out; I was in lodgings out in Rusthall, where I *had* to pay my way.

She was so kind and her response was to fill it out for me then and there...she read it through and said I would definitely qualify for  the help...and that she would make sure it was dealt with immediately.

I was grateful to hear this and rather pleased with my all achievements, but  now I was feeling dreadful; the pain had returned to a massive extent and I desperately needed to get back home, where Mrs C greeted me with a hug;

"Oh my darling, you look grey; you need your tablets and a hot drink, sit down, I won't be a moment"

I declined her kind offer of a light lunch as I had no appetite, but I joined her at the table while she ate hers.

She was delighted to hear the Doctor's prognosis, and even more so when I told her about my additional trip to the place that dealt with the sick pay.

"Gosh, no wonder you're nearly falling over. Look, why don't I help you get undressed; you pop straight into bed before everyone gets home love. You can always get up in a dressing gown for tea, if you feel better then"

She was such a sweet lady; I *was* feeling rough so that was a most welcome idea. I quickly went to sleep in the quiet of the almost empty house.

I was gently shaken awake by Mrs C quietly telling me my next tablets were due; it was gone four o'clock...I'd slept four five hours!

She was preparing food and offered me again;

"Thanks so much Mrs C but I'm still really not hungry; is it okay with you if I just settle down again?"

"Of course it is love...I honestly didn't think you would get up again. You stay there and have a good rest; you'll feel tons better in the morning"

With her usual kiss on my forehead, she left me to sleep.

# CHAPTER 27

"Well, all I hope is, she isn't going to spend the whole blooming weekend in bed"

*Blimey*, Mr C talking about me...in a *very* loud voice; I was suddenly wide awake.

That comment was followed by an extremely loud "*shush!*" from Mrs. C; followed shortly after by a gentle knock to my door...it was Brian.

"May I come in for a mo?" and with a nod from me, he sat on the end of my bed.

He looked at me sadly;

"You heard that didn't you love...I can tell from your face; don't get upset though Sue...that's just my Dad. About sixteen months ago, on his way to London, he was involved in an awful train crash; more than ninety people died. He suffered a bad bang to his head, and had multiple bruising from being thrown about. He was in hospital for quite a while; his recovery was slower because he's such a big heavy man. He did well, and went back to the City as soon as he could; he loves his work. In a short while though, Mum noticed these loud outbursts of shouting; she believes half the time he doesn't even know he's doing it. Sometimes he has the patience of Job…as he always did, and then there'll be a time when he has a storm…like you just heard love. He takes tablets every day, but they can't stop it completely"

For reassurance, Brian held my hand in his, giving it a very gentle squeeze; he gave me such a lovely warm smile.

With that, the door was flung wildly open; Mr C stood there, looking like thunder.

"I *told you* when you first came here young lady…I was *not* going to put up with any of this canoodling behaviour. *Brian get out of this girl's bedroom…now!*"

I looked at the monster in the doorway…and began to tremble inside.

His voice and contorted face were horrible; Brian was clearly embarrassed and livid with rage, shouting his denials in response. Then silently Mrs C arrived to guide them away; I closed my eyes to shut them out, and lay silently while they continued the *fracas,* back through the hall and into the kitchen.

It seemed to go on for ages.

I heard the footfalls on the stairs as the boys went quietly up to their room; poor little devils, an early night through no fault of theirs. A short while later the back door slammed shut; I strained to hear the footsteps…it was definitely Brian.

I decided to take the tablets beside my bed and lay back down; for a while, all that was audible was a low murmuring conversation, no more shouting.

I heard my door being gently pushed open; I stayed stock-still, feigning sleep. Whoever it was came to the end of my bed for a moment, then left again.

I was not ready to talk to anyone; I wanted to think.

I very well understood about the head damage *and* the terrible affect it had on poor Mr C. I understood that he could have shouting fits, or 'storms' Brian had called them. BUT…what I couldn't come to terms with was this; you can only shout out…*what is already in your head*!

My being in bed when he got home had upset him…*but why*?

Had he *never* trusted Brian and me?

It was only forty eight hours since the accident; I was certain some of my weariness was due to a bit of shock, not just the running around. The pain killers too were making me sluggish…and I was in bed at Mrs C's suggestion anyway!

*"Gawd...he'd have got in a right old rage if I'd gone through for tea in a dressing gown!"*

In addition to his first outburst was the disgusting accusation against Brian and me; that was dreadfully unfair. We had talked over the situation on a couple of occasions; I actually admitted to him one day that I was *much* more comfortable with being just friends. His manly pride was touched a little initially, but he soon realised what I meant.


I next awoke to the clinking sounds the milkman made; he always stopped his float right outside my window. Strange though, there was no sound from the kitchen of Mr C getting ready for work; then I realised…it was Saturday.

Eventually I heard the familiar sounds of the kettle, and Mrs C moving around; no voices though, so I got up and joined her. We had a most subdued talk about the previous evening; she apologised profusely, but I said I knew what the trouble was…Brian had told me.

"I'm glad he did that but my goodness, I don't think I've *ever* seen him so cross …he was *furious* at what Alan accused you of"

251

I made no comment, mainly because I didn't really know what to say; she knew it was wrong though, so I settled for that.

I saw Mr C only briefly; he had been down in the garage for most of the day. I went out for a walk after having a sandwich at lunchtime; I saw him later at supper. Conversation was rather stilted it seemed; I thought he looked a little embarrassed but no references were made…so that was that.

Brian was up early on Sunday; I was always up, washed and dressed… but he usually enjoyed a long lie-in.

"Sue love, how would you fancy a bus ride out to see Meg? I've not been out there for *ages*; she'd love to catch up on your state of health"

I didn't need to be asked twice; it was quite clear Brian had no intention of lasting through a 'brooding' weekend. There was still an atmosphere indoors which couldn't be helped I supposed.

"You two go off when you're ready; I'll do you a roast for when you get back. Goodness knows what time the buses are, but make sure you check on the return one; it's too long a walk if you miss it"

Brian laughed as we strode up the road;

"Mothers never stop ordering you about do they? God I'm glad to be out of there for the day! I feel so sorry for her and the boys…but blimey he drives me nuts sometimes; what he said to us was a disgrace"

We only talked a little about the row; what we both needed was some peace and quiet and a *laugh*…guaranteed with Meg!

She was thrilled to bits to see us, even though we'd not given her any warning; Brian gave her brief details of the situation.

"What a shame love; I wish I had your Mum's understanding but I haven't, I think he just gets tired and frustrated at work, then takes it out on you lot…I do honestly Brian"

This was added because of the look on Brian's face.

"What he said to Sue must have been already in his head to begin with; he's not 'hearing voices' for goodness sake…he's being nasty! I've known your parents for years darling; he's *always* been a bully. *Bloody great lump*"

That made us all burst out laughing and rapidly cleared the air; I then had to relate all the gory details about my hand. We drank tea, chatted and laughed…a lot; I felt myself unwinding and could see the same in Brian…this had been an excellent idea!

He was extremely fond of Meg; he helped her by getting in some coal and wood, while I helped get the meal ready. We declined the kind offer to join her, explaining what Mrs C had arranged.

"Anything need doing outside Meg before we go?"

She gratefully accepted our offer, and we set out to do the watering; even I could manage that. I filled one can at a time and carried it to the greenhouse door, Brian did the rest; we were done in no time with this conveyor belt arrangement.

"What a Team" Brian chuckled as we returned to the cottage.

In bed later, I reflected upon my day.

Meg was most scornful in the way she had talked of Mr C; stating exactly my own thoughts, and then informing Brian about the bullying. I smiled to myself when I recalled the laughter that ensued!

We were both stuffed full with her 'tea and sympathy' and left on a high note; I promising to go back as soon as the stitches were removed. All the way home we maintained the same levity; we both agreed it had been a wonderful day.

These deeper thoughts made me suddenly aware of what I had allowed myself to do; simply because I felt confident that I could. Mr C had only hurt and frightened me because *I had dropped my guard*; my barriers were down.

I'd allowed myself to fall into the happy comfort of a proper home life; I trusted him and *believed* when he said he loved me being there. It did not at any time occur to me that this could become resented by him…or was perhaps a lie from the outset.

From the very beginning I had enjoyed my new way of life, and had 'fitted in' as Mrs C had described it. Over the months I'd helped in the garden as well as the house; on numerous occasions I'd taken the boys out on my bike...and we had all spent another Sunday up at Toad Rock. Nobody could have been happier at having such a marvellous family life to enjoy.

Upon reflection, they were his exact words of welcome; "*think of yourself as one of the family*"

Brian told me again on the bus ride back, how much he, his Mum and brothers enjoyed me being there. She apparently made constant reference to my willingness to help, not just her but the boys as well; she frequently repeated how grateful she was for this.

I knew that was all true…now I felt Mr C had spoiled it all. I supposed I would never know what it was all about…but I did know I'd have to learn to live with it and not to let it worry me.

My barriers were immediately back in place; he had suddenly changed everything. I knew I would also have to make changes…but this time for myself.

I felt enormous relief that I was not going to be instantly dismissed and thrown out; nor was I going to have to make a dramatic escape.

What I decided to do was to carry on exactly as I had before…but with much more care.

I would only move when the time was right…but I would definitely have to move.

## CHAPTER 28

I was buoyant when I left the Hospital; aided by the fact that ninety per cent of the pain had gone as the stitches came out. The splint was removed; a lighter dressing covered only about half way up my arm, but the hand was still fully bound.

The Doctor had suggested a plaster cast may have helped secure the dodgy knuckle; it would have been painful on the rest of the wrist and wouldn't guarantee then that it would ever sit properly. We decided it wasn't worth it and as it stood, I could go back to work in another week…*that* was the most important piece of news.

The people at the office had dealt immediately with my application for sick pay; I'd gone back in to pick up the form to change into cash at the Post office. Almost all the money I got went to Mrs C for my keep, but I didn't need much more anyway.

I returned to Rusthall; with the last couple of pennies I had in my pocket, I rang Meg with the good news. This was Friday and she told me she wanted me in for the *whole* of the day on Saturday week to catch up…I was ecstatic.

Mrs C was concerned though.

"Are you sure you can work like that Sue? I know you want to earn again but it looks terribly cumbersome to me"

"Oh I promise I'll be alright; there are *loads* of things I can do with just one hand. Brian and I managed well with the watering…and there are miles of fences to paint. Meg knows what the damage is and will take care of me."

That was probably the slowest week of my life…*ever;* I couldn't even go to TA until I'd 'signed off'.

At last it arrived and after supper, I went to my room to get everything ready; as riding my bike was a long time off, I had sadly to go to my nest egg again. I'd dipped in a little already, but it was times like this I was grateful for my prudence.

I took a ten shilling note through to the kitchen to get change for the bus fare; the conductors could get quite nasty if you produced much more than the stated amount. There was always a sign up to tell you 'PLEASE TENDER EXACT FARE WHENEVER POSSIBLE'; there was apparently no leeway if it was **im**possible!

Brian had loads of change in his pocket; he counted it out into my hand and then squashed the note back in as well. Before I could voice my protest he gave me a smile and a wink, and mouthed the words "for you".

What a smashing guy he was.

"No bike then Sue; gosh that's a heavy dressing on there still...do you think you can *work* like that?"

Meg's ebullience often showed with the rate she spoke; this was one of those occasions.

"Meg you have struggled on your own for over three weeks, I'm *sure* there are things I can do for you"

She didn't make much of a reply; I got into work clothes and we went up to the greenhouses. The vines were heavy now; I couldn't believe the change in such a short time. She left me there to do the watering; it was a dreadful struggle in truth, but slowly I managed it all.

Once completed, she asked me to go down and get the tea things and we sat down together; I was gasping by then...*and stupidly said so*.

"Well Sue love, I've been watching you; I am worried on two counts. Firstly, I think it's going to be impossible for you to manage all I really *need* you to do; it is obviously a painful struggle for you, and it will take too long. The other worry I have is when that dressing comes off. The insecticides I have to use, the tomato fertiliser as well…I couldn't risk you getting an infection. I'm sorry darling…this aint gonna work out"

I was fighting back tears…*absolutely devastated.*

I stared straight ahead and could say nothing for a ridiculous length of time; I just did not know how to respond. I think too, I knew in my heart I wasn't going to be able do it.

"Meg I am really *truly* sorry cos I love it here…do you sometimes *hate* what life deals out?"

"Believe me I do Sue; this blooming bone thing drives me mad. Maybe I'll try and find someone else…or perhaps I should take stock now…just sell up and move on."

We were both clearly, very much down in the dumps.

I thought for a moment, and then almost screamed;

"*I've* got an idea Meg. *You* can't do the fencing; you said you've bought all the preservative *and* there is urgency to get it done now. I could *easily* do that with just my right hand! Whilst I do, I could get a paper every day and see if there's work around that *would* be appropriate. I *promise* it would only take me a week"

She put back her head and laughed.

260

"Susan Davis, you are *indomitable* without any doubt! Actually that is a *great* idea…so the deal is done. I know how disappointing it is love, believe me I do…but we've got to maintain sensibility too. Your health has to come first and think; if you got that wound infected…you could be off work for *months*"

I whooped with delight at this outcome and returned the tea things, helping as best I could to clear up. Changing again to go home, Meg said she would get Lenny to have everything ready to start on Monday morning.

A week to turn my life around…*again*…was the only thought in my head.


There was genuine sympathy at my news when I got home.

Mr C seemed to have returned more to his old self recently; he was being especially kind. He voiced sympathetic understanding and made generous offers to help; he promised to buy every local paper he could. Brian would check any display boards in shop windows and Mrs C was going to make an extra trip into Tunbridge Wells, to the office that dealt solely with local jobs. I couldn't have asked for more.

Meg got me 'arranged' as she called it for doing the painting; she bound my arm across my chest, to keep it out of the way and to offer me a little more comfort. Adorned with an over-large coat she explained had been her Dad's, I was covered quite literally from head to toe…and set to work.

My bad arm was really comfortable in its strapped position; I worked like a Trojan. Being extremely right handed was fortunate and I managed to cover a huge area each day. With such clement weather, I was in no doubt it would all be finished by Friday…or Saturday morning at the latest.

I finished it by Friday; Meg was delighted…and said so.

"I didn't doubt your pledge Sue, but gosh you've gone some to get that completed…and doesn't it look posh! Well done darling…Gawd, I wish you were *staying*" she gave me a hug.

It was mid afternoon; we went up to the cottage for a late cup of tea…did a tidy round outside…and that was me… *unemployed*!

I made the tea while Meg pored over the paper.

"Wow Sue…listen to this"

'Female wanted - to work as Petrol Pump Attendant'

She read out all the other details and I thought for a moment, trying to imagine the role.

"I reckon I could *do* that with one hand…and the other is getting better by the day; what do you think Meg?"

"Well it's rather a long way out, on the other side of Tonbridge; that would be…um…about twelve or thirteen miles from Rusthall. I reckon you could do the job physically. And another thing love…I'd give you a fantastic Reference"

"Oooh Meg! What a break …*I wonder*"

"Well young lady, there's only one way to find out"

She went to her phone; I had butterflies in my tummy while it rang.

When it was answered, she simply got on with it.

She explained the job was for someone unavailable to speak with at that moment; a girl just under nineteen, strong and very efficient…but there is one, very temporary draw-back.

She told them about my hand, making special emphasis of the fact that it was suffered while attending a local Territorial Army Meeting…she gave me a

263

knowing wink when she said that. I had worked for her with total satisfaction…and she would recommend me to any employer.

"Yes, yes I'm sure that will be agreeable with Sue. If for any reason it is not possible, I will ring and let you know. So that's ten thirty tomorrow morning. Well thank you, thank you very much indeed"

We just stood and looked at each other in utter amazement!

# CHAPTER 29

The amazement duplicated itself at home; Mr *and* Mrs C had seen exactly the same advertisement! They were fascinated to hear that Meg had already arranged the interview.

"It *is* a long way Sue…but you'll be fine once you can ride your bike again"

Brian looked at me in sympathy…and then with inspiration.

"I know what Dad! I've still got those old straight handle-bars in the garage. It's the drops that are going to be awkward for ages"

He then turned to me;

"If I fit those for you love, who knows, you could be riding again in no time"

I smiled my thanks, and then my thoughts turned to getting there in the morning; Mrs C knew all the bus routes and numbers, so that was soon sorted.

I could only afford to ride one way; I wasn't prepared to raid my nest egg for a blooming bus fare. I'd do like the racing car drivers did and 'walk the track' to familiarise myself with the hazards of riding in when I was fit enough. About halfway through the journey, I seriously wondered if that had been the most sensible decision I'd ever made in my life; it was not only *miles* away…the hills were amazing…up and down like a switchback.

I was relieved when we made it in to Tonbridge town; and as *un*relieved when we continued out again…and seemingly miles more down the Hadlow Road…the address was Hadlow Stair.

At last I was there…"D.Vinell & Son"…that was it.

I faced a small forecourt housing three petrol pumps, with a kiosk to the right; two more pumps stood on the wall of a large engineering workshop, which formed a rear back-drop. I confidently made my approach to the small side door.

"Good morning Sir, I am Susan Davis. I hope I'm not late but the bus seemed to take ages"

"You are almost spot on time so don't worry. I am Mr Vinell senior…I'll take you to meet my son, Andrew"

I was in their engineering workshop; a huge building with the 'Vinell Lathes' all around me, in varying stages of manufacture. From the office emerged Andrew, who looked more like a vicar than an engineer! He was charming and shook my hand.

He explained the manufacturing plant was still the main concern of the business; they had the empty space at the front and by popular demand, had installed the pumps.

We went on to the forecourt, all new and gleaming in the green-and-yellow BP livery; the kiosk on the right housed the till and a shelf for sweets. At the rear of this building was the small oil store; piled up were cartons of glass bottles, about half each of pints and quarts, these were filled by a hand-operated pump.

In the same colours were watering cans and buckets; he explained I would check customers' cars for oil and water, and clean the windscreen when required. The Air line for pumping tyres…and the Diesel and Paraffin pumps were set to the rear; we passed these to end the tour, and went back to the office.

I was aware the 'interview' was conducted in conversational terms during the walk around; he had even mentioned the wages, they were *excellent*.

"Right Sue, you seemed extremely interested in all that; you clearly like cars and get on very easily with people…but do *you* have any questions?"

"I would just like to reassure you that after having looked around, I have no worries about actually operating with just one hand for the moment. It is healing very fast, and should be top form in about a month"

"Well that's ideal; we have a start date of four weeks on Monday. Would you please wait here while I just pop out and get my father?"

Four weeks?

What on earth would I do for money till then?

Oh well, at least I had a positive to look forward to; it appeared they were going to offer me this job and I'd love it here. Perhaps something would turn up; I decided not to panic…at the moment at least.

They returned and both were smiling; Mr Vinell snr again shook my hand;

"Well young lady, you are just the quality of girl we were looking for; if you would be happy to start work for us, we would be delighted to have you on the team. Next week, you will receive a letter of confirmation from us; this will outline what is required of you, your start time on the first day and the shifts thereafter…and details of your promised wage"

Now we were *all* smiling; I thanked them profusely.

"Are you going straight back to Rusthall now Sue? I have to be in Tunbridge Wells in a half hour…can I take you to there to shorten your journey?"

"*Shorten your journey*" is the understatement of the year I thought…as I swept down the road at the rate of knots, in Mr Vinell's Daimler.

Once home again, Mrs C and I were sitting in the kitchen when the back door flew open; Brian stood there and, almost shouting, said

"Guess who *I* saw today and guess what I *heard*!"

"Hang on a minute son, Sue was describing her new job"

"Oh I *am* sorry Sue, but look; I've *got* to go to work this very moment so let me tell you quickly. Bill's just told me we are going to TA Camp… for *two weeks.* I'll tell you more when I gat back"

"When Brian?"

"Tomorrow week, AND my boss has *got* to give me the time off, it's the Law. Blimey Sue…will you be *able* to go if you've only just started a new job?"

"I don't start for four more weeks!!"

There were "Yippees" all round…especially from me.

# CHAPTER 30

On a hot summer's day, the MOD 7- tonner trundled down the road towards Folkestone. I sat back and reflected on my good luck at even being there, it seemed to be nothing short of a miracle; I could not fully take in how rapidly the whole thing had developed.

Because of my hand and Brian's work, neither of us attended the previous week's meeting…but Bill Stracey had.

He lived just up the road in Rusthall; when he and Brian had bumped into one another, and Bill casually mentioned Camp, he could not *believe* we didn't know. Clearly, our dispatched letters of information had simply not arrived.

The rest of the details were given out at the next Wednesday meeting; we had a complete itinerary of where to meet, what time, where we were going and so on.

During the break I went to see Sarge in her office.

"Sorry to trouble you Sarge; I wanted to tell you I am not able to do the Nursery job any more. I went back for a week, but sadly it proved impossible. She thought the risk of poisons in the wound was too high; however…I start a new job shortly after the end of Camp. My hand is healing fast and I just want to be assured I can go, even though I know already I won't be able to participate in all the things on the list you gave us"

"Private Davis; this is going to be an experience I want you to have more than *anybody else here*. I would take you with me in any shape or form…barring yer bloody coffin! I will be there; we can work around any difficulties…so go off and *enjoy*"

After studying the routine and plans for the fortnight, the excitement was building fast. One of the best bits of news for me personally; we were to be on full Regular Army pay for the whole two weeks…when I faced Idleness and Destitution.

"*Yes… there is a God*" I decided…for not the first time in my life!

Eventually we came to a gentle halt and alighted from the back of the truck; I immediately realised this place wasn't called 'Tin Town' for nothing. Neat rows of low green huts stretched into the distance for as far as the eye could see; there were acres of well-mown grassy areas and miles of dead straight pathways, running to and around each hut. Everywhere was *immaculate* of course, this was the Real Army.

We lugged our kit bags to where Sarge was standing; we got 'fell in' and she did a brief inspection.

"Right you lot. Firstly welcome…and I wish you all a really happy, beneficial experience. Remember you are not on holiday *per se* but that does not mean there won't be fun; there will be as much as any of you lot can handle. The first thing to do now is go to your hut…so "About Turn – Quick March"

We marched in perfect order, as a unit we were good at Drill and this felt incredibly special; once inside Sarge said she had watched the others…ours was the best performance bar none.

I had one brief nauseas moment as we trooped in, with flashbacks to Barnardo's dormitories; identical bedsteads and mattresses, all laid side by side in the same rows. It was harsh but momentary; I quickly snapped out if it to listen and follow the orders.

First was to make our beds; having made my own from being only knee high to a grasshopper, the regulation neat hospital corners to sheets and blankets was absolutely no problem. Even with only one and a half hands, I completed mine in double quick time. I was asked to help the others; one left-hander couldn't 'get it' at all…and we were all falling around laughing in no time.

Prior to leaving we had each been given extra kit; this we stowed in our bedside locker as ordered by Sarge. Besides our own uniform skirt, shirt and battle-dress jacket, we found boots, slacks and gaiters…and khaki, Army Issue shorts.

These I held up in front of me…and immediately my vision of half the hut disappeared. Each leg must have measured *at least* eighteen inches wide, and they would clearly come down well below my knees; to top it all they had turn ups…and a pocket!

The waist band was about four inches deep; this held three small buckles with which to do them up.

Raucous laughter rang around the place; Sarge came in, obviously to see what was going on, to cries from the others;

"Get 'em on Sue…go on…let's have a look…oh go *on*!"

"Aw Sarge, these have *gotta* be a joke…we can't possibly wear these"

She looked at me with that wicked twinkle, and laughing with us said;

273

"They are all there are girls…and you just thank God they recently stopped issuing knickers…now they *were* a sight to behold, I promise you. The MOD reckoned they cut down unwanted pregnancies by 99% when they were in yer kit"

They had left out nothing in said kit; everything was there, even all the toiletry requirements…I was rather surprised not to find a khaki toothbrush!

Once all was put away in its correct order, Sarge did another inspection; then we could sit on our beds, while she outlined what we could expect of the fortnight.

She explained it was virtually 'Army Basic Training'; not quite as rigorous or harsh maybe, but close. We would be shown how to salute, when, and to whom; how and when to correctly address an Officer and so on. This was essential to learn and follow; it was after all, a Military Establishment.

We were to undergo 'Instruction' of varying sorts each morning, but would enjoy 'Relaxation' in the afternoons. Except for organised trips, Town was 'Out of Bounds'; the perimeter fence was our boundary. There were NAAFI stores on Camp; one where we could shop for essentials and the others in which to relax. .

"There is no need to be constantly marching, but please go about the whole area in an orderly, respectable manner. I'm in charge of you, but there are Senior Officers everywhere; they will observe *you*…and therefore judge *me*…at all times. I trust you implicitly not to *ever* let me down. Now look across that path there; the building at the end is the NAAFI. You may now leave…in your best order please…and get some deserved refreshment. Back here in twenty five minutes"

We unanimously agreed we had the best Sergeant of them all; she was kind, patient *and* concise.

The NAAFI was brilliant; there was a whole variety of hot or cold drinks, cakes and so on. One side of this vast room housed a couple of table tennis tables and a Juke Box…which as we entered was playing 'The Theme from a Summer Place'.

It was a beautiful piece of music by the Percy Faith orchestra and was in the Hit Parade; we all knew it and unanimously decided it would be 'our song' with which we would associate this Camp!

We got our drinks and relaxed while absorbing what had happened to us; it had already been an amazing day.

The precision of that 'twenty five minutes' order from Sarge had not escaped our attention; we returned on time…exactly.

Prior to lunch we found our way around our immediate vicinity; toilet blocks, wash areas and so on. After a smashing meal, we learned how to 'bull' our boots, press all our kit…and how to properly get into the slacks…and gaiters.

"I'm sorry Sarge, I've given it my best efforts, but my wrist is still too sore to cope with the strength of the new webbing, it just won't do it"

"That kit is only used for driving in Sue; it is expected everyone else will still take their opportunity, but don't worry, I think it would be impossible for you to steer or change gear anyway; it's still early days. I'll find you some spuds to bash, or some other equally scintillating occupation!"

"No wonder we all *adore* you Sarge" I responded, to more laughter.

We were allowed then to relax on our beds; some dozed a little, others chatted quietly…I lay and reflected.

The farms had been quiet, isolated places compared with London, where I'd previously lived and I worked.

I'd mixed well with my colleagues, but a social life had been out of the question through a complete lack of spare money. It took me all my time to keep body and soul together; this pressure was the main reason for moving to the countryside, and to live-in posts.

Much of the farm work was carried out virtually single-handed; I saw no-one who was not in some way connected to the farm environment. Once my long hard work day was finished, I sat alone before crashing into bed, invariably shattered.

Now I had a full, proper life.

I recalled how exhilarating my first TA meeting had been.

The noise level was overwhelming, primarily because it had been such a very long time since I was around so many people in one go. The new faces and conversations, the quick wit and laughter, the Drill and the fun; all this had made for a genuine excitement. This was a great crowd…and this was going to be a great two weeks.

Sarge re-appeared;

"Right then you lot, the schedule for the rest of the day. You are all due Lunch in twenty minutes; have what you like but don't overdo it cos it's blooming 'ot out there! On your return, you are to get out your new kit; I want you to use your button sticks and do all the brass buttons on your jackets. Then polish your shoes and new boots with the 'spit and polish' method I showed you earlier. I will then inspect you, wearing your full uniform; tomorrow is Church Parade and you will be officially inspected by one of the big-wigs. There is no need at all to be nervous; concentrate…get it right…and help any of your colleagues who are struggling. You're a good crowd; if you listen to me…we will win the 'Best of Camp' award…I have *every* confidence in you"

I coped well with the buttons; awkward to get started with my weakened wrist but eventually I made it. I just sat and looked for a while at the next task; covering my knees with a cloth and holding a shoe tightly gripped between, I completed that to the desired level. I'd done the boots too even though I wasn't going to be able to drive; it seemed right because the others had to.

We compared results and examined what each of us had done; it looked pretty good to me…and we felt that Sarge would be happy…or hoped so.

"This is only the first of these procedures, but I must say I am delighted. If you can turn out like that tomorrow, I'll be proud of you. Go over now and have some tea…then does anyone fancy a run-around?"

There was a cheer that rather said it all; we trooped over to the NAAFI with the promise of a game on the sports field after.

"But Rounders I think…not cricket ay Sue?"

As we re-grouped, Sarge came over and asked how I was coping, stressing that she was more than happy; I said I was fine. I explained I was a little concerned about throwing myself all over the field in my present state, and demonstrated how Meg had bound my arm across my chest to make sure it couldn't be used instinctively.

She copied the idea exactly and I had a great game; I could bowl *and* bat without any pain whatsoever. I'd always had a good throwing arm and was placed out to 'deep field'; I could still throw in okay, hampered only slightly by the binding.

I'd enjoyed the burst of energy for a change; my hand was improving but it was beginning to feel like it was taking too long, it was becoming a bore. I was a strong, fit individual; I wasn't used to, nor did I like, this stricture to my freedom.

The first week sped by in the same extremely enjoyable manner; the weather had stayed sunny and hot. As a group we were forming friendships between ourselves; all this and the benefits of learning new skills. We learned far more quickly because we shared any problems between us; there was someone always ready to help out.

Although we regularly attended TA meetings together, this new camaraderie occurred, simply because we were suddenly living side by side.

Sarge wandered into the hut; during the chatting and laughter, she mentioned the following day was St.Swithin's Day.

"If it rains then…it will rain for forty days and forty nights"

There were groans all round but I realised; the day after that was my birthday…my nineteenth.

Most Birthdays experienced in the Homes had been pretty horrible affairs.

Every year we each received a card and gift from the 'Round Table Association' which was brilliant; my mother never ever sent to me. Once Uncle Tom and

Auntie Dodd were gone from my life, there was no-one else to bother.

I'd been moved up to Lancashire when I was twelve years old, with the dreaded matron Miss Boagey; she made sure I was always 'punished' by being sent up to the dormitory to bed…it became an annual event!

Most of the places I'd worked didn't even know, and thus it became just another day that came and went; this was going to be no different, as again I hadn't told anyone.

"*Happy birthday to you – Happy birthday to you*" etc was my wake-up call!

The whole hut was singing, led by Sarge who *had* made a note…and informed them all! There was a mountain of cards, one from each of them, *and* an Invitation to a Party in the evening; I couldn't make up my mind whether to laugh or cry…what a fantastic gesture! It seemed almost everybody on camp knew; I'd never heard as many greetings in one day…*ever.*

We washed and changed into the best of our 'civvies' for the party, and all trooped over in high spirits; the kitchen staff had laid on sandwiches and sausage rolls, and there were many more cards. Brian came over and gave me his card…and a quick peck on the cheek; we'd hardly seen each other socially, it was good to have him near again.

We started with our usual coffee, but then someone proposed a 'Toast'; for this, Brian bought me my first drink, a 'Babycham'.

I'd only ever had a little sip of cider before; in all honesty I judged that to be preferable…but the 'Babycham' *was* in a prettier glass.

The juke box was blasting away; we were all up on the floor, frantically jiving to Bill Haley, Little Richard, Buddy Holly…and of course Elvis, the King of them all.

"If anybody puts on Russ Conway, I'll personally kill 'em wiv me bare 'ands" laughed Brian; we grinned at each other at the 'in-joke, remembering the wireless incident.

Later, one of the chaps from the Royal Green Jackets asked me for a slow dance, he was good-looking and a blooming good dancer. I had been a couple of times to the Victor Sylvester Club when I lived in London; it was nice now to have a chance to enjoy the outcome of that instruction. I did glance across to Brian but he was utterly engrossed, enjoying himself swooning with one of the girls from the next hut.

He introduced himself as Les, and after a couple of dances suggested, as it was so hot in there, we should go out for some fresh air; immediately outside, he held me very tightly…and kissed me!

He wasn't at all gentle like Brian; it seemed to me like he'd lost his chewing gum in my mouth…and was trying to find it with his tongue! At the same time he was roughly groping me, which I found utterly disgusting.

A bit shocked, I broke away…and hurried back in to the others.

After I'd found and joined him, Brian asked with concern,

"Are you okay Sue?"

His dancing partner was on the floor with someone else, so I wasn't disturbing him. I nodded, and then told him very briefly about what had happened; he held my hand and told me not to worry.

He chuckled loudly when I described what I thought of the kiss; that's when I learned it was a 'snog'… *strange word as well as act…* I thought.

Once back in the hut I made a little speech, conveying my surprise and sincere thanks for a wonderful birthday. After all the excitement it took us ages to settle down; long discussions ensued about who liked whom, and the many and varied experiences of the evening.

I still felt a bit cross and slightly embarrassed about Les…so didn't contribute much to that conversation; there was however complete agreement… it had been a brilliant night.

With so much to learn, and with the relaxation that new friends bring, the days simply flew by; already we had reached the last afternoon. This held enormous significance; this was the ultimate 'Inspection' we had been all working towards.

We mustered a full assembly on the Drill Square, with all the other different troops…together for the first time ever. I was especially smartened up as I was appointed our 'Right Marker'. This *was* an honour, but it was mainly to save me from swinging my arm while marching with the others; any one of us would have done it perfectly well.

I was making the 'Mark'; the target to where the others would march, and line up in the straight line demanded. My responsibility was to be the lone soldier, standing to full attention, eyes straight ahead and remaining absolutely motionless; the scorching heat made it more difficult, but it passed off perfectly.

Once lined up, we received our Final Inspection; I didn't know who the dignitary was, but she had enough 'scrambled egg' on her shoulders to be at the very top of the ladder. Once that process was completed, it was she who was to make the announcement.

With the immaculate turn-out of today…and all the other efforts and successes…we were indeed pronounced as the 'Best of Camp'.

Sarge maintained her sense of gravitas while still on the parade ground, but did an unbelievable '**whoopee**' once back in the hut!

She was beaming and punching the air…absolutely thrilled to bits; we burst into "For she's a jolly good Fellow" followed by three *sincere* heart-felt cheers.

Many congratulations were given and received, but then it was straight down to the packing…for our return home the following day.

There was a darned sight more noisy conversation on *that journey*; we were now friends as well as colleagues, and happily refreshed our days, almost one by one. We recalled the many ups, and very few downs…and the apparent non-stop laughter over the whole two weeks. It was agreed again, we had a *brilliant* Sergeant; we had seen most of the others by then, and we weren't impressed!

I again expressed my thanks for my much appreciated birthday cards and party; everyone had enjoyed it…and they demanded I promise, that in future I would celebrate every year…and remember the Camp one forever!

They explained further;

"Sarge told us the date; amazingly you were the only one to have one while we were away; usually you could count on a couple at least. She said she doubted you'd had much to celebrate as a kid, and gave us free rein; we bought the cards on the one day we were allowed into town in the first week"

That brought on another round of reminiscing; there was no doubt we had gained an enormous amount of learning from just two weeks…and an undoubted lifetime of memories.

Once back home, our welcome was a positive 'Event'; all that was missing was the bunting in the street! Brian and I were both bombarded with questions at ten to the dozen. By the time we had described it all, there was full agreement from the twins that they would join up as soon as they were old enough.

We luckily arrived in time for supper as Mrs C had laid on a meal bordering on the quality of a Christmas lunch; to my surprise, we ate sitting around the dining table in my bedroom! The Best table cloth, crockery and cutlery were arrayed; there was much more space than in the kitchen…it was perfect.

The evening passed into night, and we were still chatting. Mrs C and I cleared up and rearranged my room; but then we joined everyone else to continue the Camp stories, and catch up with their news.

Eventually the party died away and we made off to out beds; it was really late but I found it difficult to sleep.

Reflecting on the fortnight, and relating the details to the Chandlers, made me realise just what there was in life now I could actually afford to be a part of it. I had learned what really close friendships could mean…and expected the trusting bit would come more

287

easily now; I felt deep pleasure and pride in what I had managed to achieve.

After having enjoyed such a 'growing-up' experience…I felt I could welcome the future with far more confidence.

But I had one persistent thought that was keeping me awake.

My Barnardo's Uncle Tom was an Officer in the Army; he would have been so thrilled and proud of me…and I wished so much I could have shared it with him and Auntie Dodd. Tonight's thoughts were tempting me to change my mind…to try and find them again…but I think I knew really. I would be happier in the long run keeping to the decision I'd made in that field; it was correct for me then…and I knew deep down it always would be.

*But God, I miss you so very much*…was my final thought…before a deep welcome sleep took hold.

# CHAPTER 31

The Hospital appointment arranged before Camp was happily to be my last.

All the dressings were removed; the healing was superb underneath, and there was nothing to show from the recent exuberant activity…especially on the sports field. They supplied me a great roll of padding and plasters, with directions in how to apply it before working; this was for extra protection from the petrol and oil.

Before leaving there finally, they sent me off for a session of 'hot wax bath' physiotherapy. I plunged my hand in to  warm melted wax; once lifted out into the cooler air, the wax  'set' on my skin. It was like wearing a very soft warm glove; lasting for about an hour it was an experience of absolute, painless bliss!

I was supposed to have gone back for more, but it couldn't be arranged because of starting work.

WORK; what a wonderful word that was…I could hardly wait.


"There's a letter here for you Sue"
I ripped it open in excitement;

289

"Oh brilliant news! It's from Andrew at the garage to say they are looking forward to my start on Monday, and there are more details too. Apparently my colleague is called Pat; each day is split into two shifts, and we do a 'change-over' halfway through. We are to work alternately each week, mornings and afternoons. Gosh! I can hardly believe it's nearly here now"

The next evening, Brian and I went down to his Dad's garage to change the handle bars over on my bike; the difference holding the straights was amazing. I could not have managed with my wrist twisted underneath the drop handlebars; straight in front of me was perfect. I did a practice run up the road and with minor adjustments to the height…I could ride again!

The short time left before my new job was the ideal time to get used to cycling again, so I went over to see Meg; she was delighted to see me so tanned and fit. I told her about Vinell's, but she already knew; in response to their request she had sent a great reference for me, exactly as she'd promised.

I helped her around the Nursery for a while and then went in for tea; she wanted to hear everything about Camp. She was a delightful lady and relished hearing about the birthday…and the Best of Camp award.

As I left, she thanked me for everything I'd done. She expressed again her disappointment that I couldn't have stayed at her job… and she wished me all the very best in my new one.

After that trip out, I made sure I rode for a few miles every day and gradually restore strength to my hand; this gave me the confidence to cycle the thirteen odd miles to work on Monday.


It was a chilly but bright morning, and I relished the ride on the near-empty roads. I was due to start my shift at seven o'clock; being a stickler for punctuality I'd roughly worked out the time…plus a little extra. As I braked on the forecourt, Andrew emerged from the small side door of the workshop.

"Good morning!" we hailed each other cheerily.

He showed me the best place to leave my bike; where the wash room was, and where to find the uniform coat I was to wear. It was white with the BP green collar…and their badge on the breast pocket…very smart.

"You made excellent time Sue; I like good timekeeping because it shows an added interest. In your case too I imagine, it's not just a 'first day' thing"

I assured him it most definitely was not; it was a particular of mine, and conversely, I could not bear waiting around for someone to arrive.

The 'opening up' was common sense, and very straightforward.

I read the numbers on the pumps even thought no petrol had been served; it was what would happen on every changeover in the future, so may as well start now. I filled the forecourt cans with water and placed them on the petrol pump 'island'; I then carried out the two sand buckets to deal with diesel or paraffin spills.

My very first customer was Andrew himself; he brought the car to the pumps and I filled up as requested. He then left it there until the first 'real' driver arrived, obviously tempted in by the 'customer' already at the pumps.

*Clever stuff,* I thought.

Halfway through a fairly busy morning, I felt the same thrill as I had experienced at Camp; the amount of people and conversation was stunning…I was going to *love* this job! My hand was giving me no problems at all; bound up in the plaster it made quite a talking point, and I heard details of many similar experiences.

Andrew and his Dad occasionally popped out to check all was going well; they were as delighted as I with the first morning's sales. Almost all the customers were 'locals'; it was they who had persuaded them to open the place…a big risk but it seemed it was going to be worthwhile.

Lydia, the secretary also came to the kiosk with a mid-morning cup of tea; she added sweetly, that if the men had forgotten to discuss food requirements, she had packed some extra sandwiches for me just in case.

"I doubt you had breakfast before your long ride in; it will be almost mid-afternoon before you're home. You can't possibly go that length of time without something to eat and you're welcome to share; I'll bring them out to you when the forecourt is quiet"

I was touched by her kind thoughtfulness; she was a small dumpy lady with a happy ready smile. I imagined she was of a similar age to Mrs C…and clearly just as motherly…a real sweetie pie.

The morning shift was from seven until one thirty, the afternoons from one o'clock till seven thirty; this gave the half hour changeover…and my first opportunity to meet my new colleague, Pat.

We got on immediately; it was clear from the outset we would be a happy working team. She lived just a mile away and knew of the Vinell family; apparently they had seen loads of applicants, and she was as thrilled as I that we were selected. One of her aims she explained was to find a millionaire with a Rolls-Royce; so we agreed to see if we could find one for each other!

"My Dad says it's good for the soul to have ambition…and that's mine… glad you approve" she added with a cheeky grin.

We went over the procedures together as it was the first day; she agreed with me it was straightforward enough.

Once back home, there was only Mrs C waiting for me; the holidays were almost at and end and the boys were off somewhere with their school friends. She wanted to hear every last detail and was genuinely pleased it had gone well.

In answer to her enquiry, I told her about the sandwiches Lydia had supplied.

"Silly me…I didn't think about food until you were gone this morning, but in future I will. Are you starving now or will the usual time for tea be okay love?"

I assured her it was perfect…at her insistence I then went off for a long relaxing bath. There I mused over the long journey; it had created no problems at all…in fact I'd loved it. With my competitive nature I was pleased with my times both there and back.

There was however one part which was going to present me with a challenge.

It was a steep 1 in 4 hill just outside the town; it had been brilliant whizzing down there this morning, but returning upwards was another thing entirely, I'd had to dismount almost at the beginning. I decided I'd count how many journeys it would take for me to pedal non-stop from bottom to top; quite a few I imagined.

The day of that achievement eventually arrived; at last I'd ridden non-stop… all the way to the top. I almost fell off the bike…my legs had 'gone'… thigh and calf muscles were on fire, and my chest was ready to explode…every part of my body seemed to be shaking.

Utterly barmy…but I'd enjoyed the mastering of such a challenge.

After the necessary rest at the top, I was in high spirits when I again set off; a few miles further on, I free-wheeled down the gentle slope to the village. A short distance ahead I could see a little lad standing on the pavement; about four year's old he was clad from top to toe in full cowboy outfit.

As I approached, he lifted his little plastic 6-shooter pistol and pointed it straight at me; I drew closer and he flicked the gun, while making loud guttural sounds in his throat to mimic the sound of shooting.

Immediately I let go of the handle bars; clutching my hands tightly to my chest...where I had just been shot...I let out a dreadful gasping *urrgh - urrgh* sound and fell on to the road.

When I rolled over to see where he was...he was gone!

My last sight of him was his little legs going ten to the dozen, charging like lightning down the road to his Mum.

When I related this to Mrs C she was in stitches.

"Poor little tacker bless him, he won't forget that in a hurry...I can hear him going indoors and yelling...'**Mum**...*I just shot a lady off her bike*!'

Andrew was thrilled with the rapid progress being made; he actually said as much which, after the farms, was so refreshing. It was what Meg always did and created a warm happy atmosphere; I found it encouraging…and make me want to do even better.

Those harsh times of the farms were now truly over; the constant angst about the frailty of my accommodation situation…my personal need to work too hard just to be liked…they were long gone.

I was at last being appreciated in my own right and was already a popular member of staff…Andrew had said so more than once already. It was going to be easy to work hard here with these sweet people.

It had been stressed that in addition to the petrol, the other sales were equally important; engine oil, windscreen washer sachets, and so on.

Unless there was a line of cars waiting …unusual at the moment…I would always attempt to sell more; something I loved to do.

"Shall I check under the bonnet for you…and when I've done that, if you pull over there, shall I check your tyres?"

Most were delighted with this service and readily agreed, especially the lady drivers; often their reaction was hilarious. They considered you to be a 'Mechanical Genius'…because you knew where the dip-stick was!

Some of the men could be no more familiar with engines.

One morning a gleaming black Daimler pulled in; the gentleman stepped from his car to unlock the fuel cap…he was *immaculate* in every detail. Well-pressed striped three piece suit, pristine white shirt with Old Regimental tie, and highly polished black brogue shoes.

I studied him as I filled the car; definitely a Company Chairman or better I decided…clearly a well-educated, successful man.

He was grateful for my offer to check things over; I always did the radiator and battery water first, as that was free to the customer…afterwards I checked for oil and the other sales items. Having removed the dip stick from deep inside the vast engine housing, I showed it to him, adding he needed a quart of oil to top up to the proper level.

He peered at me through extremely clean, very posh gold-rimmed spectacles…and solemnly said;

"Thank you but I think I will just take two pints for the time being"

I quickly caught his eye thinking he had made a joke, but no; this specimen of great success standing before, me didn't know that two pints *was* a quart!

My first shift of afternoons brought visitors in the shape of the local Constabulary; they went in to see Andrew then all came out together to have a word. They were asking for our assistance in the form of Observers.

I was handed a printed list of about twenty car numbers; these were known as stolen in their area. I was told to study it frequently in a covert manner; not to put it on a notice board for instance. If we subsequently found a 'matched' car, we were to tell someone immediately…and the police would pursue if possible.

I never found one of theirs…but did, in a way, go one better.

A few weeks later, one mid-morning, a pale grey Morris Minor drove in; it was highly polished and in the most beautiful condition. As I approached I immediately 'felt' there was something not quite right.

My first concern was the driver; in his late twenties, he looked the wrong age, this seemed to me to be an older persons' car. He mumbled his request for four gallons and I went to the rear to fill up; I couldn't because it was a locking petrol cap. These were not fitted as standard on the Moggie, and were an expensive rarity anyway.

I returned to his door and asked for the keys, which initially confused him; he removed them from the ignition and handed me the whole bunch... obviously with no idea of which one was needed.

I put the petrol in as slowly as I could without alarming him; I tried to catch the attention of Lydia, but she was not looking out of her window at that particular moment.

The price of petrol then was 4/11d per gallon; almost all customers took four gallons, and left as a tip the four pence change from a pound note. The Moggie driver handed me his note; he then waited patiently for his change...another oddity.

The moment he drove off I was in the office; I gave Lydia the number and a short while after her phone call... the police screamed by like bats out of hell with their bells ringing.

We were surprised when they rang before Lydia finished work, to thank us for our co-operation; the car *was* stolen and they *had* made an arrest.

I was even more surprised when a couple of mornings later, Lydia brought out a letter…addressed to me by name.

*Sevenoaks.*

*Dear Miss Davis,*

*The Police gave me your details and I write to thank you for your observational skills, which allowed my car to be returned to me  before I even knew it was stolen.*

*I park daily in Sevenoaks station and catch the train to work in London. On Monday I had dashed back having left some papers behind, and unwittingly left my keys in the boot lock. I was amazed when I received the telephone call from the Police, telling me my car was found.*

*The young man concerned was a sailor who was late for the return to his ship; he saw the keys and just helped himself. He was en route to Chatham when apprehended.*

*Before the day is through you will receive a bouquet of thanks.*

*Yours…….*


This was read by all of course, with appreciation that he was so grateful and had demonstrated this by going to the trouble to write to say so; with my permission it was pinned on the office board.

The beautiful flowers, my first ever bouquet, arrived as promised; I gave them to Lydia to say 'thank you' for her help in it all. The finale to this saga; the police called in to add their thanks.


I quickly discovered I had quite a talent for selling; being of such a competitive nature, I found it a challenge. The oil really sold itself, but I added to that in many ways.

As cars drove in I would make sure their indicator bulbs were working; when I told the customer I had checked, they would be quite happy to switch on all the other lights as well, and I would replace when needed.   As I washed a windscreen, I would surreptitiously check the edge of the wiper blade for wear, then sell and fit a replacement.

I had suggested the replacements idea to Andrew, saying I felt sure it would work; he was fascinated with having to re-order so quickly because it did…and was clearly well received by the regulars. I was as pleased as he from a business point of view, but there was an unexpected and very pleasing spin-off…in the form of tips.

By the end of my first months' work, I was almost doubling my wage in this way, as indeed was Pat. We agreed an arrangement; the tips from the petrol we 'pooled' by leaving in a tin to be shared out occasionally.

This was fairer as those sales were largely dependent on the different shifts; the mornings were mainly much the busier. The rest was down to our individual efforts, so we kept them for ourselves on a daily basis. I had more money than I'd ever dreamed of…but I decided to still save and add to my nest egg…to have cash there when I needed it.

That need came more quickly than I could have imagined.

The autumn days were rapidly changing to winter; my cycling trips to and from work were becoming tiresome due to the colder, but especially the wetter, weather.

On a visit to Mrs C, Meg had brought with her the blue working trousers bought for the Nursery; she thought these would be more comfortable on the bike. A few days later I arrived soaked to the skin for the afternoon shift; they were nothing near to being rainproof.

I always made sure I had time to change ready for work, but it was all the fiddling about I was getting fed up with. I dried myself off, changed into my skirt and took the wet clothes into Lydia; she draped them on radiators, so when I set off later I'd be warm and dry...at least to begin with.

I went to the kiosk for the changeover.

"You looked like a drowned rat Sue love, come in and we'll sort things out"

Pat was a kind girl who loved to chat, often staying a half hour longer than she need; but this day we really got things sorted out.

"Look Sue, it's all very gallant riding in like you do, but why don't you do like me and get yourself a Vespa scooter?"

"Wow! I don't think I could afford that Pat, I've got to pay my lodgings and even with the tips, I don't have a lot to spare"

"Well, I've got a friend who is having a baby early next year; she wants to sell hers and she won't be asking the high shop prices…just have a think about it"

Being so cold and wet I did just that; when Andrew came out later I asked his advice.

"I must say I worry about the onset of this awful weather; even at your age that amount of soaking doesn't do you any good. You would most certainly save hours over the week in travelling, and you certainly wouldn't get anything more economic to run"

Once home in the evening and talking it over with Brian and the others, their response was a unanimous yes. I was more than warming to the idea…except for the financial problem of actually buying the blooming thing; I didn't have *that* much saved up…I decided to forget it until I had.

Andrew came into the kiosk a couple of days later.

"At the risk of being very cheeky and pre-empting any decision you may have reached, I've had a word with Pat. She has given me the facts and figures; my father and I have a suggestion for you. We are promised this scooter is in excellent condition; the lady is going to have it serviced and the road tax is valid for eight months. What we would like to do is this; we will pay for the bike in full…you pay for it over a 12 month hire purchase arrangement…but with no interest charges"

I gawped at him in amazement;

"Am I allowed to kiss the Boss?" I asked with a cheeky grin…he blushed!

"Andrew that is absolutely *marvellous*! I'd love to do that and I promise I'll pay every penny back to you. *I know what*! I could let you have all my tips each week…I'd still have enough to pay Mrs C"

"That is more a kind gesture than a good idea Sue; I'm certain you will be able to pay the instalments *and* have some left for petrol and so on. I'll work it out and we'll go from there"

And that's what he did.

Pat let me have a few goes on hers as a trial; I took to it like a duck to water. By the end of that week….thanks to all concerned…I had wheels!

The biggest bonus was, I could now get to TA *every* week, albeit a bit late; better than not at all because of the extra cycling miles.

# CHAPTER 33

The arrival of a new garage had created a considerable amount of interest, and a rapidly building *clientele*; Mr Vinell had been very shrewd by listening to local demand. He'd planned well the use of the rather ugly empty space at the front of his engineering workshop; apparently it had been had been a familiar sight for years.

Further interest was created by Pat and me.

In most small garages one would find the Attendant to be a fairly elderly man, with equally elderly baggy trousers held up by an over-large brown leather belt, or piece of string; oily shoes with matching flat cap…black nail-bitten hands clutching a greasy rag…that would complete this vision.

Being professionally and politely attended, by a pair of not unattractive teenage girls wearing cheerful smiles and gleaming white coats; this had proved to be quite a draw.

Besides the admiring glances and flirtatious chat from many of the male customers, we had lorry drivers 'beep' the hooter when passing to attract our attention; all were responded to with a smile and a wave.

Pat and I had very similar personalities, we liked cars and enjoyed meeting people; we found it easy to make conversation, and both had a quick wit and sense of humour. There the likeness ended; I was short and athletic, with hair as black as coal, while Pat was very blonde, built like a rasher of wind…and with legs up to her arm-pits!

Because she lived locally, and from meeting so many people through work, we built up an excellent social life; she knew I was in lodgings and frequently I would be invited to her house for tea after the later shift.

Every other fortnight we would meet up with a group of her friends and go to the coffee bar in town; here we would meet a bunch of lads and invariably the evening would end with a whole crowd of us ambling along by the river. Occasionally there would be someone hanging behind for a quick 'snog'; even I was finding the *'searching for the chewing gum'* a more pleasant and frequent experience!

Then we discovered London, or rather Win did; she worked in the local Sainsbury's and had gone up with a group of workmates one Saturday.

She lived just around the corner from the garage and would call in for sweets and a chat while waiting for her bus; her dad came in for petrol and the Vinell's knew her, so they were quite happy with this, and she didn't stop us working.

She explained about her outing, saying they had been to a great place off The Strand; there were brilliant bands with plenty of dancing and only a shortish walk from Charing Cross station. Once discussed over our coffees, that was deemed to be the desired venue…as soon as could all muster together.

It was wonderful to be able to join in with a crowd; except for the TA, my social life had been virtually zero. Finding the freedom to enjoy different things, and having the funds to manage, was really increasing the fun in my life.

The new possibilities were almost entirely due to the way Mr Vinell had worked out the payments for my scooter; once they were met, and my lodgings paid, I still had some spare in my pocket. The forecourt was increasing trade week on week; as I continued to sell the extras, so the amount in tips increased. I could easily pay for my train fare to London for instance; this gave me a completely new lease of life.

I still had the nice clothes given to me ages before; they had remained with me, but were unused because the opportunity had simply not arisen…I never went out. That meant I didn't have to splash out on buying the appropriate dresses and so on…and they were all 'new' to my friends anyway.

It wasn't long before we arranged our London trip; on the first occasion we numbered about a dozen…all girls. The train journey took under the hour to Charing Cross; it was when we enquired about return times we found a small problem.

The last scheduled train left ten or fifteen minutes after midnight; missing that meant catching the 'milk train' at around four in the morning.

Win took charge;

"After we collect our coats, we can add another fifteen minutes at least to walk to Charing Cross from the dance hall; what I suggest is this. As long as no-one minds arriving home at some *ungodly* hour in the morning; if any of us is dancing, snogging, or whatever, we stay till midnight…enjoy the Last Waltz…and catch the milk train back!"

A loud cheer greeted this decision; I cannot recall one occasion when we *did* leave early enough to catch the midnight train…or miss the best dance of the night! We would noisily walk back to the station together, with a new bunch of lads each time; there we sat on the freezing cold seats, laughing and joking and waiting for the 'milko'.

On these nights, Pat's mum invited me to stay with them in Tonbridge; this extended the fun, as I didn't have an early morning ride home on the scooter in my good clothes.

But Mr C was full of disapproval…and repeatedly said so.

This made me sad because I *wanted* my new life; I was harming nobody and needed desperately to escape the privation and unhappiness that had haunted me since leaving Barnardo's.

I was growing up; not too fast and in an amazingly controlled manner… but growing up for all that.

There were two customers who came almost daily for petrol; brothers who were building contractors and lived very nearby in Estridge Way. When I got my Vespa, it was they who stored my bike for safe keeping in their garage; they were full of fun and teased us both unmercifully, but in the nicest of ways. They were holding a party to which Pat and I were invited.

It was going to mean a late start as my shift didn't end until seven thirty; Pat's brother drove her down to help speed things up a bit...she did the till while I did the mucky stuff. I'd brought my change of clothes and, with Andrew's permission, washed and changed in the workshops.

There was wine, music and dancing and we all had a great time; Pat's mum *had* said I could stay with them, but I preferred to get back, as I could then have a relaxed lie in on the Sunday morning.

Time was getting on, it had been a long day; I said cheerio to Pat and told our host James I was on my way home...but he would not hear of it.

"You can't ride all that way on that egg whisk apology for a proper motor bike...it's blooming freezing out there; leave it here. Ian doesn't drink at all, so we'll run you back in no time. Get your coat quick...before I change my mind"

Ian had a beautiful black Jaguar; the engine made barely a purr, the dashboard light was coloured violet...and the deep-cushioned seats were cream leather... absolute luxury!

He didn't like a front seat passenger so James and I sat in the back; the car cruised along and we were there in no time. I thanked them profusely for the trip…and the brilliant party…I said it was wonderful.

We had been parked for mere moments; James kissed me goodnight in a rather tender but avuncular manner and I left, quietly closing the door so as not to disturb the sleeping neighbours.

Mrs C left out a back door key for such occasions; I removed it from the hiding place in the outside toilet and I let myself in with barely a sound. I glanced at the clock; *nearly midnight – blimey no wonder I'm tired*, I thought.

As I got to the door of my room, from the corner of my eye I saw Mr C standing at the top of the stairs; he was glowering again…I pretended I hadn't seen him…and silently got into bed.

As I lay there I decided; my personal 'Jar of Ointment' was of a pretty high quality; the 'Fly' there-in though was most definitely Mr C.

His initial outburst was largely forgotten, but he continued with these niggling little things; even Brian had noticed.

# CHAPTER 34

Everyone at TA had become much more close and friendly since Camp; we had established, more by accident than design, small cliques who broke away and met up frequently on a social level.

This had started with the meeting up of one of our lot; after TA she was joining her sister for a 21$^{st}$ birthday drink in a pub in town. We always met in a coffee bar; none of us ever went to a pub…as the boys used to say…"That's where yer dad goes"

Everyone had been invited, but only a dozen or so of us arrived; we immediately formed as a group of Special friends. It was a good laugh…but we mainly drank lemonade; one of the boys had a beer, but from the grimaces being made, he wasn't enjoying it much!

Brian had arranged a lift home in Bill Stracey's car…I rode my scooter and we met up at the garage at the bottom of the road. As we walked back up to the house we saw his Dad…striding down towards us.

"*What* time of night do you call this…you're *not supposed* to ride pillion till she's passed her test…I'm not putting up with much more of this…."

We didn't hear any more; Brian tightly grabbed my hand, and we all but ran past him, still ranting behind us.

"What on *earth* is going on out there?" Mrs C enquired anxiously;

"He's been like a bear with a sore head since he first came in from work; but never mind anyway…where did you two go…did you have a good time?"

"I don't care *what s*ort of bloody time they had!" *boomed* out from the back door…I just stood there in shock.

"Dad…for goodness sake…just listen to me for *two minutes*…you have *no idea* what you're talking about. We were out less than an hour over our usual Meeting time…*and I came home in Bill's car.* I can see you don't believe me but do you know what? *I honestly couldn't care less*! I'm straight off to bed…and so is Sue"

With that he grabbed my hand and rushed me to my door; he gave me a peck on the cheek…and stormed off upstairs.

Terrified to go to the bathroom, I changed very quietly, and got into bed.

But I couldn't sleep.

I felt close to tears having witnessed the horrible row between father and son, knowing too I was somehow the cause of his apparent anger; Brian was enraged at the further unfounded accusations. His father was victimising me for some unknown reason; what that could be, I had no idea. I closed my eyes…lay very still…and pondered; I could feel exactly what was happening to me.

To stop from drowning, I was frantically swimming in a rough sea that seemed to signify Life; I had to keep swimming because I didn't have a boat.

*Other* people had boats; represented by parents, grandparents and siblings…these were their safety that kept them afloat above the swell. I felt I had nothing more than my ability to swim…with or against, the tide.

For all of my childhood in Barnardo's, I had kept afloat on mental strength and guile; out here were new, extraordinary and very different challenges. All the people who had ever hurt me were themselves bullies; now they swarmed like sharks, apparently determined to sink me.

Mr C was clearly a bully, and had set out to hurt me; he could do that **so very easily** because my vulnerability forced me to swim alone! I had nothing and nobody to help me stop him…but he *knew* that…in exactly the same frightening manner as the women on the farms.

*Will it always be like this?*

*Will I ever have a safety boat?*

*Even if I ever got married… will it sill be the same?*

I decided it would…I realised then and there, that any chance to have safety around me *had never existed…*I had already been deprived of any opportunity.

*My father had died too young.*

*My mother had no love or need of me.*

*The only home I had was where I lay my head.*

*There would always be someone to take advantage of that.*

*My Life was going to be a **very** strange journey.*

I drifted off in a sleep disturbed by very strange dreams.


I felt better on waking; I always recovered quickly from my ponderings as it was what I'd done it all my life.

I loved Sundays; with a six day working week behind me, I really made the most of the arrangements Mrs. C always planned. In the warm weather we invariably went out; now the colder days were upon us, it was lovely to sometimes just stay indoors and enjoy the warmth of the fires in the grate.

A distinct air of normality prevailed, despite the outbursts of the previous evening. I had a happy morning helping with the vegetable preparation for lunch; Mrs C and I kept up a cheerful banter that made the time fly by.

Brian and Mr C had walked up for the Sunday papers and sat reading, interspersed with as many cups of coffee as we were prepared to offer. I'd safely retrieved my bike, and the boys were out on that, with strict orders to be extra careful…and to make sure they were on time for lunch.

The meal was to her usual high standard and once everything was tidied away we all contentedly sat down around the fire, having a "good old natter" as she put it.

During the conversation, she mentioned that someone they all knew had just got engaged to be married next year.

"Well Brian, lets hope *she's* not a bit of rubbish from Barnardo's"

The silence was tangible, ultimately punctured with the pistol-like outburst from Mrs Chandler,

"ALAN – *how **dare** you!*"

I felt the dreadful familiar pain in my chest; the two younger boys rushed over crying, and pushed themselves into me in an embracing hug. Sitting beside us, Brian was shaking…but silent.

The weight of the boys and the grip of their hands in mine was welcome relief; I held them very still…and focussed my attention on the floor in front of me. I was breathless.

I heard rather than saw him get up and leave the room.

The strange silence prevailed for a moment longer…broken at last by the boys, in an anxious whisper,

"Are you alright Sue?"

Still staring at the floor, I nodded my reply; with a last gentle squeeze of my hand, they returned to the table to sit with their mum. Brian moved up a space; placing a comforting arm across my shoulder, he kissed my forehead and repeated the same question.

Very quietly Mrs C asked;

 "What on earth was *that* all about?"

"I don't know mum, but it's got to stop. He's attacking Sue at the moment because she's a soft target for his bullying…but will *we* be next?"

"My son, I can't answer that. Look…why don't you all go for a walk while there's still enough light? It'll blow away the blues and I'll go up and see what he says while you're gone"

We were all relieved at this offer of respite from that dreadful atmosphere; the moment we left the house we were talking nineteen to the dozen. We could only go over what had occurred; none of us could come up with answers or reasons, but it had helped enormously just to talk.

"Listen to me boys, when we go in, if dad is downstairs he apologises to Sue immediately. If he doesn't I am going to take her out…so I don't want any protests okay? We are *not* going to sit with him while this is somehow resolved…I've had enough…but more importantly…so has Sue"

As no apology was forthcoming, we enjoyed a welcoming quiet evening in Bill's place.

Bill was a year older than Brian and worked hard as a postman; there was talk at TA he would probably join the Regulars. A really likeable chap, he lived in a 'prefab' with his parents; I had never seen one before and was amazed at the space inside.

The sitting room was huge, and the roaring fire in the grate made a warm cosy atmosphere; his mum and dad greeted us as warmly and offered to bring a drink through.

Bill had his own bedroom, also large; this is where we sat drinking our coffee and chatting. Brian didn't give him *all* the details, but enough to keep us going for a good while, trying to sort out the ridiculous behaviour of some adults.

Walking home was peaceful; the night was very still and cold, with a beautiful star-lit sky. Brian didn't want to go back until bedtime, so we sat on a nearby wall.

He held my hand and we continued our quiet discussions; I found the darkness emboldened me a little.

"The *madness* of his attitude Brian is this; I told you I was happier being a friend rather than a sweetheart. I'm not daft; I know as much as the next girl what life is all about…*however…* there I differ. I'm not a pious moral soul by any means, but there are two things I want to tell you…with reasons I don't want to discuss right now.

Emotionally…I am totally unready to have a relationship with *anyone* that would be deeper than the friendship we have.

Physically…sexually if you like…I am also unready; should anything go wrong, I could not live in an unmarried mothers Home for anything"

"Sue, you are one of the kindest sweetest girls on earth; I don't *need* to hear any details, the sensitive sincerity in your words is enough. I wish I could promise for nothing again to *ever* hurt you…but there is no recipe for that"

He put an arm around my shoulder and held me close to him; it all seemed so terribly sad.

"Brian love, I've been thinking hard lately that I had better go from your house; I love your family, but my presence is upsetting apple-carts for some reason. If he continues his nastiness when I'm not around…your mum will know that Meg is right; he's a bully with a problem *or* the train crash has damaged his head. Maybe resolving that issue would be worth it"

"That's such a great shame Sue but I expected it…I knew it was coming; I can't blame you and nor will any of us. I'll miss you like mad but we can always catch up at TA and I know where you work. Just don't lose touch with us ay?"

We stood up close together in a comforting warm hug; I couldn't have cared less if there were a *thousand* Mr Cs looking on.

Innocent friendship was a pure and beautiful thing…but with all his suspicion and mistrust he would never know that joy.

"Better be getting back kid. I've got my key so we'll go through the front door, you go to your room and I'll go straight upstairs. I can't bear to set eyes on him tonight"

CHAPTER 35

I was on the early shift; it was an enormous relief to leave that awful day behind and go to work.

On the journey, I tried hard to get rid of the depressing thoughts about having to moving house...*yet again*. I'd brooded on the previous evenings' conversation...but concentrated mainly on what Brian had said; he'd be sad for me to go...but he understood the reasons.

With his endorsement I made the decision to sort things out as soon as I could.

Monday morning was always busy, so I had no time to think; when Pat arrived I didn't rush off...I stayed for quite a long time to speak with her.

"Don't you worry Sue; there's always someone looking to let a spare room round here. If you have to pay more rent, but move closer to work, you may only need your push bike; that would save petrol money for you. Nothing's all bad love. Go in and see Lydia; she knows 'the world-and-his-wife' locally...ask Andrew too. They're all lovely people love...keep your chin up...we'll have you moved in no time"

Later that day…after I'd gone home, Win called in to chat to Pat; as a mutual friend she described my plight.

"You're *kidding*! My brother Clive's moving out *next week*, he told us yesterday at lunchtime. Dad's taking him to our Aunt who lives in Ashford; he's got an apprenticeship there that he couldn't get here. Mum almost immediately said, maybe jokingly I'm not sure, that it was a good thing…'cos we can let yer room'. I'll talk to them later so tell Sue to wait here until this time tomorrow; I'll let her know one way or the other... let's hope Mum meant it!"

That snippet of conversation I eventually heard from Pat; in the meantime all sorts of behind-the-scene shenanigans were going on.

Pat left a note for me to find in the morning, explaining what so far had transpired; I inwardly groaned at the tension of the long wait to find out…it was going to be quite an ordeal.

I hadn't however taken Lydia and Andrew into account.

Apparently Andrew made a telephone call to the Manager at Sainsbury's; it was by no means a large shop, so everyone knew each other very well. He then rang back and had a word with Win during her break. The first time I was made aware of all this was when Andrew came to the kiosk with a cup of tea…and a very broad smile;

"I have some wonderful news for you Miss Davis…you have new accommodation…with Win!"

I must have looked positively idiotic in my response; I just stared at him, not understanding any of it. He then explained that the conversation between Pat and Win had been relayed to him and Lydia, and it all evolved from there.

"All you have to do now is wait for Win; she'll take you to meet her mum. Be rest assured though Sue; the room is *definitely* yours. Good luck…you deserve it"

After my shift, Andrew invited me to stay around rather than go home and back. Firstly I cleaned my scooter, he then allowed me to clean his car inside and out.

It was a cream and green A-line, Armstrong Siddeley 'Sapphire'; his pride and joy. It was a beautiful vehicle and he deserved it; he'd worked extremely hard to acquire it. There was plenty of it to get through; the concentration of achieving perfection made the time fly by, with no anxiety whatsoever.

"Win's fifteen minutes away Sue; clear up now and go to meet her at the bus stop"

I was trembling with anticipation and relief when she stepped off the bus.

"Hiya Sue…how about *this* then love; are we gonna have a laugh *or what*? My mum's already heard loads about you and now she can't wait to meet you. Poor old Clive was funny last night; he thought she was only joking about the room…she may have been had Pat not spoken to me"

Chatting as we walked along, totally unaware of my surroundings, I was more than a little surprised when we stopped at a small wrought iron gate…we were there.

"Blimey, that's only about five minutes from work!"

"Perfect innit Sue?"

Everything was; my welcoming greeting came from yet another cuddly, motherly lady who clearly adored her family.

She let Win show me round and we trooped upstairs; the room was fairly small with space for a single bed, but I was only going to be sleeping in the darned thing. It looked very cosy.

Returning downstairs, and in response to Mrs Gallagher's quizzical look…I assured her it was perfect…and I couldn't wait.

She *beamed* and said how pleased she was adding…

"And you must join in…and live as one of the family"

Where had I heard *that* before?

"*Oh God…please, please let it be true this time*"

# CHAPTER 36

When I gave Mrs C the news she didn't know whether to laugh or cry.

"I'm delighted it's been so straightforward for you love, but a diabolical shame it has to happen at all. It has made a huge difference for me, having a girl about after a houseful of men for so long; you have been like the daughter I never had, and such a blessing. I appreciate so much all the help you have given me.

The youngsters *love* you; you've brought them and Brian out of their shells with your humour and sense of fun. I realise now how hard sometimes it's been for them in the past; Meg is right...he has always had the propensity to bully. Maybe the train crash made it worse, I really don't know; I'll watch him now like a hawk and if he continues, I'll get some help for him"

I was close to tears; I felt so extremely sorry for her...but I couldn't stay.

I could see ahead already to that help becoming necessary; I couldn't imagine him giving up his current behaviour that easily. The train crash perhaps, had just given him an excuse to lapse into what would be his 'normal' attitude. I couldn't work it out …but I also couldn't make it my problem.

"I'd love a last afternoon in town Sue if that's possible"

"I'm on mornings all week; if I don't stop and chat with Pat, I could be here with plenty of time to get a bus with you…I'd really enjoy that"

Thursday found us in town; Mrs C offered to buy me some shoes for going out in, as the only best pair I had were black and a bit low-heeled. I chose white patent leather…and then she bought me a small evening bag to match.

"That's so kind Mrs C and now I'd like to buy something for all of you"

She chose an enormous tin of biscuits; they enjoyed sweet things, and she added…Mr C wouldn't feel left out…they would *all* share them.

"It's a good sized tin too; I'll keep the home made cakes fresh for ages in that"

The week passed by surprisingly quickly under the circumstances.

It was especially good being home for when the boys came in from school; I made certain I spent all the time I could with them. They were lovely kids and repeated constantly they didn't want me to go.

"I'll make sure we meet up one day; I'll get your mum to meet me in Tunbridge Wells…we'll go swimming and then have tea somewhere"

I made a mental note that this promise was to be kept.

Brian was his usual attentive self; we walked miles to get out of the house and to talk everything over, never getting any nearer a solution to his father's behaviour. On the Friday he treated me to a Show in town.

I had attended orchestral performances as a kid; I played violin in a Youth orchestra, and it was part of the education. This was the first live 'Pop' performance I had ever seen; it was 'Emile Ford and the Checkmates'. Absolutely enthralled, I knew that was definitely not going to be my last live theatre visit…I was hooked!

I'd arranged with Win to make the move to my new home on the Sunday; with no work for anyone concerned, it was by far the easiest plan.

I had a rotten last night though; feeling a wearisome sadness at having to leave these dear people and the home they had given me…and anger that Mr C had forced it upon me.

I experienced a weird mix of emotions about it; the boys had been tearful at bedtime which was sad…and yet I felt pleasure in the sweet way they showed they cared so much.

Brian was clearly *very* low; once the boys had gone to bed, we went up to see Bill Stracey and his family. This was to say 'goodbye'…but also to get out of the dreadful atmosphere in the house. We took the opportunity to tidy up all the arrangements for the next morning as Bill had kindly offered the use of his car; this was going to make things so much easier.

The day dawned cold and very wet; I lay for a while with hands behind my head, listening to the gusting wind blowing the rain against my window… I'd always loved that sound.

Shortly, there was a gentle knock at my door; Mrs C stood there smiling, carrying a tray of tea.

Both in low moods, we sat together while the rest of the house slept, having a quiet girly chat…albeit for the last time. We made a joint agreement to stay in touch;

Brian would impart my news after TA, and we would definitely meet in town.

As arranged, Bill arrived prompt at ten thirty; it was still absolutely pouring down. Brian suggested I travel in the car with my belongings and he would ride my scooter over, to save me getting a drenching…he was such a sweet man.

Bill kept Brian in his sights and we drew up in Estridge Way together; there was a gathering of the whole family to greet us.

"My god…well just be looking at you…soaked to the skin you are. Come on in boys…and you Sue…let's get you by the fire and warm up"

She had the softest gentle Irish accent, and a singing manner in which she put her words across; I could have sat transfixed at her reading from the telephone directory!

We took our dripping wet things off in the rear porch, then she steered us into the sitting room; a roaring fire disappeared half-way up the chimney and the room was like an oven. She set off to the kitchen with Win, returning with a tray laden with cakes, biscuits and hot drinks.

"I'm not doing roast till late today Sue; dad's not taking Clive after all. His aunt is coming about two o'clock…so we'll eat after that"

"The bed should have cooled down by then Sue" Clive responded…with mock rancour.

"Don't be so cheeky you…make yourself useful by taking Sue's case up and be showing her where to put everything"

"Well …I suppose we'd better go now"

With the bustling noise all around, Brian's quiet tone shocked me; there was a genuine deep sadness which touched my heart. I moved over to him; he put a strong protective arm across my shoulder as we made our way to the door for his departure.

I whispered gently;

"I'll see you on Wednesday Brian, *and* every week after that. We'll *never* lose touch love… *I promise*".

He then said, very quietly and clearly with a degree of considerable pain;

"I can't *believe* I've just helped move you away…having you there was a *marvellous* thing for all of us. Take lots of care Susie my love; I'll see you at TA on Wednesday"

He held me tighter, heaved a huge sigh, kissed my forehead…and was gone.

"Clive, sort Sue's things out now love, give her time to get unpacked Win, and then go up; the room's not big enough for any chaos"

I was grateful of the few moments to myself; I felt such a mix of sadness and excitement.

Brian's manner had been a revelation; what a darling man he was.

No one could have done more to help me over the latest hurdles in my life; escaping from that dreadful farm, the accident to my wrist, and now his blooming father.

We'd keep in touch though…that was a comforting thought.

CHAPTER 37

A concrete path had led from the small gate up to the house, and to the apparently smiling arch at the front door; it continued down the left-hand side, and to the back door. Neat lawns lay on either side of the path; the whole was protected by equally neat hedges.

Inside and out looked lovingly cared-for; I sat quietly while I could, taking in my new surroundings. I already felt an encouraging sense that it *would* become a happy home.

The room was long and narrow, with my bed tucked neatly behind the door; a sturdy chest of drawers and dressing table were on the opposite wall. To my left was a window with a view stretching far across open fields; I was at the back of the house, and it was hard to believe there was a large busy estate built up all around. The back garden was enormous; this though was grass, rather than lawn…with clear signs of football and other pleasures being enjoyed out there.

"Well Sue…what do you think?"

Win had noisily bounded in to help put the last few bits away; I responded by saying it was *marvellous*…and I meant it.

I then described the dreadful apology for a bedroom I had on the farm, and told her I called it my *boudoir*; I had her in fits of laughter about the dowel wardrobe, and the state of the bathroom.

Later, we ate a huge roast beef meal, sitting together round the kitchen table, then all mucked in to clear away. It was still pouring with rain, so an adjournment to the sitting room was the perfect antidote to the misery outside.

Relaxed around a cosy fire, we chattered away for hours about nothing in particular; it was very clear, from her constant reference, Mrs G was going to miss Clive a great deal. She was proud of him for moving away to better himself; she talked highly of her son and his ambitions, as did his father.

Mr Gallagher exuded a kind gentleness which was utterly endearing; when first introduced, he asked me to call him 'Gally'...

"Been called that all me life...an' I don't wanna change it now"

He worked for the Council, in one of the rather lowly areas as far as I could make out. Not very tall but a strong man; with hands like shovels, and a heart of similar dimensions I guessed. He had helped and

338

encouraged Clive with his learning, and longed to see 'his boy' have the better things in life.

He worked hard for long hours and this was taking its toll; his breathing was poor, and his weather-beaten face made him look older than his years. He explained he needed the overtime money to live well; he was a sweetie-pie…as indeed was she.

"You two girls ought to go upstairs now; give your dad and me a bit of time to ourselves, before the new week begins; get anything for Sue she doesn't have Win"

Then followed hugs…and a cheerful exchange of "Goodnights"

Win came with me to my room to check things over as her mum had asked
"You gonna be okay Sue? It's not late, and if you're not really sleepy yet, come to my room and natter some more"

Win's room was nearly the same size as her parents', which she had shown me on my initial tour. She snuggled down onto the big double bed, while I got comfy lying on the eiderdown on the other side; I felt comfortable but animated…and nowhere near sleep.

"Win, I've loved my day…I truly have; this is a dream come true being here with your family. I was absolutely *dreading* having to make yet another fresh start, perhaps alone, and in horrible surroundings. It's all happened so *quickly*…I feel I need to pinch myself to make sure it's real. I'm just so grateful to you all"

"Ah…but remember Sue…these things works both ways. With you paying for your room, perhaps my dad could finish work at midday on Saturdays now…that would be great for him and mum"

That was a refreshing thought.

We went on then and shared a long girly chat; I heard all about her family, to whom she was clearly very close. She too would miss her brother, and said as much; she related numerous amusing tales of them growing up.

I laughed when she told me that from birth he had been known as 'Little Gally'…it was so inappropriate now, as he was considerably taller than his dad.

She asked about my life in Barnardo's; with someone I barely knew I found it difficult to talk in detail. Instead I imparted the barest of information about my mother, and some of the funny stuff in the Homes, which was enough to satisfy her curiosity.

I told her a little about the two farms and the disaster they turned out to be, but I didn't want to spoil the mood, and made it as amusing as I possibly could.

There was a gentle knock on the door…to quietly tell us it was time to go to sleep.

"I'm alright Win; I don't relieve Pat till one o'clock"

"Huh! Okay for some …I'm in at eight-thirty"


On the first night in my new home, it felt strange to be in a proper bed, in a proper bedroom…and on the first floor; but I soon dropped off.

Even after the late chat I woke early, after a deep refreshing sleep. I still heard a milkman somewhere in the distance, but not right outside my window like at Rusthall.

I was contented to just lay there and relax.

I could hear the comings and goings as the household awakened slowly to the new day…and felt a deep sense of warm comfort at the expectancy of these sounds becoming a familiar in time.

Mrs G very gently tapped my door and came in.

"I knew you'd be awake love and I'm grateful you gave me the opportunity to get everyone off to work.

341

You get up now if you like; join me in the kitchen and I'll get you some breakfast"

I explained I couldn't eat that early, and received a gentle, motherly admonishment; I was soon downstairs for a cuppa though. We sat together and I gave her the details of my work shifts. She promised to make sandwiches, and even with the differing finishing times, would cook me a good meal to come home to.

I was anxious to do my share, and offered to help her in any way I could; at first there was a decisive 'no'.

Upon my insistence however, we agreed a routine; I'd help with the housework when I was home in the afternoon, and on the other shift, I would do errands. She explained how the shopping took too much time from her morning; on my scooter I could get into Tonbridge and back in no time at all.

As well as being so economic, it was great having such a short journey to work; five minutes brisk walk saw me onto the forecourt.

"Hiya Sue...blimey, don't *you* look like the cat that got the cream!"

That was Pat's welcome and I had to give her the complete rundown of my move; she was thrilled to bits

342

for me, and it showed. The whole story was repeated for Andrew, and then again for Lydia; they were all so sweet and delighted on my behalf.

In answer to Pat's question, I assured her I was going to TA on Wednesday. She asked could we all meet up afterwards; she would ride and bring Win on the pillion... then we could ride home together.

I wasn't too grubby at the end of my shift; a quick splash to hands and face was sufficient...and I drove straight off to the Meeting.

# CHAPTER 38

"Well…look who's here bright and early" was the general cry; I'd got away with arriving late when cycling, but arrived in no time on the scooter. I immediately fell in to what the others were doing…and then enjoyed the tea break.

Brian came directly over and gave me a quick hug.

"Gosh our place is *awful* without you there, it's utterly dead; it's only been a couple of days but it's like a *morgue* in there! Dad has quietened down, but mum's watching his every mood; I hate it. I'm thinking of moving out quite honestly; Stracey and I were talking about it after we delivered you on Sunday, we're considering sharing somewhere, a cottage or something"

"I can't say I blame you love; there's a big wide world out there for the taking. But that's what you have to do…take it. No one will come and place it in your lap; if you *want* it enough…you'll *get* it"

"God you're wise for someone two years younger than me, but I suppose that's what comes of fighting for your survival"

*Oh indeed…and that's the battle to fight…and win.* I thought.

Pat and Win were awaiting our arrival when we all trooped in to '*Fortes*' coffee shop; the chatter very soon filled the place, and the little matronly lady who served us had to ask us to pipe down on a couple of occasions. They got along fine with everyone, and the culmination of the chatter was to arrange another London trip.

Once that was decided upon, some bright spark came up with, what she thought was a good idea, a challenge for the Sunday coming. Two teams on bikes…to cycle the sixty odd miles…to Brighton and back!

"You've got to be *barmy,* that's much too far"

"Nah…they do it every year in the Vintage Rally…from London!"

"They're in blooming cars though"

"There's less problems on a bike"

"I ain't even got a bike"

"Well *borrow* one"

For something received with so much dissent…I was ready and lined up on the Sunday morning…with the other dozen or so who'd agreed to this madness.

With unanimous agreement, one rule was altered, two teams competing was utterly daft. Far fairer we each look out for each other; especially as with Win, who was totally unused to any exercise whatsoever…except for her manic dancing on a Saturday night!

The early March weather was kind to us; it was only eight o'clock in the morning and rather cold, but there was promise of a sunny day. We soon warmed up naturally with the riding; we didn't race, chatted throughout, and took a rather sedate pace… we had all day to do it in.

Half-way we stopped for refreshments; we had brought drinks and food with us to save buying that sort of thing out. We all felt a little sore in differing places, but unanimously agreed it was an absolute lark…and loads of fun.

I was in the leading three as we pulled up near the promenade; then I heard an awful scream.

Rushing just a few yards back I saw Win…flat out on the ground with a nasty graze to her knee; at first I thought she'd been hit by a car, but nothing as dramatic. Poor devil; as soon as she'd stopped pedalling, suddenly got a massive cramp in her left leg…it had brought her to an abrupt halt.

It was clearly painful…she was desperately trying to mask her embarrassment for the tears.

"Don't worry about *that* Win love; I pulled a hamstring once which stops you in exactly the same fashion…and it's agony. You've been amazingly sporting just taking part. For the moment, get masses of drink into you, and I'll go with someone to get our fish and chips…can the others help Win down the steps to the beach?"

"I'll come with you Sue"

Any food in the open air is enjoyable…'fish and chips' is simply wonderful!

A few of us left the others lounging around, to go down to the shore line; for an hour or more we walked, threw stones…and then paddled in the sea until we were in danger of cutting off the blood supply to our toes.

"Blimey" That's *freezing*!"

We were warm again by the time we returned, but there was a problem, a big problem; Win could barely walk, let alone pedal a bike.

After a long discussion it was decided…I would stay with her; the others would ride home, with us two following by train. Poor Win protested but there was simply no alternative…I couldn't have left her to try and cope alone.

She was a smashing kid, and I should have realised it was possibly too much for her; when fighting fit yourself though, these thoughts aren't necessarily uppermost in your mind.

She was comfortable inasmuch she was leaning against a wall; she'd had food, plenty to drink, and showed no signs of shock, so I had to make a move.

"Look Win, you'll be okay here; I've no idea where to go, but I'll have to find out how we'll best get home. I expect it's a train...but I wouldn't know for sure with it being a Sunday…I'll be as quick as I can"

"Leave your bike Sue; I'll look after it"

"No…I'll take it with me; if I have to go a long way, it'll be quicker to ride back"

It was already established Win had sufficient money to pay for her ticket, but I knew there was not enough for me too. I had nothing to spare after buying my lunch, which was pre-arranged…but a train fare hadn't been.

I was still very cautious about spending. I never took out more money than I needed, thus was never tempted to impulse buy simply because I had sufficient in my purse.

I rode along the promenade and up into a side street; I'd spotted a fairly large group of uniformed chaps, by what I thought was a garage of some sort. They were really kind when I explained about Win's accident and the desperate need to get her back to Tonbridge; they assured me the train was the only available option.

"Look, I hope this doesn't sound too mad…but I haven't the fare to get my friend home. Do you know anyone who might buy my bike?"

I was feeling a little sick when one of the chaps immediately showed a genuine interest; he tested the brakes and went all over to check its condition. They had told me roughly what the train fare would cost; as long as he was fair and the offer covered that…I would be ok.

It did…with a little extra as well.

I thanked him profusely…but was a little shocked at the rapid transaction; I turned very quickly and walked off…before I had to watch him wheeling it away.

I felt ridiculously low and very near to tears…but then reflected.

It was my first ever purchase with my own hard-earned money…I'd enjoyed mile upon mile of pure freedom, with never a hitch…it was almost the sole reason for my sanity and good health.

Now it was gone.

"Never mind; Win was worth it"

Getting her to the station cheered me no end…it was hilarious.

I managed to get Win up and onto her saddle; I told her to hold on, but to dangle her legs away from the pedals. She was a good six or seven inches taller than me however; the struggle to keep her and the bike upright was drawing some very amusing glances from the passers by.

It was also giving us the most terrible giggles.

My left arm was helping to steer in a fairly straight line, but because of the height differential, I was trying looking up *and* ahead…from the area of her rear end.

We were exhausted, both from the laughing *and* the effort when we eventually made it…still in one piece.

Next day, when I wasn't there to hear, Win apparently explained about my bike to her mum and dad. They immediately wanted to give me the money for a replacement. I thanked them of course, but assured them I was quite happy; I'd enjoyed it while it lasted…but those days were now gone.

Two weeks later Win was still off work; she didn't have a straightforward cramp at all, but had a badly torn calf muscle.

She made light of it by saying,

"Its so blooming swollen now…it's more like a *cow*"

# CHAPTER 39

A few weeks later, Brian exploded a veritable bombshell; he was going into the Regulars, as indeed was Bill. Sarge was very proud, but we were all a bit nonplussed. It would seem a very different prospect if they weren't there; both enormously popular, they were going to leave quite a gap.

At break we managed to have a quick chat, and arranged to meet in town to catch up on all his news. It was a beautiful early spring afternoon so we went down by the river; once settled on the bank, Brian explained.

The atmosphere indoors was not improving; he seemed constantly to be protecting the rest of the family from his father…but it was beginning to get him down. He could see no future there any longer; the 'Army Catering Corps' was where he would finish his butchery apprenticeship, and have far superior instructors than in civvy street.

"You made me think hard after what you said the other day Sue love; life *is* there for the taking. I need to take control, to take responsibility for my decisions and actions, to take the opportunities as they present themselves and have the courage to carry them through. Then I'll be a happy man"

"You'll go a long way Brian Chandler, of that I'm certain; I am so grateful for knowing you, and having you as my Extra Special friend. I was reflecting the other day on all the things we've done together. I know you'll be gone in a very short while now, but let's make a promise. Let's *never* forget each other…but don't let's make daft pacts or promises we'll probably never fulfil"

He laughed in a rather ironic way, stood up…and gently pulled my arm to get me to my feet.

"You are a cracking kid, and I know one thing Susan Davis, I'll never meet anyone *quite* like you *ever* again in my life; and I mean that more than you will ever know"

"Well I'd thank my lucky stars for that if I were you!"

He pulled me to him for a long time, in a comforting warm embrace; then kissed my forehead. We left the river bank hand in hand, and went into the town for some supper.

They only attended a couple more evenings, and then they were gone; the stark reality of Brian's actual departure brought a lump to my throat. I almost regretted we agreed to no letters or other sentimentality, but I knew we would never forget one another; that much I would treasure.

A few Sundays later found me *en route* to visit the Chandler tribe; with only a couple of miles to go, I changed my mind. I was not ready to face *him.* I headed on the other road, to Meg; she never minded a visit without prior notice.

"Hey Sue…what a lovely surprise…*love* the scooter…don't you look *well*… come in and sit down…give me all your news"

Wow! What a welcome; her exuberance literally bubbled!

We caught up on the generalisations then she said,

"You remember me saying I may move on after losing you? Well, that's the plan. I've had an offer I can't refuse for this place; regrettably it's to a builder who will probably develop the land, but I can't be bothered with that Sue. I'm exhausting myself here…I've had it! I'm going to the coast somewhere, probably Eastbourne or Bexhill. I'm so glad you came out before I leave"

"Everyone is on the move it seems" and I told her about Brian and Bill.

"Brian came over to see me last week; he said he was enlisting, and I already knew about you being almost forced to leave there. That was absolutely shocking; they were all terribly unhappy about it you know. Brian however, *never* came to terms with the things his father said to you; he hated him for it, and it was one of the main reasons for him leaving his home.

You are such an *innocent* little bird aren't you Sue…did you never realise that Brian was absolutely *head over heels in love with you*?"

I stared straight at her, frowning, but both her voice and face were deadly serious.

"His father stopped you 'going out' when you moved in; fair enough, but it was early days then, and as he explained, it was fairly easy and he respected your preference to be good friends. However, the longer you stayed there, the more he got to know you, so his feelings for you became stronger. I know this because he told me so last week. He loved you *so very much* Sue; so much he didn't dare tell you"

Initially I was stunned at this comment; almost disbelieving in fact.

355

Throughout the entire journey home, I found myself going over what she had said; I found myself questioning, almost arguing.

*Why hadn't he told me?* ...Because it could have spoiled what we had.

*Would I have taken him seriously?* ... Of course I wouldn't.

*Could I have admitted to feeling the same way?* ... I wouldn't even know if I did.

It was a shock to realise, and to recognise yet again, the extremes of my naivety; by the time I arrived home I felt a need to talk to Win. It was a lovely surprise to find Pat there as well; after hearing what amounted to a desperate plea for advice, we settled down to chat.

Having planned in my head what I wanted to say I quickly outlined the problem as I saw it; *how could I have no inkling of being loved when it was staring me in the face?*

I became very tearful when I told them about Uncle Tom and Auntie Dodd; I explained they were the only people in my life so far who had bestowed any sort of affection on me. I added that I *did* know *they* loved me, and I *knew* I loved them; no doubts either way at all.

356

"It's so very different for us Sue; we are lucky because we've always had our parents around and have never had to doubt they love us. *You* can't imagine that…but I can't imagine your side either love; it seems your situation is the complete reverse of ours"

"Do you remember meeting my Aunt Alice Win? She was *awful* Sue; rude to my mum, scorned my dad…and would smack me and my brother pretty hard when no-one was looking. I hated her, and I can see a parallel. I had one person who hated me in a world surrounded by love…you have had one person to love you in a world full of hate"

We drew all sorts of analogies to give me some comfort and hope.

Win actually told me she *knew* I was special to Brian, in the few short moment she had seen us together;  Pat also saw it that night we got together in '*Fortes*'.

We talked quietly in that vein for a long time; it was good therapy but I wasn't sure I'd progressed much. One thing they totally agreed upon; if I hadn't moved to the Chandlers' to live…if Brian and I just stayed dating normally…I *would* have seen for myself.

I couldn't bring myself to speak to them of the other doubts. I knew I still had the barriers in place to protect my emotional self, I wasn't ready for more pain and hurt yet, I would do better when I could trust again.

In the first place, I'd found it impossible to believe that I was even lovable, and it didn't seem to matter much anyway. Since leaving the Homes, my only two concerns had been…working hard to keep myself from being homeless…and trying not to starve.

From being very young, I'd always considered myself to be ugly; maybe because of the physical abuse and emotional torment in the Homes…but I'd never considered it as particularly important. I accepted it for what it was, and felt my ability to work hard and get on with people, to be of far greater benefit.

I felt very plain and ordinary compared with a lot of my current peer group; they appeared automatically to know which clothes and hairstyles suited them, and how to enjoy being girly girls.

I'd read newspapers, but only the pieces that interested me. Advertisements for hair and beauty products become pretty boring; with no money to buy them, and without anywhere to go to wear them, it was all a bit futile.

To discover Brian had been *in love* with me…that was something entirely different.

Slowly I allowed that thought to become acceptable…all I had to do now was to actually believe it.

Thanks to Meg for disclosing her conversation with Brian, I did become a little more positive about myself; the next thing was to become comfortable with that.

I achieved one new, *very* clear personal understanding; after the years and years of longing and endeavour… I felt I was now a *true* Outsider…at last!

No longer did I wear the heavy mantle of Dr Barnardo's Homes.

I was *me,* Susan Davis…w*hat a revelation that was*!

# CHAPTER 40

I had settled quickly, and thoroughly enjoyed my new home and life-style; no long rides to work, a peaceful relaxing atmosphere in the house, hours of good conversation…and even more fun.

I could sit and talk with Gally for ages; he loved to relate the stories from his war. These he delivered, not just with the expected gravitas, but always with a humorous anecdote. He said one day;

"You've got a dirty little laugh Sue; but your eyes don't half twinkle as well. You've got lovely eyes altogether; they've lived a life…and show it"

I blushed; totally unused to hearing comments such as this; Win heard too and suggested;

"Come up to my room Sue; let's have a girly evening…let me make you up"

Without second bidding, we charged up the stairs.

She brushed my hair back and then 'set to' with the contents of her make-up bag.

She knew I had *no idea* of cosmetics and explained every detail as we progressed with the transformation. That's exactly what it was when she finished; I gazed back at myself in the mirror in awe.

"Good grief! What a difference. Let's go down and show your mum and dad."

I got a wolf-whistle from Gally as I entered the room; he stood up and caught me in a mock embrace, bending me over backwards smothering me in pretend kisses…I nearly ruined my mascara with laughing!

"You look absolutely stunning Sue; we'll do that before we go out on Saturday night…and from then on, all the time"

It took a bit of getting used to but I did like the change, and it most definitely boosted my confidence. Win and I met in town and with her guidance, I bought all I needed; it was made perfect by having enough money to do so. She treated me to a little bag like hers…so I treated us both to a coffee.

While we sat drinking I told her; when I lived in the Homes we were not allowed to look in a mirror, except to clean our teeth…it was to stop us becoming 'vain' apparently…one of the Seven deadly Sins.

"Well…if you end up in Hell cos you've been vain by using make-up…at least you'll look gorgeous when you arrive!"

That was a pearl of wisdom I would never be in danger of forgetting!

The forecourt was definitely the place to meet guys and arrange dates; as much selection as for a starving man in a bakery! We could both flirt like mad and the amount of invitations grew by the day; but Pat, Win and I had discussed this to the nth degree.

We drew up a list of 'Sensible Rules'.


Never let anyone pick you up from your house, cos then they'd know where you lived.

Never go to somewhere isolated, but always to a dance hall or similar.

Never go out alone, unless you could be absolutely positive about their true motive.


"That'd be a rarity" Pat chuckled.

We would arrange to meet whomever at the Saturday dance in Hadlow, the next village up the road. It was only music from a record player, and soft drinks on sale, but it was always packed; it was a great laugh…with good dancing thrown in.

The guys who veered away from this, those who wanted to take you for a drink and meal out, they we steered away from. We just wanted to have fun; the other sort of girls could enjoy the other sort of men…they weren't for our crowd.

We went with various people…to Brands Hatch for the British Grand Prix, to Goodwood and saw Stirling Moss, frequently to the pictures, as well as visits to the coast…but not on push-bikes!

On one occasion I was on a blind date with a friend of Pat's escort.

We all piled into an old Land Rover and went to a Scramble Bike Festival.

My chap Don had ridden bikes for years; he was involved in a serious crash some years before and needed an artificial leg.

He used a trailer to tow the all his kit and the bike. When we arrived at the circuit, this had to be checked over by the official RAC scrutineer; he then got himself ready for racing. Pat and I watched in utter amazement; he pulled down his leathers, undid a strap… and casually removed his artificial leg. This he replaced with his 'racing peg' as he called it!

Once out on the course, I couldn't believe his bravery and speed; the ground was no more than a rough field, with great lumps and bumps all over the place *and* the bends were tight. He rode like a demon…and won each race he'd entered.

He was in really high spirits when we met back up by the trailer. Here he reversed the previous procedure, and showed us the leg; it seemed to weigh a ton…but the important thing was the point in the 'foot' bit.

"When I take the bends it most certainly pulls on my thigh, but then I just dig the point in deeper; that gives me the extra leverage…I've been winning rides here for ages"

He was so accepting and cheerful of his situation, I was both fascinated and impressed…but decided I'd still rather have all my own bits and pieces attached.

One sunny Saturday afternoon, a silver Vauxhall Victor Mk 2 drove in; a customer I'd not served before. It may have been the decent weather, or the fact that the forecourt was quiet, but he stayed for ages.

He was a quietly spoken pleasant chap; we only chatted lightly about nothing in particular…but he was nice. Eventually he paid up and drove away, but I found myself thinking about him; I decided the last time I had felt as relaxed with a stranger, was when I first met Brian.

As I was finishing the locking up, he returned.

"Did you forget something? We're closed now I'm afraid"

"Well, if you could say that my asking if you were doing anything this evening is 'forgetting something'…then yes…I did...and are you?"

He was smiling as he said this; I replied that I wasn't going out as it was late by the time I got home and changed. He persisted gently; and an hour later, I met him back on the forecourt.

"Would you like to go into Tonbridge for a drink?"

"Thank you, but I'm not all that keen on pubs; I do like the coffee bar on the high Street though"

In no time at all we were chatting as if we'd known each other for years; he made proper conversation which was refreshing. He was ten or so years older then me, but managed to put me completely at ease; after finishing the third coffee, he asked me out the following day.

He had already established that I loved cars and travelling, but did not yet drive. The trip in mind was to Fawley, the Esso refinery near Southampton; he asked me to navigate while he drove, as he had something to collect from there.

I told Win and Mrs R where I was going, and that it was to be a very early start. I also gave them his name, Owen, and the car number, 960 KKK …just to be on the safe side!

Mrs R made enough sandwiches for two people…and they both wished me well.

No-one else was up when I quietly left the house; it was a long run there and back, so the early start was essential.

On leaving it was cold, with early morning sun breaking through; being a Sunday though, the roads were very quiet and we were making good time. I told Owen I had sandwiches packed for a late breakfast, so he agreed to a break.

It was now much warmer, which meant we could eat our sandwiches outside; he put a rug on the ground and we sat on the grass…leaning against the gate to a field. The peace of the countryside was beautiful and the whole situation was just so easy and relaxed. He was a good driver and an even better conversationalist; we completed the remaining miles in no time.

We drove right through the Refinery after being 'security passed' at the main entrance. The place was like something out of a science fiction book. There were miles of asbestos wrapped steam pipes, blowing out their excess at all angles, the oil storage tanks rose like cathedrals above us, and we made our way, very slowly to the final destination.

Owen pulled up in front of the main office building; he loaded a large trunk into the boot, turned the car around…and was ready to go home.

That didn't seem to me to have been worth driving all those miles for…but it was none of my business, so I made no comment.

"Just a few miles out of Midhurst, is a dear little cottage place that does good food; how about we stop in their car park, have a walk to stretch our legs, then eat before we set off back?"

I still felt completely at ease in his company, and felt no qualms; it all sounded good to me, and that's what we did.

For quite some distance, we ambled along beside a slow-moving river; I was fortunately wearing flat shoes so it was easy. Gone for well over an hour, we both built up a real appetite for the lunch that followed.

I was having a lovely time; consciously aware though of feeling altogether 'different'…this was no ordinary date.

I would have felt too embarrassed to say this was my first proper meal out; I'd eaten the odd café snack, but this was the real thing, with table cloths, waitresses and so on. He was obviously utterly relaxed with it all; I felt suddenly thrust into a very new world.

Once driving again…there was a very amusing, telling moment.

He divulged he had never needed a navigator; apparently he had done this same journey on numerous occasions!

He admitted then to all sorts of things; he didn't think I would go out with him, he thought he was too old for me, and he was certain I would have arranged to be out already. I found it illuminating that for all his charm and panache, he too was human enough to have this self-doubt.

As the light faded so our day out ended; I thanked him sincerely…I *had* enjoyed a wonderful day.

"Thank *you* for a marvellous day I've enjoyed myself too, very much. Goodnight Sue, I'll call in tomorrow morning and see you in work"

"How do you know I'll be on in the morning?"

"Because I've done my home-work" he added mysteriously.

It had been a long day but was by no means late; everyone was in the sitting room and anxious to hear how it had gone. I went over the details; Gally was fascinated with the description of the Refinery, adding he would love to make a visit. They all decided he must be rather 'Important' when I explained about the travelling trunk…and the posh surroundings for our meal.

I asked then if I could have a bath as I felt grubby from the journey; Win said she'd have the water after me, so we went upstairs together.

"Did he *kiss* you?" she burst out as we got to my room.

"No…he didn't actually…and in a strange way it would have seemed odd if he had. I've never been out with anyone quite like him; there were occasions when I could have drawn parallels with Brian, but I can't explain why"

After our respective baths we adjourned to Win's room and assumed our 'girly chat' positions on her bed.

"I've had a super day too, Dave's new Dormobile is *amazing*; the guys can meet up here and leave their cars, cos there's loads of room for us all. We've got so much going on over the next few weekends you wouldn't believe it! My Dave is taking us all to Brands Hatch on Sunday; there's a special Minis Meeting we have just *got* to see. Pat's new boyfriend Lenny is taking her; do you want to invite Owen?"

"I don't think so; I'd rather go with John again in all honesty... did you see him today?"

"I did, and he's already anticipated you'll be going with him, so that's *perfect*"

"Next Saturday there's that film on that Pat wants to see; Dave and John want to go too if that's okay with you. The following Saturday is back up to London...but it may be the last one Sue"

"Well that's not a surprise really; with all of us having fairly regular dates. All that expense for one night out, and the lateness of the return, I'd happily go along with that as our *finale*"

"Let's just have one last time though...but then *finito*!"

"And I'm going to *finito* as well; I'm worn out after that bath and we've both got an early start in the morning"

# CHAPTER 41

After having Sunday off, I loved Monday mornings; the customers were non-stop, the entire forecourt had a thorough clean and the time flew by.

It was approaching lunch time when Owen called in; we went over the details of the day out, for which I thanked him again. He asked about the next weekend and looked a bit disappointed when I explained I'd made plans already.

He broached the subject of meeting mid-week; I explained about the TA meetings, bathing, hair washing and so on…so it was left that he would call in again anyway.

When Pat came in for the change-over I heard the full run down on Lenny;

"He's lovely Sue and funnily enough, he's a bit older than me, but it doesn't seem to matter"

"Well I personally think I had a better time because there *is* the age difference with Owen. I love the times we have, all of us together with our regular guys; I must say though I appreciated thoroughly the chance to be alone, and doing something completely different. And Pat…I want to talk to you and Win about something if I

371

can; nothing really worrying but want to hear your opinion"

"Well, if it's okay with you two, I'll call in after work"

I told Win about my discussion of the morning; she was a bit intrigued but was delighted about Pat calling. We'd finished our meal when she let herself in, through the unlocked back door, as she was used to doing. Mrs G always referred to her as another daughter; she and Win were such close friends, and had been since school.

We raced upstairs in no time at all and leapt onto Win's bed; at their invitation I 'spilled the beans' as they put it.

My worry, I quietly explained, was going out with John; all the while we were in a crowd he was great, but they already knew that. My anxiety arose when we all went our separate ways, and John would see me home; I always faced his inevitable question of 'going all the way' with him. I hated it... and it was spoiling everything else.

They were both shocked at this revelation, but immediately understood and shared my concerns ...and promised a resolve.

"When we're out on Sunday, either Pat or I will raise the subject in the most oblique of ways; you don't even have to join in the conversation, if indeed such a thing ensues. He has *got* to respect your feelings Sue; and does he think the rest of us go too far? Of course he doesn't. Hell's teeth…my mother would kill me if I did!"

"My mum always says 'that is what your Wedding Night is for' and I agree with her totally. Okay…there are temptations and some pretty heated moments, but blimey…to ask you outright is *horrible*; it's a blooming insult too Sue, cos he's playing on your naivety. Don't you worry though kid; your instinctive feelings are spot on. You're becoming more like us every day you know love; you are growing up fast, and out of those dreadful regimes you endured for years. You're hardly recognisable from the little waif whom we first met…you're alright you are. We know you like him but remember babe…there are plenty of other fish in the sea…*and some bite*"

Win went on to announce, she 'had a bit o' gossip'…which she frequently did.

"You know Jane down the road Pat? Well she's told a friend of mine she has lost her virginity! She's slept with her boyfriend!

"Oh my god…what's she going to do about the *baby*?"

They both stared at me with distinctly puzzled expressions.

"Don't you know anything about *protection*?"

"Well I wear a mac in the rain…and my scooter's insured…but I don't think you mean that somehow Win"

We all laughed…and she continued.

"Sue…your education quite obviously falls down badly in this area; here cometh the first lesson…with apologies to the church!"

She then explained in detail; to say I was amazed as well as educated, would be a gross understatement.

We were soon all laughing again but Pat had to get home; Win and I stayed upstairs chatting, right up till bedtime.

Owen came in again on the Saturday; in answer to his question I told him where I was going, and with whom. He had never been to Brands Hatch…or any other racing circuit either. I asked him what his hobbies were; I was amazed when he said he didn't really do much outside work.

"But I can tell you every star in the skies…both Northern and Southern hemisphere!"

"Blimey…that's the weirdest chat-up line I've ever heard!"

That made him laugh…and he explained what he meant.

He was a Navigator in the Merchant Navy, with 'Esso Petroleum', on their tankers. He had been around the world more than once and his enthusiasm was plain to hear, he loved it. He added that, with the sea time required to sit his tickets, and the study involved…there had been little space for anything much else in his life.

With the conversation continuing, I felt he didn't seem to know much about anything; I told him there was another world outside all that.

"So where would you like to go Sue, if we went out again?"

"I know something I would *love* to do in a couple of weeks; I've seen it advertised in the paper, but none of my crowd wants to go. You said you've never been very interested in music, BUT…the Bournemouth Symphony Orchestra is due to perform a wonderful

Beethoven concert. When I was a kid I played violin, and enjoy the Classics almost as much as rock 'n roll; if you went with an open mind, I'm sure you'd enjoy it"

"Okay, that sounds good to me. I'll give it a try; if I get tickets for the second week, when you're on mornings again…how does that sound?"

"Oh my gosh…I'd love it, but I can pay for my ticket, I just didn't want to go alone that's all"

"No, not at all…let it be my treat. I may be able to introduce you to something new too; have you ever eaten Greek food? It's marvellous…and I know the very place"

Everyone was fascinated when I told them later;

"We all learn something new every day Sue; the man who doesn't is a fool. Owen doesn't sound very foolish from what you have told us about him"

"Oh he's no fool; he has excellent taste too…I know cos he wants to go out with me!"

Win and I exchanged a wink at my new-found confidence.

The following morning, John, Pat and Lenny, turned up in their cars almost simultaneously; we jumped into Dave's van and were off.

We all loved Brands and it wasn't that far away; we always had time for a coffee from the flask when we arrived. During the break in the racing, we made our way back to have some welcomed food; I noticed the guys were sitting a short distance away from us.

We nattered between ourselves then all joined up to return to the bank and our viewpoint. John was his normal cheerful self…until we got back for him to pick up his car; I sat beside him and asked why he was so quiet.

"Sue I want to say how sorry I am; I should have realised I was hurting you, and how much. I'm sorry but I wanted you…I still do. I've loved being together today…but I think it would be fairer to us both if we made this the last date"

I stared down at my hands in my lap; I couldn't decide if he was making one final attempt…or if his pride was injured and he was simply being petulant.

I decided on the latter.

We spoke just a few more words; he pecked my cheek and I left him there. When he did drive off it was with the pedal to the floor…he *roared* down the road.

377

I thanked Win for her intervention and help, but we didn't discuss it any further, but her mum offered some words of wisdom,

"Don't worry about him Sue, he's no great loss. You think he left you because you didn't...I'm telling you...*he would have left if you did*"

A few weeks later a strange thing happened.

Lenny had introduced me to a friend of theirs; I wasn't particularly fussed about him, but he joined us for the Hadlow dance. We'd enjoyed the usual evening of rock n' roll and plenty of laughs...he'd joined is as 'one of us'.

He had a car and although I'd only met him at the venue, gladly accepted a lift home. We were travelling at a normal speed, chatting and laughing and in good spirits; suddenly he veered off left into a long lay-by...stopped the car... and in seconds, was across the seat and nearly in my lap!

He was almost smothering me; yet again my mind flashed back to the Homes. There was a horrible bullying member of staff, whose favourite punishment was to stifle breath; she would lift me bodily, with her hand clamped ever my nose and mouth so I couldn't breathe.

That was how I felt now.

I was shaking with that memory…and rage at him; I went loopy and started shouting…in truth, I was scared of him as well. I grabbed the door handle but he shouted back;

"If you get out…you can stay out…and blooming well walk home"

I got out….he drove off.

It was dark, raining and very cold; I was wearing light-weight dance pumps, and my feet were freezing. With a good mile and a half to walk home, I pondered the experience all the way.

He had been horrible…but worse had been the painful recollection; it was as sudden as it had been scary.

*"Oh God…when will these memories leave me alone?"*

When Pat next met Lenny there was Hell to pay; but then, through the local grape vine, we heard the end of this story.

Some days later, this chap was in a bar in town, where very occasionally John would have a beer; they were standing within earshot of one another. They had never met, so had no idea of who was whom.

Apparently John heard this chap mention 'the little dark one at the garage'; that was a term so often applied, he knew it was me. He turned and asked how he knew me, to which came the reply; he'd had a date with me.

In an extremely exaggerated and disgusting way, he then alluded to me having 'done it' on my first date…and had promised him again next time.

John only hit him once…he was out cold…and went to hospital with concussion!

Hardly worthy as a Knight in Shining Armour, but it was lovely to have had had my reputation defended…in whatever manner!

CHAPTER 42

Owen loved the concert; the opening piece was their particular *forte*, a superb rendition of the 'Fifth Symphony', with which he was already familiar. The close proximity to the sounds and the sheer *magic* of live music stunned him initially; once settled and relaxed, he just drank in the whole performance.

"That was one of the most amazing experiences of my life…now I hope to impress you as much with a wonderful meal"

And he did.

The emergence from my chrysalis was suddenly taking place; absolutely and most definitely. I was by no means, ever going to be a beautiful butterfly, but I decided I was not a moth either. I found myself becoming rather indifferent about my current social life, but only because the alternative was so fascinating.

Owen and I had been to some wonderful venues; I introduced him to opera, which for him was another new experience. He had never been to a car or motorcycle race meeting; we did that as well, with enormous fun and enthusiasm.

In exchange he introduced me to restaurants I would never have dreamed of patronising; his understanding of menus fascinated me, and he had the most exquisite taste in good food.

Some weeks later we had been out, and enjoyed yet another beautiful meal; as he was driving me home, in the middle of nowhere, he suddenly brought the car to a halt.

He gently pulled me towards him and kissed me…unbelievably he was trembling nervously. That was all it was to be; one rather tender kiss and embrace, and we continued the short run home…without a word.

"Gosh…I hope so much I haven't offended you Sue"

"*Au contraire*"…I replied smiling; kissing me gently on the cheek, he squeezed my hand…and drove away into the night.


It was established practice to call regular customers by their number plate numerals; Pat and I knew exactly to which customer we were referring, and it was easier than remembering names.

I asked her a couple of weeks later, and continually over a seemingly long period of time.

"Have you seen 960?"

She hadn't, and I decided I'd somehow spoiled things; I couldn't think what or why, and felt rather sad. Perhaps he regretted kissing me on that last evening we'd been out; I found that a rather strange notion…but who knows?

Unable to answer my own question, I simply got on with my life; less interesting now without Win and Pat around, but still good. I especially put renewed vigour into my TA activities and was seriously considering doing as Brian and Bill had done…enrol into the Regulars.

My life could become so simple.

I was perfect material according to Sgt Major Glazier; she expected I would very quickly make Lance Corporal, and go up the ranks as I wished. I would have immediately been on an amazing wage comparatively speaking, and I would never again have to worry about a roof over my head…oh bliss!

What Win and her family never realised, and something I would have *never* divulged, was the constant emotional pain I experienced living with them as I did.

Theirs was a perfectly happy home life; she was adored by her entire family. As indeed was Pat…and other people I knew who were still living at home. Hearing all these people referring to "Mum" and "Dad" still brought a lump to my throat.

I concluded…the biggest load of garbage ever uttered by anyone was;

"What you've never had…you'll never miss".

I had every day to face the living example of something I'd never had…or ever would.

There were days, but more especially nights, when I found myself so choked up I hardly knew how to disguise it…I always managed somehow.

Pat and Lenny, Win and Dave; they were items now and blissfully happy and I was genuinely delighted for them.

However, I still couldn't envisage myself *ever* trusting anyone enough to be in their blissful state.

Then I had a very timely boost.

Lydia came to the kiosk; in her 'bustling' mood so I knew there was going to be quite an important announcement. There was…but it was most unexpected.

"You've had a phone call Sue, from your pal in the Army; Brian isn't it? I've written down the message for you"

I could hardly believe it; I knew there was no bad news because Lydia would not have looked as happy as she had.

*Hello Sue – sorry I couldn't speak in person but I've got three days leave. The lady said you finish at about two o'clock - so meet me in 'Fortes' at three. Brian.*

What a surprise and what a brilliant lift to my low, confused spirits.

As I was getting changed, I worried a little about Meg's divulgence of their conversation; however, I realised he would have no idea that I'd been over there and heard about it... I set off to catch up with a special friend again.

"Good grief Brian...you're a *giant* now!"

"And you're still the same little short person...come here!"

With that he picked me up and swung me round, as you would a child. Clutching my arm we went inside; our usual lady was on duty, and out of habit we promised to make no noise. She gave Brian a pretend clip round the ear…and left us to it.

"Come on Brian…*tell me…tell me everything*"

"Sue, it's the best thing I could have ever done…oh! by the way…Bill sends his love; he's in Canada already and I'm on leave now before I go to Norway. I have already grown an inch and a half, and put on almost a stone in weight; that's partly good food, but mostly it's the training. I love it, we both do. But look love…what about you?"

We had plenty of time and the conversation just continued on and on...but I decided against divulging my consideration of joining up.

I knew he wouldn't be hurt when I said how happy my life was; I told him all about the outings, the London trips and so on, and the whole new social life I'd found, thanks to Win and Pat.

Because it was him, I knew I could also tell him about my recent misgivings and the emotional turmoil I occasionally felt.

"It's a strange old world Brian; I wanted, all my childhood life to be part of a happy family environment, and now I am I find it hurts more by the day. It seems to be just a constant reminder of what I didn't have; does that sound *mad* to you?"

"You mad my little Sue? Never...and don't *ever* question that opinion. What you are feeling is just so natural; if you want to cry, go ahead...it's the best healer in the world. You'd be amazed at how many of us guys did in the first few days; the corporals were collectively scathing, but told us on an individual basis, that it was to be expected. Please don't worry darling. Let's get out of here and have a walk by the river"

The pleasure of each others' company was equally shared; I felt too that Brian was over the 'in love' stage. All was incredibly natural and relaxed; the short time had flown by, but now it was time to leave.

"That was one of the best evenings I've had in ages. Look, I've got a BFPO address Sue if you'd like it. I'd love to hear your news and I'll reply, of course"

We parted on that happy note and caught our respective buses home...with matching happy smiles spread across our faces.

After a couple more days of deep consideration...I made my decision,

*"On Wednesday next, I'll definitely ask Sarge for the forms"*

I felt the camaraderie of an army unit would be preferable to the angst, which seemed not to go away; it was haunting me. Besides everything else, the chats with Win and Pat had largely ceased; they met their new boyfriends now without the escort of a *chaperone,* and I was seeing less of them both.

I wouldn't tell anyone for the time being, but rather wait until the acceptance had taken place; there would be plenty of time then. I was absolutely confident it was the best decision; in fact I was already looking forward to it.

I'd written to Mrs C shortly after seeing Brian, suggesting we met in town again, but this time with the boys; I would treat us all to the pictures. Her reply was swift and enthusiastic; the twins were playing football on the Saturday, but Friday evening would be perfect.

It was wonderful to catch up; they all said how I'd changed…but in the nicest possible way.

I told them all my news, including the tale of the jaunt to Brighton and the loss of my bike; the expression on the boys' faces would not have shown more alarm if I'd said I'd had a leg removed!

No mention was made of Mr. C, but Brian had already told me he was still being difficult at times...much to the concern of his mother, Meg and everyone else.

We enjoyed the film and it was lovely having the money to afford to pay for our tea; we parted in high spirits and with the promise we would do it again another day.

# CHAPTER 43

I was at work the next day; Saturday afternoons could be deadly quiet, and this was no exception. I'd kept myself occupied with cleaning anything that didn't move, and other equally engrossing activities.

I heard a car pull on to the pumps…looked up…it was Owen.

It was weeks…no months, since he had been in; my tummy was doing flik-flaks all over the place! I could hear my own heart beating like a pneumatic drill; I went towards him with what must have been the most *ridiculous* grin on my face.

The fascinating thing though…he was quite obviously experiencing exactly the same feeling…his grin too was bordering on the inane!

"Where have you *been*?"

"I've just done my five months back at sea; I didn't say anything before I left because…well I just didn't"

"It's really good to *see* you…and I *did* wonder where you had gone"

We caught up on the gossip, such as it was, then he left me to get on with my work; he wound down the driver's window as he was leaving.

"So will you be available tomorrow, for another trip to Fawley…simply to navigate you understand?"

"Errm…am I doing anything tomorrow? Course I'm not…I'd love it, and thank you"

I felt so excited about his coming in again; there was a huge buzz when I told Win and the family what was happening. Dear Mrs G made up more sandwiches…and once again, in the early morning, I quietly left the house.

The day was pretty much the same as our previous visit but with one major difference; we were both very much more relaxed.

Owen explained in more detail about his work. He had his Masters Ticket which meant he could captain a ship; currently he was serving as Chief Officer, or Mate as he called it. He'd already mentioned the five months away, adding he was now ashore for five to six weeks leave.

As on the previous journey, the miles and time rapidly disappeared; this time, conversation seemed easier, and laughter came more quickly.

On the return trip, he suggested we revisit the same restaurant for our meal; again walking the riverbank and chatting nineteen to the dozen as we went.

His academic education was *vast* compared with my own; attending a good Grammar school, then on to Southampton University to sit his Tickets.

I explained I'd attended a very good Secondary school, but subsequently had to work hard just to keep body and soul together. I made the briefest mention of being raised in Barnardo's; he equally briefly told me he lived with his widowed mother.

However, his life had been totally consumed with years of constant study and nothing else; I had, once it was affordable, really enjoyed mine to the full. As we ambled along, we entered into a discussion about who exactly was the *ingénue* in this case.

We decided it was a pretty even state of affairs; we would each introduce the other to our own particular interests.

"Sue I would love to spend more of my leave with you this time; I thought a lot about you when I was away…could you manage that within your busy life?"

"It is less hectic now Win and Pat have regular boyfriends; we still all meet up occasionally, but nothing like before. I've made plenty of friends and I'm out and about a lot…but I could be out and about with you" I chuckled.

"One thing though…Wednesday evenings are sacrosanct; nothing would stop me attending TA meetings. Other than that, I think I would love to spend more days like this one"

"Right then, that's a deal. Let's teach each other plenty, and thoroughly enjoy ourselves; for far too long I have concentrated on the interminable struggle with books and exams. I need you to show me how to really relax, and if the Bournemouth Symphony Orchestra is anything to go by, we are going to have a great leave. I can wash *my* hair on Wednesdays!"

Considering the scarcity of said hair, I just grinned.

We certainly made the most of the decision to make it a good leave.

One of the first and most memorable places we visited was the National Gallery in London.

I loved Art in school and had a brilliant teacher; on one occasion, he took the whole class to a small gallery in nearby Lytham. Here he explained how to enjoy the magnificence of original works, however humble the artist. ...but the National was something else!

Initially, while standing absolutely still, staring in awe at some of the truly great paintings, I felt he didn't seem to me to 'get it'; he was looking but not *seeing* anything. We were in front of a Constable; he said he recalled seeing it on a chocolate box...or something of equally disgusting treatment to this Great Master, as far as I was concerned.

Recalling the school visit, I reached for his hand; pulling him gently to my side I said quietly;

"Right...stand very still and focus on the sheer *size* of the canvas; now zoom in and concentrate hard on that bit of paint *there*. That daub of paint...that brush mark Owen...he did that *with his very own hand*. You are looking at a glorious moment in history; it happened once, on that canvas, and will never *ever* be repeated. That's it...history directly in front of you... worship his genius"

For a moment he just looked at me; then right there, in the middle of the blooming National Gallery, he kissed me.

We continued to hold hands; he studying with new eyes the sheer magic of the painting…I knew he'd 'got it' then.

Part of the deal, while we were in London, was a visit to the Planetarium.

"Now I hope I can show you the beauty of what *I* see in the sky; it's not just my job. As a very little boy I was already fascinated; fortunately, my father got me some books and they were read from cover to cover, and back again. That part of my Navigation exams was so easy for me; it may sound boring …but Sue it's truly not"

"I'm sure I'll be as enchanted in here as you were eventually with the paintings…come on…educate me!"

The dome was a most odd affair at first glance, but was intriguing when the lights went down; the night sky was there above, even though it was still mid-afternoon. I was enthralled and his whispered asides, imparting just a little more information than the commentary, made it a marvellous experience.

He knew every planet and star group by name; he was brilliant…and I told him so.

"Quite clearly we have founded a new branch of the Mutual Admiration Society!"

"You have a certain way with words Susan Davis and you manage to always make me laugh!"

We continued the chatter and laughter all the way home on the train; I felt a new relaxed confidence with this man, this gentle man. I'd totally accepted the fact that there was a twelve years age gap, *and* he was beginning to lose his hair. This made him completely different from anyone I had been out with in the past…and I was beginning to like the difference.

We visited more galleries and museums; enjoyed rowing on a lake, with a picnic in complete isolation on the island in the centre. Attended two more concerts and seemingly walked *miles*; there were not many days passing without we made some contact or another.

After each meeting, it became natural now to kiss me goodbye…the same gentle tender embrace…but it worried me. I was aware that he was a very different person, and not just from the point of view of dating. I found him to be straightforwardly just that…a very different person.

I lay in bed, wide awake and in positive torment; I knew this was something totally new, but I could not drop my protective shield, in fact it seemed even more firmly in place.

I reflected upon all the wonderful times we had spent together;

*Why couldn't I trust him?*
*Why couldn't I trust myself?*
*For goodness sake, my twentieth birthday had just passed in the usual uncelebrated manner; when would I allow myself to grow up?*

No answers would come however hard I tried; I drifted off to sleep, deciding that I would mature eventually…when the time was right.

Win, Pat and I, at last met up for a chat, and quickly established our rightful positions on Win's bed. I listened utterly fascinated, at the easy way they spoke of the relationship they had with their boyfriends. Nothing these chaps said or did, seemed to be doubted or questioned by them; their self-confidence was something of which I was in awe. They appeared so contented, almost in a state of bliss.

I added very little to this particular conversation; I felt miles distant from their standpoint.

*Would I ever be like them?*

397

*Would I ever have their confidence?*

*Am I yet the Outsider I believed myself to be?*

Once again no answers; I felt rather foolish and totally out of my depth...not for the first time in my new life.

CHAPTER 44

Owens's leave was at its end; we were meeting on the Sunday for a final outing before he returned to sea for another five months.

The thought of him going was already leaving a vacuum within me; I could make neither head nor tail of how I felt…or why. It was a day that at its best could be called low key; we quite clearly felt the same about each other.

The sadness on his face and in his voice simply reflected my own feelings; but those feelings still confused me.

"Sue darling, I could never have imagined such a magical leave; I have written the address where letters will reach me, I hope you will write"

"I would love to keep in touch… but will you write back?"

"Of course I will. I've written a note here I'd like you to leave until the morning to read. Please write to me…I want so much to know you will still be here when I next come home. I know it seems a long time at the moment, but it does pass quickly. Please be here?"

"Well I'll be honest and say I am thinking of joining the Regulars; you know…enlisting in the Army"

His face was a picture no passage of time could ever erase from my memory; he was utterly shocked.

"Sue…please! Oh please wait until I next come home to make that decision. I am as unsure of my feelings as you are of yours; *but I think I love you*"

Now I was the one in shock to hear those words; it scared me.

"Alright Owen, I'll wait; I never want to hurt you…but please try to understand who and where I am"

"I do know that; but remember, I too face my own dilemmas…man of the world I may be…but I too cannot be confident of what may lie ahead"

We were by now both in tears; the emotion of the conversation, and the parting of the ways; each had come into play. We were in a close embrace; I did not want to leave this man, and yet his presence was stifling me.

Again a tender kiss to say goodnight; then he was gone…into the distance for a further five months.

I could not wait until the morning; I tore open the envelope as soon as I got to my room. In his small, neat handwriting, I read;


*Dearest Sue,*

*I could never have dreamed of having the leave I have just experienced. Please be there for the next one; the empty space if you were not, would be impossible to imagine. You have made me so happy and I just pray you feel the same.*

*With fondest love*

*Owen*

*PS Please write to the address below*


I lay in my bed and cried; missing him already.

I was amazed on the Tuesday morning to find a letter for me; he had caught the post before sailing. Inside was a written request,

*Each evening at nine o'clock, please look up at the moon; I'll synchronise with the right time anywhere in the world... let's both say 'nosda cariad'... the Welsh for 'goodnight darling'*

401

There were also beautiful comments and reflections upon our time spent together; with no time to waste, I replied in similar vein.

Every day I put pen to paper, what I found to write about is a mystery; sometimes brief, but more often than not an epistle of some considerable pages long.

The postal system was a drawback in its complication; I posted daily but he didn't receive them until he reached a port. My letters went on board with the Port Agent, and he brought away those written by Owen. These were then sent by Air Mail, and eventually arrived with me.

Fortunately his first trip was to North Africa; a place called *Marsa el Brega,* an outward trip of about five days. As I had replied immediately he received two letters; the remainder were waiting by the time he returned to Fawley.

This made it important to write in generalisations; it was pointless referring to today, tomorrow and so on. The date on the heading was essential as then they could be 'filed' in order before reading; at least this made the account chronologically accurate.

From his eventual reply I knew the most important news received by him was when I told him I had spoken to Sgt. Major Glazier;

"I told her tonight I have decided *not* to go into the Regulars"

She replied in response;

*"*I bet you've met the man of your dreams"…but I didn't answer her.

His response to that was to ask me the same question; I didn't answer him either!

I simply didn't know where I was, or what was going on; I certainly wasn't ready to make any statements I could eventually live to regret.

The letters were the only form of communication available; Mrs G didn't have a 'phone, or he may have been able to make a 'ship-to-shore' call. He mentioned this in a letter, warning me it was an odd conversation; I would have to say "OVER" each time I'd finished a sentence…he would then come in with his chat. In addition to that nonsense…the radio officer would be in attendance.

I replied I'd prefer to write!

His letters were gradually evolving a pattern; the 'news' was becoming less, with terms of affection taking its place.

These words were beautiful to read, and I tried so hard to believe what he was saying. I knew by now how strong my off-guard feelings were; allowing myself to bring them to the surface was the continual stumbling block. The months progressed as the letters flew back and forth; at long last I had the one that gave me a *possible* landing date.

This would depend entirely on whether the Company 'changed the orders', which meant diverting his ship to another port from the one now designated…Fawley. What he planned was to come back to Tonbridge in the usual way, and we would do as we had before; collect his trunk on my first day off.

On the morning shift the day before he was due in, Lydia came out with a message for me…and a lovely big smile.

*Arrived Fawley on the 0400 tide; have the cargo to discharge - but as long as all goes to plan - I'll see you tomorrow late evening. Love Owen*

I held the note hard in both hands and scrunched it into my face; I was absolutely elated.

# CHAPTER 45

The hour was approaching midnight when the door bell rang. Everyone else was in bed, but Mrs G had allowed me to wait up… I *knew* he would call… whatever the time.

I answered the door; we just fell into each others' arms, and stayed there for what seemed like an eternity.

"Oh God... I can't believe we're together again" he sighed.

"Come in and have a coffee…Mrs G said it would be alright"

We talked quietly while making the drinks, and then continued once relaxed at last in the sitting room. He looked tanned and well and quite definitely happy, but also tired.

"Look Owen, I've got an early start tomorrow and you've sleep to catch up with; I ought to go to bed now"

"That's fine; I'll call in the garage late morning, and we can make plans then"

"*Nosda Cariad*" we said in unison…and he was gone.

I crept up the stairs of the silent, slumbering house; as I went to my room, in a rather loud whisper, I heard Win call my name. It was good to resume my place on the side of her bed; all thoughts of early morning starts were forgotten as we talked into the early hours.

She told me she understood completely, how different this was for me; and my reluctant hesitation in admitting to myself, how I really felt. For her, it was all so easy by comparison…to voice and demonstrate her own true feelings.

"Don't rush Sue…but don't deny yourself either darling. I know you listen and dissect everything you hear; you do it automatically, even with us. Of course I can see your reasons to protect yourself from rejection, BUT… remember this. There are people out there who think you're great and wouldn't hurt you in a million years. I know this with such certainty cos I'm one of 'em love"

I was close to tears at this sweet statement, and tried to explain.

"Win, do you recall the first time you stood on the edge of the swimming pool, with arms outstretched, trying to pluck up the courage to dive into the

406

water…that mixture of excitement and dread? Well that's where I am at the moment. I know from his letters how he feels about me; I don't understand *why* that's all. I think I feel the same way too, actually I *know* I do; I can *say* that to you…but I still can't seem to convince myself"

"Take your time Sue; you did eventually get into the pool didn't you, and you will again. You'll know when everything is just right…and that will be it! Try not to worry so much; allow things to happen and events to take their rightful course. If you wait until it's perfect for you…believe me it will be. *And* I'll tell you another thing.  I'm gonna get up early with you on the day you go to Fawley;  I'll do your hair, wear that lovely dress you bought last week… and you'll leave here looking like a million dollars!"

I did too… dear Win.


Owen opened the car door for me, as he always did; he took my hand as I slid onto the seat, and then gave a very quiet wolf whistle. That set us off laughing and we continued in the same manner for the rest of the journey. There was however, one surprise awaiting me;

he informed me his mother had invited us both to return in time for an early supper.

I heard myself say 'that would be fine' but my stomach sank. I'd only ever thought of him as a single entity; he had mentioned he lived with her but it had not really sunk in. Now I was to meet her in person and have a meal; I was immediately a bag of nerves…for no apparent reason I could see.

Theirs was a bungalow on one of the nice estates just beyond the garage; as we pulled up onto the drive she came to the front door. She wore the most expressionless face I'd ever seen in my life! No smile, no querying look, no pleasure at all at our arrival…absolutely nothing.

Owen took my hand again as I left the car; I felt a positive comforting squeeze, which was tremendously reassuring. Usually I could mask quite well any nervousness I may be feeling; I got the impression she was not convinced.

After a decidedly cool greeting, we were ushered through the hall and into the dining room on the right; all was prepared for our supper. A cream Damask cloth covered a beautiful old oak table; freshly polished cutlery and all the other accoutrements were meticulously laid out. There were fresh flowers everywhere in this rather elegant room; it was a most welcoming sight.

*"Perhaps I've misread her"* I thought.

My offer of help was politely declined; we were told to relax as she wouldn't be long. The table became laden with a delicious looking salad; she had spared no expense, and had clearly spent a lot of time with it all. I commented as much…but in response was simply invited to sit to the table.

Throughout the meal I realised Owen's conversation was becoming increasingly hesitant and stilted; his cheerful banter I was used to hearing had completely disappeared. I just chatted away in my usual manner; I wouldn't stifle myself just because it seemed to be what she expected. I was going out with her son…not her!

In conversation she admitted to being extremely surprised at how much Owen had enjoyed the concerts and opera; his father too had loved classical music apparently, but she was never interested.

When I responded to her query about where *my* interest started, there was clear disbelief when I told her I played violin, and had performed concerts in a Youth

409

Orchestra. I was beginning to be on my guard with this woman; whether she believed me or not though, worried me not at all.

We ultimately reached the end of this ordeal and left…actually we escaped! Owen asked whether I wanted to be driven straight home.

"Good grief *no*…but thank you anyway; could we drive somewhere and finish off our day out on a high note?"

I immediately wanted to retract that remark; it seemed almost rude to refer to the visit in such a derisory manner.

"It was hard going love, and I really do apologise; she has airs and graces which *infuriate* me but you were marvellous…she wasn't going to put you down was she?"

We looked at each other and with enormous relief, he saw the funny side; it lightened the moment, but he was still brooding.

So was I.

I realised how easy it had been to feel the negative animosity his mother had quite openly displayed; why couldn't I feel the reverse of that? This man had told me he loved me…I thought that I loved him; why was it then such a dilemma to admit both these facts to myself?

The bad spell was broken when Owen pulled into a small lane that led up to a farm; this lane wove its way upwards for a fair distance. As we left the car I shouted

"*Bet I can race you to that big tree!*"

It was strictly no contest, he was so unfit it was hilarious; when he eventually arrived we just collapsed with laughter. As he lay on his back, completely puffed out...I kissed him. That was a 'first' for me but it was pure impulse; I don't know who was more surprised!

Goodness knows how late it was when we agreed we were freezing, and had better get back; but what a wonderful few hours we had enjoyed. We laid side-by-side with hands held...looking up at the beautiful moonlit sky...and talked as if we were never going to stop.

He started by explaining his mother had been widowed when he was only nine years old. His father was an officer with Customs and Excise; his Will had left her, if not well off, in no way destitute. He barely remembered him as he was away a great deal. What he *did* recall of that sad time…was the insistence by his mother that he slept in her bed for comfort.

"I hated it Sue; I felt all my friends knew, which was utterly ridiculous. It gave me a dreadful sense of being different and inferior; that's why I concentrated so hard on school and studying. Being engrossed in a book took me away from the ghastly reality of her replacing me with my father. I don't mean she ever behaved wrongly with me, if you know what I mean; I was only acting as a physical hot water bottle, but I still hated it"

Only previously alluded to, I then told him more of the Dr Barnard's Homes and my life there-in; I made no mention whatsoever of the sexual abuse I'd experienced. It was neither the time nor the place; indeed I could never ever see that those disclosures would be necessary. They were buried deep within me, and nothing would bring them from that hiding place.

The explanation of his mother's attitude towards me was simple; he reckoned if he was courting the Queen of Sheba, she would not be good enough! My own thoughts I didn't divulge; I reckoned she wanted to have her son around, for her own selfish comfort as always.

We met whenever we possibly could; more of the visits to similar venues of the previous leave, including another wonderful day spent in London. Owen had to attend a meeting at Esso head office; we travelled again by train and when we arrived at his venue, he insisted I enter with him.

"It won't be a long time for you to wait; you'll just sit in the foyer where there is always a supply of magazines. But most importantly, it is where all and sundry will be able to see my lovely girl, and be jealous of how lucky I am"

I didn't read much; I reflected solely on what he had said, and the times already he had made similar remarks. I was much less troubled then at first, but I was still finding it a strange experience.

From the office we went to a beautiful restaurant; black-dressed girls took our coats, and grey-clad flunkeys escorted us to our table, this being covered with a grey and pink heavy linen table cloth. Vast chandeliers hung from the lofty ceiling and the carpeted floor completed the *ensemble*…it was pure opulence.

The menu was leather-bound, in the same grey and pink; it was also totally in French! I did try to see if there was anything I could decipher …no chance!

Owen was deeply engrossed, but still attentive. In answer to his question regarding my choice, I simply replied I would like chicken, but cooked in the way he would best recommend. He ordered the wine by name and year, completely at ease in these very grand surroundings.

Once the hurdle of actually *ordering* anything was overcome, I settled with as much comfort as he, and enjoyed an exquisite lunch.

On leaving, we were a only few yards away from the place when he stopped and hugged me.

"You were the most perfect guest Sue darling…thank you"

I cheerfully admitted to him, that I had not a *clue* we would go to anywhere as grand, and how flummoxed I was at first with the menus; he told me that was when he had first realised the magnitude of the occasion.

"But *nobody* else in there would guess you didn't frequent such places as a matter of course; you were absolutely marvellous. Talk about natural *aplomb*!"


Again, far too quickly, the last days loomed large; the sad dread between us was tangible.

"I know where I would love to return; by that bridge and path where we lay and talked…I want to talk again"

He readily agreed, but requested no race up the hill this time, and that *I* kiss *him* again; something I was happy to do…without any second bidding.

In response he whispered he loved me…for the first time I said;

"I love you too Owen"

I was shaking like a leaf, but what a beautiful moment; we were both absolutely overwhelmed with those few small words. They opened up many new doors, and once again we lay and talked for hours.

We were rapidly approaching our last few hours together, but the deep sadness had lifted; we would still communicate by letter, and for now that would have to suffice.

Those three words 'I love you' were my passport to cross the Rubicon.

I felt at last, fully grown up, and in an irrevocable situation which was bringing me an inner peace I could never have dreamed of.

The reminder "to look at the moon" was included in the letter he managed to post before his ship sailed; with the addition we both say those three words as well.

Letters now were so much easier to write; I had become used to the rather odd postal system, and guaranteed he always had plenty to read once he'd sailed. Likewise I received my share from him.

One day however, a single envelope fell on the mat; it carried a UK stamp and the frank mark stated it came via London. It was Owen's familiar writing but I was deeply puzzled and concerned; what could have gone wrong for him to be ashore?

Thoughts raced through my now confused mind as I ran upstairs to my room; I threw myself on the bed and just stared at this unfamiliar object.

With trembling hands I at last tore it open; the relief was unbelievable!

He had started the letter by saying it would be posted in the UK by one of the guys who was due his leave; such a simple solution...but not something that had occurred to me in my near panic!

What he then went on to say, almost put me back in the same state of panic.

Once his sentences of introduction were over he continued;

*I cannot wait until I get home to ask you this question; Sue sweetheart, will you marry me? Can we get engaged on my next leave? You'll be twenty one and out of the Care of Barnardo's and I want you so much. I know this is not the perfect way to ask you, but I can't* wait *another three months before I know. Please think about it darling and let me know.*

With trembling hands and feeling breathless, I sat on the edge of my bed, reading those sentences over and over again until I was almost burning a hole in the paper. I knew *immediately* how I wanted to respond; had he been there facing me, it would have been so simple!

Instead I got out my paper; without a date or any preamble...and slap bang in the centre of the page...standing alone in big block capitals...

## xxx <u>YES</u> xxx

It seemed an interminable length of time before he knew I'd received that letter; I had replied, and then heard back from him. He could not hide his absolute joy, and the rest of the letter continued with all sorts of anticipated plans for the next leave.

I had told no-one else to date, and that's what he'd hoped; he wanted to make a joint announcement and maybe have a party. This would include the celebration of my Big birthday too. He said he had masses of things to ask me, but there was one *very* important matter, requiring immediate reply…would I marry him the leave later…about February or March 1963?

"Gosh…*in only about nine month's time, I would become Mrs Williams*"

I was elated…and a further "xxx YES xxx" was included in my letter of response.

Thinking of Mrs Williams…I assured him I was regularly visiting his mother, as he had requested. I dutifully called in once a week but I hated it; she was as unwelcoming and cold, as on the day we first met.

I was longing to inform her of our plans and arrangements; *blimey she didn't know we were engaged... let alone moved on from there too!*

I didn't dwell too much on how Owen was going to tell her...or how well it would be received; that was most definitely his problem!

Owen had told me her birthday was due during this trip; before sailing, he'd left a card and gift in his room, but apparently she knew where it was to be found.

I decided to buy her a carpet sweeper; mentioned more than once by her, as something she really needed. I bought the best one in the shop; a really posh wooden affair, with a strong steel adjustable handle. It was a lot more money than I'd anticipated, in fact I could barely afford it...but I knew she'd be really pleased.

On the day, I arrived after work as promised; she showed me into the kitchen...still looking more like the Grim Reaper than the cheerful Birthday Girl! I was longing for her to tear the wrapping off my gift, and leap around the room in great joy...that's what I would have done.

 But no...she put the kettle on and made tea...got out biscuits she knew I never ate...and *then* sat down.

She carefully opened the card and read every word twice; then looking at me in her usual unsmiling way, murmured 'thank you'.

At last she opened my gift…but all she said, in a very bored voice,

"Do you know how to put it together?"

A bit put out at her manner, I asked if she was happy with it.

"Yes it's nice, but *you* shouldn't have signed the card you know. I know my son bought it before he left, so you would be able to give me a present too. That's just the sort of sweet thing he would do for me…but it's very naughty of *you t*o pretend"

"I'm afraid you're wrong Mrs Williams…I bought that with my own money…*and* I went without to afford it"

Her expression of disdainful disbelief was sickening; I felt hurt and angry…and left without another word.

I *slammed* her door, and stormed out from the drive in a high old temper…then an old Morris Minor drew up alongside me.

"What are *you* doing in this neck of the woods young lady?"

I recognised them as regular customers at the garage; I hesitated with my response, as I felt it might show disloyalty to Owen.

"I didn't realise you lived up here Mrs Speltz...I've been delivering a birthday present to my boyfriend's mother"

"What... *Mrs Williams*...are you going out with Owen?"

I assured them I was...adding that they sounded a bit disapproving of the idea.

"Oh no...not at all...he's a sweetheart! But her ... how on earth do *you* two get along?"

That frank and honest opinion from her came as no surprise; they were a lovely down to earth couple and we'd had many a laugh in the garage. He was a retired engineer and she had once been a nurse; they told me they had both been actively involved in the War, but didn't elaborate.

I gratefully accepted their offer of a lift; as they drove me home, I explained the events of the day. They were disgusted, and said so in no uncertain terms...she was as close to swearing as I'd ever heard anybody!

"Look love, do your duty to Owen and call in to see the old bat; then come around to see us, we're only a little further up round the Crescent. You don't need to put up with that sort of behaviour from her"

I agreed, and a few days later made my first visit; although young enough to be their daughter, we got on famously.

He was 'of the old school', and in many ways reminded me of Uncle Tom; a true gentleman, beautifully spoken and always immaculately dressed, even in his garden.

She was of similar ilk…but an absolute Maverick; we had long discussions about the joys this shared attitude bestowed upon us both. Mine was honed in childhood; hers, she explained, came from Nursing…especially during the War.

"If I'd stuck to all their ridiculous rules Sue, I wouldn't have got through the Training…as it was, I made SRN; I didn't go on to be Matron though…even more blooming rules at that dizzy height!"

One day while visiting, Mr Speltz asked me would I back their car up, and away from the garage doors; I said a had never driven, except for one brief occasion at TA. He took me outside, sat me in the car and showed me what I needed to do. Once successfully started, I shifted into reverse, and moved the car to where he wanted…with no problems.

"You're a natural Sue; you've *got* to take lessons. Imagine not only the fun that would be…but look at the advantages; you could go anywhere in the country to meet Owen's ships"

The end of the next days' shift found me at the "British School of Motoring" office in Tunbridge Wells.

I was a bit shocked when the costs were explained, I immediately realised how deeply they would bite into my budget. Going back outside, I walked up and down the road for quite a while, mulling over the sensibility, or not, of the whole idea.

Eventually, reflecting on the words of Mr Speltz, I decided to take the bull by the horns…and returned to make the arrangements. I was honest with them about my finances, so they introduced me to Mr Holland, the gentleman who would be my Instructor. We got on immediately, and he promised he could gauge from the outset, how many lessons I would probably need.

After my first hour session, he reckoned it would only be about twelve at most; then laughing added, he was certain I'd been a driver in a previous life.

"Maybe I was…but I want to be a driver in this one too!"

He assured me I would be, without any doubt in his mind.

I studied hard at the 'Highway Code', with Win helping out by asking me potential Test questions. The course was completed, with me feeling full of confidence; he was a great chap and I loved being behind the wheel…he made it seem so easy. He arranged for the Test date as early as possible; it was to be July 18th …just two days after my 21st birthday.

It's quite difficult arranging an event without a venue; I would have loved to throw some sort of party for the Big One, but it was proving impossible to arrange. The place to hold it in was one thing…the cost was something else!

But come The Day…I missed out on nothing.

Mr Vinell and Andrew gave me cash, as did Lydia and the boys in the Workshop; she'd organised a 'whip round' and they had all been extremely generous.

Many other gifts of toiletries and chocolates came from customers, not all of them daily regulars either; the word appeared to have reached far and wide…obviously Pat's endeavour.

By the end of my shift the forecourt kiosk resembled a card shop; each one bearing the **21$^{st}$** badge on the front… with so many kind words on the inside. Mr and Mrs Speltz came in with theirs; it was the biggest card I'd ever seen. Their gift was a gold *Ronson* ladies' cigarette lighter, upon which they had my name and birth date engraved.

Andrew took me home by car; it was only 500yds away but I was over-laden with so much to carry! Once indoors, there was even more from Win and the family; between them they bought me a cream leather vanity case…full of make-up. Pat had sweetly added to the contents, with a beautiful mother-of-pearl manicure set and some hair products…it was all gorgeous.

At the very end of this amazing day, Win and I were in our 'talking place' on her bed; she had apparently known Pat was planning to broadcast the news.

"But I bet she never expected *that* outcome Sue. Will you now at last understand what a *popular* person you are…and just how many people *know* that? My Dad calls you 'unique'…and we all agree with him; try and *feel* it though darling…or you'll miss out on so much. Right… here endeth the fist Lesson…now give us a blooming chocolate!"

Two days later, after receiving my final half- hour of instruction, I was at the Testing Centre; full of nerves until I sat behind the wheel…and instantly calmed down.

"There is a Royal visitor in Tunbridge Wells today, so the traffic will be very heavy; I cannot however, take that into consideration. If you can drive, you can drive in all conditions"

In a rather hoity-toity voice, that was the opening gambit of my sour faced, grumpy old Examiner; he looked like Worzel Gummidge on a bad day…and he smelt.

What he hadn't bargained for was my absolute determination. Besides wanting the fillip of passing 'first time'…in addition, I couldn't afford any more blooming lessons!

I felt as confident as ever, and knew I was driving well throughout the whole course. After completing a perfect three point turn, *and* with an exquisite up-hill gear change, we arrived back. He asked me to answer three or four simple questions on the Highway Code…then handed me my 'Pass' slip.

He congratulated me on an almost faultless test, and then asked me how long I'd been driving; when I told him twelve and a half hours, he said

"If I'd known that – *I wouldn't have passed you*"

We laughed all the way at that ridiculous statement, while driving back with a delighted Mr Holland…and Susan Davis!

Everyone was full of congratulations at my news; once I'd informed the family and the garage…I walked up to see Mr and Mrs Speltz. I thanked them for spotting my potential, and for their on-going encouragement; they handed me a little package…inside was a car key ring.

"We bought it days ago…cos we knew you'd pass; well done Sue"

This completed my deep sense of increasing happiness; the whole of my life was changing. Win's words of wisdom were filtering through, and I was beginning to feel it now.

That night again found us both in talk mode; she was genuinely pleased at my Pass and announced, she would be the next one. I rushed downstairs to get us both a coffee; on my return, I emptied out onto her bed, the entire contents of my new vanity case. Going through every item there-in, I was still chattering at nineteen-to-the-dozen; Win laughed,

"Susan Davis…I know why you can't settle for five minutes at a time… Owen should be home in less than forty eight hours from now"

She was spot on…the time was so close; I had the most *amazing* mix of dreadful nerves…and total exhilaration!

# CHAPTER 47

Once again the knock on the door was late; everyone else was in bed.

My nerves ceased the moment I saw him again; *God I love you,* I thought. We sat close together on the settee and talked until we were almost exhausted. We went over all the letters, and the events of the trip; eventually I said

"I didn't write and tell you, but I've been taking driving lessons; I've had twelve and a half hours…but I'm not going to do any more"

"Oh Sue…*but you must*…don't stop them now love; it would be *marvellous* if you could drive. My car sits in the garage all the while I'm away; it's such a waste…why won't you continue?"

"Because…I passed my Test on Wednesday!"

The expression on his face said it all; crestfallen with the bad news… and absolute delight from the good.

"You are even more wicked than I remember Susan Davis…but congratulations! Look sweetheart, I'd better to go now, it's terribly late; I'll be in the garage though as soon as I can tomorrow. We've got plans to make for your late birthday celebration"

And could this man make plans? I was fascinated at the detail; maybe his officer training was brought into play.

He picked me up from the house; we made a very brief visit up to his mother, who presented me with a birthday card...and congratulated me on passing my Test. I read the card; noting it was the only one without the 21$^{st}$ emblazoned...thanked her...and we were gone.

Owen described the day as his 'big surprise'; no hints at all about what or where. I was fine with that...I *loved* surprises.

He drove straight into Tonbridge and walked down the High Street, heading for I knew not where. Walking hand in hand, he guided me inside a shop...it was 'Angell's' the jewellers. I felt myself blush with a deep shyness, not experienced for years, when he explained he was looking for an engagement ring; I held on tightly to his arm.

Mr John Angell Snr. was a regular customer at the garage; in his late 50's, he was a quiet utterly charming gentleman, who was clearly well versed in how to perfectly manage this situation.

After my finger was measured, he brought out the trays; Owen and I pondered before agreeing on the one we liked most of all. It was a small but exquisite diamond; Mr Angell assured me it looked beautiful, and was the perfect choice. He took Owen's address for the account…so the transaction would remain discreet.

Once out of the shop, we hugged each other very tightly; my mixed emotions bringing me near to tears, but with an elated joy inside making me fit to burst.

The ring had suddenly made everything else a reality.

In the middle of the High St, he kissed me, and with a whispered "*Come on…this is only the start*" we were back in the car, heading for Tunbridge Wells.

He drew to a halt in 'The Pantiles' …a historic and most beautiful area of the town; I was gently ushered into one of the grandest Hotels. We were escorted to the reserved 'table for two'…for Captain Williams and *fiancé*; that was the first time I'd heard him addressed thus...I mentioned that fact, and he laughed,

"I only ever use it for Reservations…especially at short notice like this… it's never failed me yet. Was it as good to be referred to, for the first time as my *fiancé*?" I just smiled my acknowledgment.

The table was in a quiet corner of the most beautiful Dining Room; the magnificent surroundings were understated opulence.

"*Gosh, I'm glad I've experienced this sort of place before*" I thought; then relaxed to soak up every detail of this exciting day.

Owen signalled the waiter who immediately appeared with the menu…and an ice bucket holding a bottle of pre-ordered Champagne; he filled our glasses and departed.

On our own again I was presented with two cards; I first had to open the one congratulating me on my driving Test result. The other was a beautiful 'To my Sweetheart' 21$^{st}$…with a cheque included.

"You can open a bank account now darling…and make that your first deposit; it pays back all the money you spent on those driving lessons. It was a marvellous thing to achieve without me even knowing…and you deserve it"

Along with the birthday card were two small packages. One was a pretty gold watch; the other, a Siamese Silver drop pendant necklace, which he immediately put around my neck…I proudly put on my watch.

To complete this *ensemble*…and with a toast in Champagne, Owen slid my engagement ring onto my finger.

I felt an unbelievable shyness come over me again; all I could do was smile in silence at the happy face opposite. He came around to my chair and, with not a care for who may be looking, kissed me gently and whispered "I love you"

I gazed at the array of gifts on the table;

"Owen I have never *seen* such beautiful things, I am *thrilled*…I thank you far more than can be ever expressed in words"

"You don't need words my sweetheart…your eyes say it all"

Returning to the car he said;

"This was not in the plans, but you only had one glass of wine, I had the rest! As you can drive now, would you do the honours to be on the safe side? I feel ok…but maybe not sharp enough to drive far"

I readily agreed. I thought I'd have felt rather nervous, but no; as soon as I was in the driver's seat, I was totally confident.

"Like Mr Speltz said darling…you are a natural"

Neither of us wanted our day to end yet; I drove to the little bridge and path, now a firm favourite. Owen got out the car rug…and we finalised my special day, together in the blissful peace of rural Kent.

# CHAPTER 48

Informing everybody of our plans brought about a fresh set of cards, but 'Engagement Congratulations' this time.

The entire leave seemed to be taken up with arranging our wedding; Owen explained he had to do all he possibly could before returning to a ship. He planned the day, for about ten days after the due date for his next leave; around January 24th. He was worried about finalising with the church for that arrangement...so he rang Esso in London.

They were wonderful, and managed to put the planning on an altogether different level.

"I can hardly believe it Sue; the Rule of 'five month on – six weeks off' is changing. A little prematurely of the full system, they are bringing me on *as from now*. I go back in mid August...take my four weeks leave in mid November... then return in mid March for our wedding! It's the sort of date we first hoped... it's absolutely perfect!"

I never imagined Owen could be so excited...he was almost jumping up and down...but only to copy me! It was fantastic news; all the pressure was off. He no longer needed to arrange *everything* to the nth degree…but he still busied away doing all he could.

The vicar was young, as vicars go; tall and slim, with black-framed heavy spectacles…and an absolute loony! There was an instant *rapport* we all felt; although the three obligatory 'talks' were suitably sombre…the rest of the time we spent laughing and joking. The vicar booked the date of March 27th at 11am; with complete confidence, knowing Owen would definitely be home.

After Owen's return to his ship, I set about organising myself; I went straight to see Mrs. Speltz…I knew she would help. I sadly related the dreadful comment Mrs Williams had made to me, when told of our arrangements.

"And are you *eligible* to have a white wedding?"

"Well that's typical of her sort I'm afraid Sue; I wonder, did she realise she was also slurring Owen's integrity, with the suggestion you had already slept together? I know you two well enough to realise what tripe that is…but I'll tell you one thing darling…you most certainly don't *have* to be in white anyway. I'll show you my photographs"

Although her album was only in black and white, she proudly showed me the lovely dresses. Her own beautiful gown she had made by hand, as well the dresses for the bridesmaids. She went on to explain they were all Peach coloured…in varying shades from light to dark.

She told me too, who all the people were; there seemed to be *masses* of them…and that made me concerned about my own situation. The vicar had explained the 'who does what' roles, and that made me realise how sparse was my choice.

"Mrs Speltz, you know I don't have family for bridesmaids or anything; please would you be my Matron of Honour…and make *me* a beautiful, colourful wedding?"

"I would be Honoured!" she agreed, laughing.

I spent many hours with them and their kind guidance, but it seemed, every time I visited Mrs. Williams, there was yet another snide comment.

"You do realise it is *your father* who should be paying for this…not my son"

She made other dreadfully hurtful comments in the same vein; one of which particularly upset and

437

worried me. I related this to Mrs Speltz…adding, I wasn't even sure the statement was accurate

"The right side of the church is for the Groom's family and friends *only* …you have the left side for yours"

"What a miserable old mare she is…but technically she's right. Don't be down-hearted though Sue; you have more friends than she's amassed in a lifetime, just look at all the birthday greetings you received. You leave it to me darling…she'll wish she'd never said that…you'll see"

With so much to do, the three months sea trip flew by very quickly…for me at least. Unlike the previous occasions, Owen was due to arrive at a respectable time of day; I had sufficient warning to arrange a change of shifts with Pat. This gave us the opportunity to meet up for an early supper, in a small restaurant in the countryside.

The time apart was quickly gone; it was wonderful being together again and catching up on the progress. He seemed though, to be in a particularly *animated* state…so I asked was he hiding something?

"Okay little engaged person…last time I came home, you threw your driving test bombshell at me; well I'm about to blast you to the heavens high!"

I could not *believe* what I had just heard…and so he repeated…grinning from ear to ear;

"I <u>said</u>…we will go from the Reception… *directly to our very own home*! I've bought a bungalow in Warsash, where I did my Merchant Navy Tickets; we'll be living next door to Bill, my chosen Best Man"

How I managed to stop myself from passing out one moment…or dancing around the tables in utter joy the next…I know not.

Owen then explained with further details.

Bill was also at sea; on ship-to-ship radio, Owen had spoken to him about his anticipated role at the ceremony. Their leave dates almost coincided, and he agreed he would; that was easily arranged. However, he'd then gone on to tell Owen, that his neighbour was about to sell up…and move permanently abroad.

Owen had made many visits to Bill and Sylvia in the past; they had known each other for years.

Bill had become fond of Warsash when he'd sat *his* Merchant Navy Tickets; when he married it seemed the obvious choice of a place to settle down. They had been very happy there; they knew that Owen liked their bungalow…it seemed a miracle that the adjacent one should now be for sale. Owen had a talk with the owner; the deal was done verbally in less than twenty four hours…with Completion anticipated within two months.

"Sweetheart, I'm *sorry* you haven't seen it, but I know you'll absolutely love it. We'll have two bedrooms, a lovely large sitting room and a kitchen…of your very own. Fawley is only about seven miles from Warsash; it's only a small village with a few shops, two pubs and the 'Clock Tower' garage right in the middle. I was very unsure about not discussing it together, but I had to strike while the iron was hot. I couldn't lose the unbelievable opportunity; I was confident you'd love it…I had to go ahead… I wanted so much to surprise you"

I cupped his face into both hands; while gently stroking his brow with my thumbs, I laughed at him quietly.

"Don't look and sound so *worried* darling…and 'to surprise me' would be the under-statement of all time! I *know* I'll love it. I think our tastes match as far

440

as rural living is concerned...gosh I can't begin to take it all in...*me in my own home*...it's like a dream!"

We agreed it was best for Owen to have a couple of days down there on his own; he could stay with Bill and Sylvia, and get the necessary papers signed.

He wanted time to thoroughly look around the place, to measure the rooms and windows for curtains, that sort of thing. It would be difficult for me to arrange two days away from work...and I truly felt more than happy to see it for the first time...on our Special Day.

If the three months at sea had seemed to pass quickly, I couldn't believe the four weeks leave!

We had a marvellous time but he was gone again.

# CHAPTER 49

At work a few weeks later, a most unusual incident occurred.

I was locking up after a bitterly cold January day; I could already see and feel the warm fire awaiting me. The forecourt lights were just switched off, making the dark night even more pronounced; from the gloom at the far entrance to the forecourt, a gentleman appeared.

When I went out to tell him we were closed, I could see immediately his considerable state of distress; he was having difficulty standing upright, and was gasping for breath. I managed to sit him down in the kiosk; a little more relaxed, he explained he had run out of petrol about a half mile down the road.

He was clearly in no state to sort this out for himself, so I took over. Filling the can he had carried up with him, taking his keys so I could drive the car back, I locked him safely in the kiosk…and set off.

I wasn't gone long, but by the time I returned, the poor man was looking ashen faced and rather ill; I was becoming more than a little concerned for him. He explained his house was only in the lane opposite, and he *was* feeling slightly better; although still wobbly, he promised he could cope to drive that short distance. He was stronger when he stood up, and warmly shook my hand; with a parting shot of extremely grateful thanks, he drove away.

Mid-shift the following afternoon, a lady walked onto the forecourt making a bee-line for the kiosk; clearly with the intent of talking to me.

"Hello dear, I know you are Sue, as Andrew told me on the 'phone this morning.I have come to thank you so very much for putting yourself out on such a freezing cold night to help my husband yesterday. He suffers a serious heart condition, and the stress of the long walk up to you was bad enough; to have gone back as well, carrying a heavy can, could *easily* have been too much for him. I can't personally thank you enough Sue. While talking with Andrew he told me you are to be married soon… *and* you have a bungalow to move in to. Well dear, my husband is a Director of 'Cormar Carpets'; he asked me to come, not only to sincerely thank you, but to offer to lay new flooring throughout your new home. It is the only way he can think of to demonstrate his gratitude for your extreme kindness"

She stayed for a little while and talked some more, she was a charming, elegant lady; I thanked her courteously for this wonderful gesture.

Immediately I arrived home, I wrote the wonderful news to Owen; his response was of overwhelming delight. In the same letter he explained where to find the floor measurements he had taken when he visited Warsash. I was to get them down to Mr Cormar Carpets, and tell him that he would be in touch with Bill's wife Sylvia; she would arrange to be there for the fitters, on the arranged day.

Owen understood when I said I was not in a financial position to do a great deal…but I wanted to buy us a really good cooker. Being in the Homes, then Lodgings meant I never got to cook any meals; I watched a lot though, and knew once in my own kitchen, it would be something I was going to greatly enjoy. To buy my cooker, I established a 'one-woman' car cleaning service; it was a great success. Andrew was my first customer; because he sang my praises to all his friends, it built up quickly from there.

I would scooter out to whomever, mainly at the big houses on the Hadlow Road and Cuckoo Lane, so not too far to travel. Everyone was pleased with the result, and I had mainly repeat business; it didn't take long to have sufficient money in my new bank account for my cooker…plus some spare.

I tried when I could, to buy something for our new home each week; one day found me decidedly strapped for cash…but I still looked around the small hardware store I'd visited on a weekly basis for ages.

The owner was a sweet man, full of fun. He worked long hours in his small but well-stocked shop; always wearing the same brown linen coat, which was far too large for his height and small frame. He had got to know me as a regular customer and I'd told him I was amassing my 'bottom drawer'.

I wandered around the solidly packed shelves, with the problem of finding something useful…with what amounted to peanuts!

At last I saw the perfect thing; a potato peeler, a small but vital item still on my Needs List. In response to my query as to the price he said;

"One shilling and threepence"

"*How much*?"

"Well, it *will* last a lifetime"

"For that amount…I'd wanna take it with me!"

For my cheek...he gave it to me as a gift!

445

I had been so industrious, once again the time had slipped by; Owen was safely home and we double checked all the arrangements.

He had not seen my dress; Mrs Speltz explained, the Groom would see me fully adorned, only once in Church. Mrs Williams had though…she was furious! On Mrs Speltz's insistence, together one day, we called in to see the old moo…it was an unforgettable experience, to say the least.

With a flourish, she removed from a bag, the material for our dresses; mine was turquoise, hers was a deep red, both in brushed velvet. Mrs Williams looked as if she'd just seen a ghost; all she said, in a rather shaky was…

"What is she wearing on her head?"

Having already discussed my positive hatred for hats…and deciding if we were going to be different, we may as well go the whole hog; Mrs Speltz simply replied;

"Nothing…but her bouquet is going to be very pretty"

Satisfied all was complete...at last our day arrived.

Uncle Affie, Owen's father's brother, was to give me away; he was a wonderful character, and a perfect stand-in for my late father. He'd had an unbelievable life, and loved to relate the stories to me when I visited him.

He enlisted in the army at the very start of the First World War; in a little over a month he was in France. Being a tall lean man he had manage to fool them all; they only realised he was underage when, along with other brave kids at the time, he didn't join the 'Shaving Line'. He was too young to shave! Before he reached his eighteenth birthday, he'd had his fore-arm blown off *and* was blinded in his left eye from the shrapnel.

He was sent home of course, and made a good recovery; only twenty one years later, he enlisted for the Second World War. Invalid though he was for front line duties, they took him on in an office capacity *and* he completed the full term of the conflict.

His prosthetic arm hindered him in no way at all; he successfully carved out an excellent career in the Civil service.

447

What a man!

Full of nervous excitement, I took his arm and we walked into the beautifully decorated church, full of flowers; as my eyes adjusted to the different light I looked ahead…and could not believe the sight.

On the right hand side were the two rows of pews holding the Groom's family and friends…as ordered by Mrs Williams.

Instead of the anticipated emptiness…'my side' was at least fourteen rows deep!

Unbeknown to me; the garage was closed for an hour at the direction of Mr Vinell Senior and Andrew, they were there with their families. I could see standing with them, dear Lydia and the boys from the Workshop…and dozens of my regular customers.

In addition were Pat and all her family; Win, with not only the family, but many of her colleagues from Sainsbury's…plus a host of their friends!

I was completely overwhelmed.

They all turned around as I slowly walked down the aisle, to stand at last beside my man; he touched my hand and  smiled at me…he looked so handsome in his full uniform.

All continued without a without a hitch; the vicar gave us a beautiful but cheerful service and at the end he moved away. He then turned around by the door he was approaching, and called out for Mrs Williams to go to the vestry; she appeared at Owen's side.

"Not you madam…I need the *new* Mrs Williams"

Her *chagrin* and personal humiliation were etched on her face; this new title was obviously going to take some getting used to, for both of us!

Immediately we had signed the Register, she came straight up to me, and in an exaggerated, extremely loud whisper said crossly;

"I hope all this lot aren't expecting to come to the Reception….."

Before she could say any more, Mrs Speltz interjected, announcing at full volume,

"*Everyone* is welcome to join Sue and Owen at the reception; if there is an additional cost to pay, my husband will arrange that with the Groom"

Mrs Williams was clearly livid, and the gathering of people around was totally unimpressed with her obvious mean attitude towards me; not everyone came back of course, as most of them were taking the short

449

time off from work. Those who did loved it…and made it an enormous success.

I looked across at my new mother in law; she cut such a pathetic figure. I felt a deep sadness for her; she *was* devoted to her son, but tragically viewed me as the interloper; I couldn't imagine she would ever change.

I was a little sad too; I once thought that if anyone ever did want to marry me…I would have my own family…his family. That wouldn't happen in this case; but I was more than happy with my own particular lot. Mr and Mrs Speltz had expressed clear a desire that we all keep well in touch…and I knew we would.

At last, we returned Mrs Williams to her bungalow, where we quickly changed out of our finery; with the car already loaded to the gunwales with my 'bottom drawer' …we were on our way to our own bungalow home.

CHAPTER 51

The journey sped by as we reflected upon every detail of our day; Pat had told Owen she and Win were going to invite friends along, but neither of us could believe the lengths to which they had gone. Owen was clearly aware of the comment made by his mother, and the sheer volume of guests being the resulting outcome; but it wasn't mentioned.

We had made excellent time and at last approached Southampton; the excitement was building for us both…then, just before reaching Warsash village, we entered a lane to our left.

"We're nearly there now darling" Owen said quietly.

He pulled the car over and gave me a quick kiss; as we continued slowly along, there were bungalows to my left…with acres of strawberry fields on the opposite side of the lane.

"It's the next one"

We drove through the decorative wrought iron gates, and up the drive to the rear of 'Hove-To'; the existing name of the bungalow, and something we decided we would keep.

My excitement soared…for the first time I was about to enter my own home…with my own wonderful husband.

We left the car, and for a few moments he held me tightly in his arms. Digging deep into his pocket, he removed with a flourish, a set of door keys. These were already attached to the key ring given to me by Mrs Speltz, when I passed my driving test.

"My darling Sue…these are yours and yours alone…the two Front, Back and Garage door keys to your very own home. Never again will you be Homeless…this is yours…*and I know you are going to love it*!"

He handed them to me…I stood motionless; I was stunned at the most marvellous revelation that crowded my head…*I had my very own door keys!*

I realised then the enormous difference between *having somewhere to live*…and *being in my own home;* it was a breathtaking moment.

Owen clearly realised the effect this was having and, placing his hand over mine, together we opened the door; he held me in his arms again and, with choking emotion said,

"Hello wife…welcome home"

452

We stayed in that warm embrace until the emotion left us both more stable.

Roaring with laughter, we left that door; grabbing his hand, we scooted around the path to the front of the bungalow. I unlocked both the porch and main doors…and because I could…locked them up again. Excitedly I did the same to the garage, and then back to the kitchen; I was utterly elated.

Still grinning with amusement he said,

"Come on sweetheart, let me show you round…I've seen it…you haven't yet"

I was amazed at the sheer size of the place; it was going to be wonderful living here. The first difference Owen could see from his original visit was the carpets; they were marvellous.

The fitters had laid light grey tiles in the kitchen and bathroom; the small dining area, the lounge hall and bedrooms… all were laid with rich, top-quality carpet. As if that was not enough, propped up on the window sill was a card from "Mr Cormar" himself; inside were his personal congratulations, and wishes for a long and happy marriage.

Bill and Sylvia had left the Reception early; they didn't drink, and said they needed to hurry back...it now transpired why.

Owen had organised with them, to light the small boiler in the kitchen; everywhere was cosy and warm...except the Champagne...this they had placed in an ice bucket in the garage, along with two glasses.

In fine style, he carried this into the sitting room, where he popped the cork...and we toasted our own happiness, in the peace which was our own home.

Completely relaxed now, I asked Owen about the furniture already in situ .

"We've got Bill and Sylvia to thank for a great deal; they instigated the sale as you know, but then wanted immediately to be good neighbours...all to be kept secret from you..

The settee is a spare, on loan from them, but I sorted out the purchase of the bed...with their help of course.

They made a personal recommendation, and found the exact one in Southampton. I sent them the money and arranged for delivery, the day after the carpets were laid.

That perfect arrangement was also down to them; it was they who had the keys to let the fitters in. They've also loaned the sheets and blankets for the moment; we'll go to town…and you must choose just what you want"

It was amazing how quickly the day had gone; we extracted from the car our immediate kitchen and toiletry needs, kindly packed separately by Win and the family; but decided to leave my other purchases until the morning.

With the evening rapidly turning to night…we finished our bottle of Champagne…and turned in.

# CHAPTER 52

Jumping with nerves, I went to the bathroom to get ready for bed; I wanted this man so much, but I also wanted to make the waiting for our wedding night to be as perfect as it could possibly be.

I had gone through first, and was lying very still when Owen slid into bed beside me.

In the quiet room, he gently moved towards me; I felt his hands on my body... *I immediately freaked out...absolutely terrified*!

I was aware of nothing else...just hands in the darkness.

The most horrific of my childhood flashbacks had burst like lightning into my head. My mind was being bombarded, with the graphically detailed recall of horror, pain and revulsion. I instantly recoiled, and rolled myself into the familiar ball I had adopted then...so I could be hurt no more.

I was as silent as I had been at the time; my body was trembling uncontrollably...and was absolutely freezing cold. I had become once more, the tiny abused little child I once was...in a state of mental and physical agony.

The raging storm in my head brought back memories of a bedtime when I was about six years old; already in my nightdress, two female members of staff had scooped me up from the landing. I wondered where I was going as they laughed and jogged me down the landing…to an empty sluice room.

Water was already run into the shallow sink; they stripped my clothing from me and with amazing force…they raped and sodomised my tiny body. If that was not enough to satisfy them, now covered in blood, they washed me in the freezing water…then pushed me feet first through the mangle.

It took me a considerable length of time to recover from the shock…but the worst thing had always been…I did not know this enemy…I could not recall their faces. The only things I *could* remember were their giggling…*and their hands in the dark*!

I recalled as well when I was fourteen; another member staff came periodically to my bed for her sexual gratification…once again it was *hands in the dark*.

Poor Owen was horrified; I couldn't respond to his questioning of what was wrong, his voice seemed far

457

away in the distance. I was in a blind panic; shaking all over, and feeling physically sick.

Without touching me he pleaded,

"Sue my dearest darling, *listen to me*…there is *nothing* here to hurt you. I'm here, and I'll make it better I promise you. Calm down darling *please*. Can you get up sweetheart? I'll get a dressing gown to try and make you warm; come through to the sitting room and please talk to me. Come on sweetheart *please*…do it just for me"

In total silence, still trembling and confused, I allowed him to cover me with a blanket; he gently took my hand in his, and with a strong arm across my shoulders, led me through to the sitting room.

With every light turned fully on, he held me tightly in his arms for what seemed like hours; he kissed and caressed my forehead and stroked my hair. Very very slowly, the nightmare scene left me, and the trembling ceased; his continuing strong support, was acting as a comforting balm, he never once let me go.

Gradually his tenderness gave me the confidence and trust to explain the horror of the sexual violations; the memories of which being locked away somewhere in my deepest psyche. I had no reason to think they would ever recur; I was as shocked as he that this dreadful situation had taken place.

I tried to explain; at no other time in my life had that same scenario occurred, bringing to life those terrifying recollections. For the first time since leaving the Homes, another person was in my bedroom...at my bed; the hands and the darkness had been the trigger.

I added that too, that shocking recall would put my childhood forever behind me; to be buried again, never to re-emerge. My liberation as an adult was finally complete; for twenty-one tumultuous years I had waited for this moment...I would never again regress.

In his quietly considerate, understanding way, he eventually restored me to some sort of calm. We sat for hours through that night, and talked it all out of me; we drank coffee and brandy...and eventually, in the early hours of the morning, we returned to our bed to become man and wife.

In the morning I woke, still in the embrace of my darling tender husband sleeping peacefully beside me.

I felt fulfilled as a woman...and cherished as a wife.


When eventually awake sufficiently to talk to one another, I did ask Owen the question...just once.

"If we had slept together *before* our wedding night…if you knew then what you know now…would you have changed your mind about marrying me?"

"Sue my angel, I love you with every fibre of my being; nothing on this earth would allow me a moment of regret. If anything, your disclosures have brought me even closer to you; I feel privileged you fell in love with me, and sufficiently entrusted yourself to my love and care. I will *never* forget the trauma of course, but nor will I ever forget your surrender to my love. I will treasure that moment…and you…forever"

I felt deeply in love…and in total peace.

CHAPTER 53

Owen had put the car into the garage the previous evening, still stowed with all the necessary accoutrements I'd bought to help make up our home. We had a marvellous time unpacking, as he had neither seen nor heard about any of it.

He did know about my wish to buy the cooker. Once the money was saved and the selection made, thanks to more intervention from Sylvia, my very own cooker was installed…it was a beauty.

He was intrigued at how much else I had managed to accumulate while he was away; putting the new towels and flannels into the bathroom, I explained I'd bought white, for fear of clashing with any existing colour scheme.

Almost everything else was for the kitchen; we had great fun finding places for it all to live. He laughed heartily when I took out the potato peeler, and told him why it was a gift. After an hour or more of this busy activity, we were both ready for our first breakfast.

The pans were unpacked and I had the wherewithal to cook; what we lacked was a dining table.

One of my kind garage customers was a carpenter; for my wedding present he'd given me a hand made ironing board of some considerable size. This I put up in our dinette; adjusted to the lowest level it proved to be a perfectly satisfactory alternative. Covering the ironing surface with a table cloth, I placed the hot tea-pot on the asbestos panel at one end; *hey presto* ...a table of the highest quality!

Bill and Sylvia were our first most welcomed visitors; they were suitably impressed with our dining table. They admitted they weren't as organised as Win had been; she having packed a separate box with kettle, cups and so on ready to use. They admitted to using jam jars found in a cupboard for their first cup of tea...from a flask and only luke- warm!

We were clearly going to be great neighbours; I told Owen we could invite them in for a meal...when I could cook properly!

There weren't many days of the leave ahead of us, but we made the most of every single one; they were enjoyed in a state of utter bliss. We were an established married couple, living in true contentment, by the time Owen returned to sea.

This parting brought incredible pain to us both; however much expected, this was unavoidable. I was able to drive him to Fawley, and promised I would collect him from wherever he docked to come home. Passing my test had been fun at the time; now it was proving to be the making of a far easier, happier time, than otherwise it might have been.

While he was away I found I had not only the desire, but quite an aptitude for not only gardening, but also decorating; by the time of his return, both the sitting room and our bedroom had been repapered...furthermore *he noticed*!

He'd already told me that, as his wife I was allowed to sail with him; upon his return he informed me my first trip was to be in November...we were both absolutely overjoyed. He added that because of the Charter Company, it would probably only be to North Africa.

*Only?*... I thought.

I reflected then on a question Mrs Speltz once put to me, on their return from a holiday in France.

"Have you ever been abroad Sue?"

"Mrs Speltz...I haven't even been to the Isle of Wight!"

Now I was going to be high-tailing around the world with the ship's Chief Officer! I wrote them one of my long letters, to tell them the brilliant news.

The evening before I sailed, we visited a few friends to say our goodbyes; one couple in Locks Heath happened to be watching their television when we turned up. Within moments of our arrival, the BBC gave the harrowing news of the assassination of President J F Kennedy.

The shock to us all was immense…matched almost by the immediate continuation of "The Harry Worth Show", the comedy broadcast interrupted by this dreadful revelation. The television was immediately switched off; we stayed long after the anticipated time of our visit, coming to terms with the gravity of what had happened.

I did do the anticipated trip…and for the next five years, sailed with my man; the near Continent, North Africa, Malta and South America.

The most memorable trip was down to Australia; and being fascinated with actually passing through the engineering feat of the Suez Canal.

It was a fantastic, oft times unbelievable experience; to be able to live so closely together in the luxury of beautiful ships. Our cabin was huge; we had a proper double bedroom…with en suite bathroom.

Because of the constant movement of the ship, the bath had very steep sides; this meant you could indulge in a good depth of water without it slopping over the side. As I was so short, Owen roared with laughter when he first walked in on me; from the door he could only just see the very top of my head!

I never tired of any of it.

I loved to see the flying fish sweep out of the bow-wave in their swift, darting dance. The dolphins swimming alongside for miles, communicating with us on-board humans; we would mimic their sonar sounds, and they would squeak back in response.

I saw the depth of the seaweed in the Saragossa Sea…sailed through the still, almost static area known as the Doldrums…and was given a fabulous 'Crossing the Line' ceremony as we sailed through the Equator, bound for Melbourne.

On one trip,we were in *Marsa el Brega*, North Africa; coincidentally where Owen was heading after we had first started our courtship.

At the end of each day Owen would pour a drink; we'd sit relaxed together in the peace of our cabin and talk. We frequently enjoyed long, profound conversations...but this one was very different.

Owen suddenly announced we should start our own family...that we should have a baby.

I was really surprised at first as there was no inkling he'd been thinking along those lines. We discussed all the changes this would make; the effects of a completely different life-style. My trips with Owen were enjoyed as a wonderful experience...but far more importantly for the extra time we spent together; I would miss that dreadfully...and said so.

He went on to explain; having served his time with BP, he spent many uninterrupted years at sea...far more than he would with most other Companies. This quickly accumulated his 'sea time' and enabled to him to study for his Tickets. He was only twenty eight when he got his Masters; a wonderful achievement then...but one that had its drawbacks now.

He had more than once been appointed Captain of a Dry-dock, but having his own ship permanently was a case of 'dead men's shoes'; there were too many older men in front of him for this to happen in the near future.

What he hoped for...as soon as knew I was pregnant...he would search for a shore job; he wanted to share all the new experiences, and ultimately see his son or daughter grow up.

Before the evening ended, we were in total agreement…a family we would be.

We weighed anchor and set sail for England; this was to be my last trip…I was *Homeward Bound.*

THE END

Lightning Source UK Ltd.
Milton Keynes UK
UKHW011846230821
389352UK00001B/35